ISSUES AND CRISES DURING MIDDLESCENCE

ISSUES AND CRISES DURING MIDDLESCENCE

Joanne Sabol Stevenson, Ph.D., R.N.

Associate Professor
The Ohio State University School of Nursing
Columbus, Ohio

APPLETON-CENTURY-CROFTS/New York

To Bob, Jay, and Mike
and to all who wish to grow throughout their life-span

Library of Congress Cataloging in Publication Data

Stevenson, Joanne Sabol, 1939-
    Issues and crises during middlescence.

    1. Middle age.   2. Adulthood.   I. Title.
HQ1061.S83   301.43′4   77-9405
ISBN 0-8385-4409-6

77 78 79 80 81 / 10 9 8 7 6 5 4 3 2 1

Prentice-Hall International, Inc., London
Prentice-Hall of Australia, Pty. Ltd., Sydney
Prentice-Hall of India Private Limited, New Delhi
Prentice-Hall of Japan, Inc., Tokyo
Prentice-Hall of Southeast Asia (Pte.) Ltd., Singapore
Whitehall Books Ltd., Wellington, New Zealand

Text design: Steven Abramson
Cover design: RFS Graphic Design, Inc.

PRINTED IN THE UNITED STATES OF AMERICA

Contents

Introduction

A friend is one who knows you as you are,
understands where you've been, accepts
who you've become, and still, gently
invites you to grow.
                                    Author unknown

Increasing numbers of professionals and lay persons are beginning to look with interest at the heretofore undifferentiated middle years of the life cycle. Although some material is beginning to appear, there is still a relative dearth of literature specifically concerned with the stages of adult development between high school graduation and late life. The amount of literature about the aged has grown enormously during the past 15 years; it is hoped that the next life stage to be the focus of scientific and literary attention will be middlescence.

Lack of interest in the middle years is both understandable and paradoxical; the middle-aged are the most hidden age group and simultaneously the most conspicuous. Although they comprise a minority of the population, they are the economic providers for the other population groups. Perhaps one reason the middle-aged have not been the focus of much attention is that only groups defined as being troublesome or having problems troublesome to society are studied and written about. Further, it is the middle-aged who define problematic groups: the middle-aged defined adolescence as a life stage needing study several decades ago; the middle-aged defined the elderly as a group with special problems requiring attention; and the middle-aged defined the youth of the 1960s as a problem group. Ironically, the truth about these so-called problem age groups is that they caused problems for the establishment, and the establishment is made up of the middle-aged.

Some concerns relevant to the personal lives of the middle-aged have been studied and reported, such as difficulties with marriage and family life, problematic occupational issues, and financial distress. Very few books have been published that deal with middle age in toto as a distinct life phase. But middle-aged people have not defined themselves as a target generation for scrutiny. As noted earlier, only "problem age groups" are studied in depth and written about conspicuously.

The primary intent of this book is to serve as a text for college students. It could also be useful to middle-aged persons as a frame of reference for what they are experiencing, with the added bonus of some ideas about how they might enhance their continued development. Special emphasis is given to situations and problems that have particular relevance to nurses and other health service professionals. Part I has two chapters. Chapter 1 is a discussion of the historical development of the middle years since the dawn of recorded history, with particular emphasis on the emergence of middlescence as a specific life stage in the mid-twentieth century and an explication of developmental tasks for youth or young adulthood, middlescence I and II, and late adulthood. Chapter 2 presents the theoretical framework and basic concepts underlying the approach taken in the subsequent chapters. Part II has four chapters, one each on the central components of the life space for adults: work and leisure, family life, community participation, and human maturity. The first three chapters of Part III are relatively detailed discussions of arbitrarily divided substages of early and middle adulthood: young adulthood, middlescence I (or the core of the middle years), and middlescence II (or the new middle years). The last chapter is an epilogue. It contains some implications and recommendations for social institutions such as education and the mass media. In addition, recommendations are made both for those who are currently middle-aged and for their children, who should learn early on that human development is a lifelong process.

The approach taken in this book is to present research results in a manner that nonresearchers can comprehend. Research findings are used to back up generalizations whenever feasible. Each chapter is followed by two bibliographic lists. The first contains the references cited in the chapter. The second is a suggested reading list, which readers can use to pursue special interests in more depth.

This book is not an objective statement presenting the range of opinions about adult life. Actually, most of the writings about adult development and aging do not represent a range of opinions. By and large they all present aging as a downhill process. The specific value emphasis in this book is a positive developmental bias about human adulthood. This admission is made without apology; a positive, self-fulfilling prophecy must be better than the negativistic attitude that has overshadowed Western thought and society for so long.

Many people contributed directly or indirectly to this writing project. To Barbara Smith, Helen Lafferre, Ellen Langham, Martha Steinmetz, and my research assistants, D. J. Lafferre and Ann Yersavich, I am grateful. Dr. Mary Irene Moffitt's editorial assistance was invaluable, but perhaps even more valuable was her consistent encouragement about the content. I am also indebted to the news reporters from local television stations and the area newspapers who reported my views about adult development to the general public and thus opened up an opportunity for serendipitous validation by many middle-aged viewers and readers even before the manuscript was published. I am deeply indebted to my family, colleagues, and friends, who put up with my mood swings, headaches, neckaches, irritability, impatience, and preoccupation. I am grateful to my mentors; some professional women have not been so fortunate as to have wise and generous mentors.

My symptoms of stress were worse on Thursdays than most other days because that was writing day. Whenever possible my work schedule was arranged so that I could write at home on Thursday. When people ask how long it took me to write this book, I usually startle them with my response that it took 117 Thursdays plus a few other days between semester breaks. There are probably many wrong ways to write a book; I can testify that writing it on Thursdays is definitely one of them.

Nearly everything has some advantage. The advantage of the one day per week writing schedule was that it took nearly three years to complete the work. During that time, some new literature became available; one such book was *Passages, Predictable Crises of Adult Life*, by Gail Sheehy, which was most welcome since it appeared in print just about the time that I was working on Chapter 7. The other advantage was that, over the course of the three years, I was conscious of my own growth and the growth of people close to me. This direct observation was helpful; it sometimes provided validation for hunches that were simply not treated in the available literature.

All the vignettes and illustrations are of real people, although sometimes two or more actual incidents were blended together to make a particular point. I am grateful to my students, to their client-families, to my research subjects, and to my own client-families for what they have taught me over the years about adult development, chronicity behavior, and the damning effects of negativity. When I was a youth, I transacted in the world with sarcasm, biting humor, and negative thinking. More recently, I have discovered that these old habits are my worst enemy. At present, I am attempting to train myself to view the world with a more positive orientation. I have tried positivity, and it really does make a difference. I invite you to try it too.

Joanne S. Stevenson
Columbus, Ohio, 1976

I

HISTORICAL AND CONCEPTUAL BASES OF ADULT LIFE PHASES

"Middlescence" is a term that originated in a facetious comment about the age group in the middle. Someone considered adolescence on the one side and senescence on the other and quipped that middlescence is in the center. The facetious remark does have utility.

Chapter 1 presents an extensive look at the manner in which developmental stages are specified according to the cultural milieu of the times. It traces the lengthening of human life from the Bronze Age life expectancy of about 18 years to the current life expectancy of well over 70 years and the projected life expectancy for people born nearer the twenty-first century of 120 or more years.

Four stages of adulthood are introduced, and the developmental tasks postulated for each stage are presented. The four stages are youth or young adulthood, which occurs between the ages of approximately 18 and 30; middlescence I or the core of the middle years, between 30 and about 50 years of age; middlescence II or the new middle years, which last from 50 to roughly 70 or 75 years; and finally the late adult years of 70+ to death.

Chapter 2 presents the theoretical framework underlying the content of this book,

1

namely, a social system's perspective of human relationships. Chapter 2 includes a rationale for the utilization of systems theory, some definitions and discussion of major concepts within the framework, and an explication of the significant systems processes used throughout the subsequent chapters. It also contains a discussion of role theory as it is used in this book. This approach to role is not in general use. Although many readers may prefer other approaches to role theory, this one is used because it fits well with social systems theory and helps to define social system dynamics at the dyadic and single-person levels. The section on role contains definitions of the major terms and a few examples of their use to illustrate the way that these terms are used in the remainder of the book.

1

INTRODUCTION TO MIDDLESCENCE

Through practically the entire evolution of human beings, only two distinct phases of life were recognized; infancy and adulthood. Middle childhood, adolescence, young adulthood, and late adulthood are all inventions of the past three centuries. Actually, most of these phases postdate the Industrial Revolution. This book focuses on another developmental phase in the life cycle of man: middle adulthood or middlescence. These two terms are used interchangeably throughout the book to refer to the period of decreased physical but rapid emotional and intellectual development that occurs between young and late adulthood. The terms "young," "middle," and "late adulthood" seem preferable to specific chronologic age ranges because the latter are often misleading. One person of 20 years may already be working on the tasks of middlescence, while another may still be moving through the struggles of adolescence. The same is true of two 40-year-olds or even two 70-year-old persons—one may be dynamic, intent on further personal development, and perhaps highly valued in the environment, whereas the other may have "retired" into himself and perhaps has been labeled chronically ill or even senile. While this book focuses on the middle years, some attention is given to both young and late adulthood because they are the neighboring phases; that is, the middle-aged person comes from young adulthood, moves through middle adulthood, and then grows into late adulthood. It is useful to have some basic indicators of the developmental tasks that are relevant during the neighboring phases, and these are included later in this chapter. It is also useful to under-

3

stand neighboring phases since the middle adult group has responsibility for the needs of other people to a much greater extent than any other age group. They are, on the one hand, parents to children, adolescents, and young adults and, on the other hand, are caretaking offspring to their own parents, who are moving into late adulthood.

HISTORICAL OVERVIEW OF THE HUMAN LIFE-SPAN

In this section an attempt is made to portray the gradual differentiation of the life-span into specific phases or stages through history. This differentiation evolved as a natural consequence of the gradual lengthening of human life and occurred within the context of changing societal needs.

The term "Bronze Age" refers to the third period of human development. It follows the Old Stone Age and New Stone Age, which are also known, respectively, as the Paleolithic Age and the Neolithic Age.[1]

Bronze Age man lived between 4000 B.C. and 1000 B.C. These figures differ somewhat depending on the source, but in general there seems to be agreement that transition from the New Stone Age to the Bronze Age took place in the Near East about 4000 B.C., occurred in Greece and Crete about 3000 B.C., and then moved further north in Europe about 2000 B.C.[2-5] This age is difficult to study because the prevalent custom for disposing of the dead was cremation. Numerous urns have been found containing calcined bones and ashes, but this leaves minimal information about clothing or physical traits of the people.[6] Some skulls have been found in Asia Minor from about 2000 B.C., and much of what is known comes from this period.[7]

The life expectancy of Bronze Age man is said to have averaged about 18 years and, from all that scientists can determine, two stages of life—infancy and adulthood—were sufficient. A person was born and cared for by very young parents who produced several offspring in a few years and died, leaving their young to be cared for by other members of the tribe. The tribes did have elders. Experts say that they lived well beyond the eighteenth year, but just how long these elders survived is not known. Perhaps 50 years was an exceedingly long life, or perhaps a few survived well beyond 50 years. Several centuries later, in the Golden Age of Greece, the life expectancy had changed minimally from the Bronze Age; it was still only 20 years. The impulsive actions of the Greek and Trojan heroes and, a little later, of the Roman heroes might be viewed differently with the knowledge that today we would label most of these heroes teenagers. The wise men of that era were few in number, but they lived into their seventies and a few may have reached 80. Statistics from ancient Greek and Roman times are not available, but experts report that a few hardy people have always far outlived their contemporaries in every society through the millenia. This was so rare, however, that such persons were considered seers, prophets, or oracles, and their advice was widely sought by the younger adults.

During the Middle Ages, a time of rapid human development in France, England, Germany, and other European countries, the life expectancy was still a mere 31 years. Some authors report that it was really closer to 25 years; the difference seems minimal to us but probably was important to the people living in that time. Most children were parentless by the age of 12, and the youngest child in the family was frequently still an infant when one or both parents died. Orphans were a prevalent part of the culture.[8]

The concept of childhood was still not known in the twelfth century.[9] Infants were nursed in swaddling clothes until the "age of reason," which supposedly occurred at 6 or 7 years, and then they immediately became small adults. They moved completely into the adult world and dressed accordingly. The adult-styled costumes can be seen in portraits painted in the Middle Ages such as Holbein the Younger's *Edward VI as a Child*, DeSilva's *Don Baltosar and His Dwarf*, or Titian's *The Vendramin Family*. These and other paintings show the figure of a child in miniature adult clothing in the elaborate and ornate style of the Middle Ages. These young people were married between 10 and 14 years of age. Several European kings took the throne at the age of 12. Most of the decision making was done by influential family members or by members of the church hierarchy because the monarchs were so young.

Children finally began to appear in special clothes that came to be defined as children's clothes in the sixteenth and seventeenth centuries. During the late seventeenth and the eighteenth centuries, pressures from a few powerful religions began to bring childhood into focus as a distinct phase of the life-span. Adults were told that they had a moral obligation to care for their children. Slowly the societal expectations of nurturance and education of children by parents or parental substitutes became established.

Life expectancy rose during the eighteenth century to 37 years, and again there were notable exceptions; that is, some people lived for years beyond the age of 70. The reader should keep firmly in mind the fact that persons who did live past 60 constituted somewhat less than one-half of a percent of the population. Childhood became an accepted developmental stage during the latter years of the eighteenth century. However, the other developmental stages had not yet begun to emerge.

The Industrial Revolution began in earnest during the early nineteenth century. Many changes began to occur in society, in technology, and in all the sciences, but particularly in the health-related sciences. Some diseases that had plagued man for thousands of years were diagnosed and appreciably subdued. General nutrition was improved, and people began to grow larger. It is an interesting experience to look at the shoe sizes in a museum display from the eighteenth and early nineteenth centuries and discover the vast degree of disparity between the foot size of, for example, a 4-year-old child of that time period and the shoe size of a 4-year-old today. Longer lives for a larger percentage of the population followed the general improvement in nutrition, the decline in epidemics, and the decreasing hardship of life-styles.

The percentage of persons aged 65 or older was up to 2.5 percent in 1850 and grew to 4.1 percent by 1900. The average life expectancy had taken a considerable jump, from 37 to 50 years, by the early 1900s.

Remember that the increase from 18 to 31 years had taken a thousand years to accomplish through the process of natural evolution. The increase from 31 to 37 years took 600 more years. But the jump from 37 to 50 years occurred in just one century.

Life expectancy in the Western nations is currently over 70 years. In the United States, the average life expectancy for late adults is 74 years for women and 70 years for men.[10] The more than 20 million U.S. citizens who have survived to age 65 have an even longer life expectancy because their death-prone contemporaries have dropped out of the statistical computations. A female who survives to age 65 has an average of 16 to 17 years left to live, and her male counterpart has about 13 to 14 years to live.[11, 12] This brings the average life expectancy of the elderly elite to approximately 85 years. Anyone who looks through the list of ages of persons in intermediate nursing homes will quickly realize that a surprising number of residents are between 84 and 104 years old. The mean age of admission to intermediate-care facilities is now about 82 years, and the mean age for admission to skilled-care facilities is about 78 years.

In 1960 there were an estimated 3700 centenarians in the

TABLE 1. Evolution of Human Longevity

TIME	AVERAGE LIFE EXPECTANCY IN YEARS	PERCENTAGE OF POPULATION OVER 65
Bronze Age	18	Unknown
Ancient Greece	20	Unknown
Middle Ages	31	Unknown
1600–1800	37	1–2 percent
1900	50	In 1850, 2.5; in 1900, 4.1
1975	72 (70♂ 74♀)	Greater than 10
Born in 1965	Approximately 80	Projected to 16
Born in 2000	120+	Projected to >20

Compiled from a variety of sources but most notably the Encyclopaedia Britannica *and the United States Bureau of the Census.*

United States.[*,13] In the 1970 census the reported number of persons 100 years or older was 29,000, which seems grossly exaggerated. There were 7000 documented centenarians receiving Social Security benefits, but this would not take in the total centenarian population. A conservative estimate is that centenarians rose from 3700 in 1960 to 10,000+ in 1970. This is a substantial increase over a one-decade period.

The percentage of people over 65 in the United States is 10 percent, while in France it is almost 20 percent. The percentage of older people in Western societies almost tripled between 1900 and the middle 1970s.[15] Always, some people have lived to be very old; however, the important point for the present and the future is that the average number of years lived, the absolute number of persons who survive to old age, and the percentage of such people in the society have greatly increased during the twentieth century. Table 1 contains a summary of several statistics mentioned in the foregoing discussion.

The twentieth century has been characterized by accelerated evolution in nearly every aspect of human life, and the specification of several additional phases of the life-span is but one of these aspects. The phase called adolescence began to emerge during

*The figure of 3700 is a corrected figure based on the 1950 census and earlier census data because the number of centenarians reported in the 1960 census was 10,326. Several authors have reported the existence of age exaggeration in persons near 100. The Metropolitan Life Insurance Company reported that projected population estimates remain close to self-reports on the census under age 95, but beyond that the self-reported ages are much in excess of the projected ones.[14]

TABLE 2. Evolution of Human Longevity with Life Stage Differentiation

TIME	AVERAGE LIFE EXPECTANCY IN YEARS	PERCENTAGE OF POPULATION OVER 65	LIFE STAGES*
Bronze Age	18	Unknown	Infancy and adulthood
Ancient Greece	20	Unknown	Infancy and adulthood
Middle Ages	31	Unknown	Infancy and adulthood
1600–1800	37	1–2 percent	Infancy, childhood, and adulthood
1900	50	In 1850, 2.5; in 1900, 4.1	Infancy, childhood, and adulthood
1975	72 (70♂ 74♀)	10	1930s, adolescence; 1940s, late adulthood; 1950s, middle adulthood 1960s, youth/young adulthood
Born in 1965	80+	Projected to 16	Unknown
Born in 2000	120+	Projected to 20	Unknown

Compiled from a variety of sources but most notably the Encyclopaedia Britannica *and the United States Bureau of the Census.*
Stages partially from Aries[9]

the 1930s. The study of gerontology, geriatrics, senescence, or, as this author prefers, late adulthood was initiated during the 1940s. Although there were a few people interested in this field of study before that time, the American Gerontological Society was started then. The study of the middle years is of more recent vintage, with seminal work being done in the late 1950s and a general increase in interest occurring after 1970. To date, young adulthood or youth has not been well documented or researched as a separate stage. During the youth uprisings of the 1960s, some persons focused on these years as a separate life phase, but work has not proliferated in this area as it has in the other life phases.

Table 2 shows the relationship between the evolution of life expectancy and the evolution of life stages.

In this book the general assumption is that the life-span becomes divided into phases when the society's awareness is heightened about the uniqueness of a life phase. Generally one phase has emerged out of the total life-span and has somehow become highlighted. During the early course of evolution, only two life phases—infancy and adulthood—were highly noticeable, useful, and worthy of differentiation. In the sixteenth century, childhood became an object of interest, and the differences between infants and children and between children and adults became accentuated. Thus, childhood emerged as a separate phase with separate developmental tasks and a set of norms and expectations for how adults were to act in relation to children and how children were to behave in relation to adults and each other.

Following a similar pattern, adolescence and late adulthood began to be acknowledged and treated as separate stages of life when the following events of the twentieth century occurred: The average life-span increased by 20 years; the population capable of work expanded beyond the capabilities of the employment market. Economists and others reasoned that people needed to be kept out of the work force longer and to be retired from it proportionately sooner in order to maintain balance in the work force and keep unemployment rates low. This is a grossly oversimplified claim for the emergence of adolescence and late adulthood as developmental stages, but an attempt at synthesis frequently results in oversimplification. This pragmatic approach can next be extended to the short-lived focus on youth. The majority of the work on youth occurred during the years when young people between the ages of 18 and 30 were highly visible and vocal.[16] As they have become resubmerged into the general category of adulthood, the focus on youth as a distinct life phase has decreased appreciably.

Adulthood has existed as the undifferentiated whole, apart from infancy, since the dawn of humanness. What, then, of the current trend toward specifying different developmental stages within it? Adolescence completely replaces the average adult years of the Bronze Age. Late adulthood has always existed, but the chronologic age-span at which it now occurs is higher, and ten times the number of people live to reach it. The most significant outcome of the rapid change in life-span is the amount of time that now exists between adolescence and late adulthood; it is currently 52 to 55 years. While some readers will find it difficult to believe, a great deal of growth, development, and change takes place during those 52 + years in the middle. The belief that people are completely grown and developed by the end of adolescence has been shown to be grossly inaccurate by research on the adult years.[17] Indeed, a basic premise underlying this text is that growth and development continue to occur up to the time of death in old age. Kübler-Ross has recently published an edited work that promulgates this concept. Her philosophy is ably demonstrated in the title, *Death, The Final Stage of Growth.*[18] Contentions about the nature of lifelong development, adult learning, and emotional maturation are presented at some length in the section of this chapter on developmental tasks, but in actuality the whole book is dedicated to this end.

Life expectancies for certain bench marks in history are presented in Tables 1 and 2. Now consider a few projections for the future. Actuarial experts have projected that children born after 1964 will live upwards of 80 years.[19,20] The projected life expectancy for people in the twenty-first century is over 120 years. Some experts deny the accuracy of this projection unless something is done to alter the basic course of aging.[21] Others argue that the elongated life-span will continue because of observations that 60-year-olds of today resemble 40- or 50-year-olds of a century ago in terms of the aging process as evidenced by muscular agility and strength, skin turgor, and other indices of youthfulness versus senescence. The second-oldest human being in the world was alive in the United States in 1976.[22]His age was 133 and he was diagnosed to be in good health. Medical examiners called him a "totally authentic survival machine." To what extent this type of occurrence will increase in frequency is unknown, but as noted earlier the population of people over 100 years has been increasing in the United States for the past few decades. Many of these 100-year-olds are still physically active, self-reliant, and cognitively adequate.

It is well beyond the scope of this book to judge the correctness or incorrectness of the projections about elongated life-spans presented in Tables 1 and 2. However, it does seem reasonable that the life-span will increase at least a few more years in the next century, although probably not as dramatically as it did in the last century. But even if the life-span only stays where it is now, there is ample justification for studying and discussing the growth potentials that exist during the greatly expanded years in the middle. Add no more longevity, and the middle still encompasses over 50 years. What are the dynamics, the properties, and the processes of this lengthy middle?

VALUE ORIENTATIONS

Another important theoretical frame that deserves explication before we discuss the stages and developmental tasks is the concept of value orientations. Kluckhohn and Strodtbeck defined value orientation as follows:

> Value orientations are complex but definitely patterned (rank-ordered) principles, resulting from the transactional interplay of three analytically distinguishable elements of the evaluative process—the cognitive,

the affective, and the directive elements—which give order and direction to the ever-flowing stream of human acts and thoughts as these relate to the solution of "common human" problems.[23]

Kluckhohn and Strodtbeck maintain that there is ordered variation in the value orientations of all human beings regardless of cultural origin. They further maintain that there are a limited number of common human problems for which all people at all times must find some solution. These problems in the form of questions are listed below. The phrase in parentheses after each question is the title for the value orientation emanating from each question. The five value orientation titles are used to label the five rows in Table 3.

1. What is the character of innate human nature? (human nature orientation)
2. What is the relation of man to nature and supernature? (man—nature—supernature orientation)
3. What is the temporal focus of human life? (time orientation)
4. What is the modality of human activity? (activity orientation)
5. What is the modality of man's relationship to other men? (relational orientation).[24]

Reading across the human nature orientation in Table 3, one can see the three major categories of evil, the split middle cell called neutral and mixture of good and evil, and finally good on the right. These human nature orientations are further differentiable depending on whether it is believed that each is alterable or not. For example, one can believe that man is evil and mutable (changeable) or that man is evil and immutable (unchangeable).

In the man—nature—supernature orientation a few comments should be made about the distinctions between subjugation, harmony, and mastery over nature. Subjugation is a fatalistic approach in which nature as the supernatural is seen as definitely in charge without any possibility for alteration by man. Harmony with nature implies that there is no real separation of man, nature, and supernature. One is simply an extension of the other, and wholeness derives from their unity. Fragmentation derives from their separation. The mastery over nature orientation implies that it is part of man's nature to overcome obstacles and that natural forces can be put to use by human beings. The control in this orientation rests with man, the ruler of the world.

The time orientation is fairly self-explanatory. Those with past orientations tend to dwell on ancestry and the meaning of historical events. Present-oriented persons are concerned with today—

TABLE 3. The Value Orientation Paradigm

VALUE ORIENTATIONS

DIMENSIONS	DON QUIXOTE	LIVE AND LET LIVE	"GREAT AMERICAN DREAM"
Human nature	Evil (Mutable / Immutable)	Neutral (Mutable / Immutable) — Mixture of good and evil (Mutable / Immutable)	Good (Mutable / Immutable)
Man–nature–supernature	Subjugation	Harmony	Mastery over
Time	Past	Present	Future
Activity	Being	Being-in-becoming	Doing
Relational	Lineality	Collaterality	Individualism

Adapted from Kluckhohn and Strodtbeck, Variations in Value Orientations, 1961. Courtesy of Row, Peterson

24 hours at a time. The future oriented are concerned with weeks, months, or even years from now; they are planners and dreamers.

Next, let us consider activity orientation. The person who believes that human nature is evil will subjugate himself to nature or supernature. Such a person is concerned with the accomplishments of the past, and his activity in the present consists of simply being. The glory of his present existence rests in his capacity to imitate the heroes of the past and to maintain his honor in this imitation process. Modeling oneself after heroes leads to salvation. This is essentially a nondevelopmental conception of self-expression in activity. The being-in-becoming orientation puts paramount stress on the development of all aspects of the person as an integrated whole. The doing orientation emphasizes measurable accomplishments achieved by acting on persons, things, or situations. Success in the doing orientation is stated in terms of measurable products.

Relational orientation refers to the definition of man's relationship to other human beings. Lineality refers to the like-mindedness of homogeneous groups. The belief systems among members of the same group must be rigidly alike. There is little room for variation or flexibility. Collaterality means that the person is important primarily as a part of the total social order. Individuality speaks for itself and implies heterogeneity among the societal members. It further implies that individual needs and rights take precedence over the general social order.

The contents of Table 3 can be used to assess the dominant value orientation of family, friends, or nations. It is particularly useful for health care professionals to use as a guide for assessing the value orientation of clients. Simply follow the items down the columns.

It would be helpful to learn to use the paradigm, so a few illustrations will be presented to familiarize the reader with the technique. Those persons who fit the model of the so-called Great American Dream would follow column 3: Man is basically good. The relationship of man to nature is mastery over nature by harnessing energy, building roads, bridges, and sturdy buildings, and enhancing the physical capacities of man with technology. The valued activity would be doing. And the relationship between people would stress individualism: "I do for me; you do for you. We cooperate if it will benefit each of us." This is generally recognized as the dominant value orientation in the United States.

Certain variant groups follow the middle column, which is labeled Live and Let Live. Such persons see themselves as mixtures of good and evil; they strive for harmony with nature, are present oriented, view themselves as being-in-becoming, and stress collateral (interdependent) relationships with their fellow men. Among these groups are some tribes of American Indians and many people in their late adult years. Other groups of Americans who come close to the middle column or straddle the middle and right columns include the Mormons, the flower children of the 1960s, and some self-help groups such as Alcoholics Anonymous, Gamblers Anonymous, Overeaters Anonymous, Emotions Anonymous, and Child Abusers Anonymous. Still others include certain religious organizations and the ministry. It is pointed out in Chapter 9 that many persons who believe in the Great American Dream value system change to the Live and Let Live value system later in life.

The value orientation paradigm presented in Table 3 is referred to over and over again throughout this book. Hence, the reader is encouraged to become familiar with it and to come to understand it.

DEVELOPMENTAL TASKS OF THE NEW LIFE STAGES

Erikson[25] and Maslow[26] did the classic work on the explication of developmental tasks beyond adolescence. Pikunas carried their work further and developed fairly specific tasks for early, middle, and late adult years.[27] Pikunas published his tasks in 1961 and again in 1969 with strong implicit values of traditional marriage and family life-styles. He had a section in the 1969 edition of his book called Late Adult Years, but it contained no developmental tasks.[28] The age range he used is inappropriate in light of the facts presented earlier about the lengthening of of the middle of life. Hence, in the discussion below the chronologic age range between 50 and 70 years has been shifted to a phase called the new middle years. This serves to formalize the actual shift in prolongation of the mental and physical attributes of middle age within the elongated life-span. It is an error to visualize the additional years of life as tacked onto the end. Rather, we should think of them as slipped into the middle. Thus, the tasks that appear below emanate from the work of Maslow, Erikson, and Pikunas, but they have been changed significantly to reflect a philosophy of positive growth and development throughout life, from conception to death.

The developmental tasks are expressed in the "ing" form to connote that *each task is a process* and is ongoing throughout the stage. In some instances, a task will continue to be worked on in subsequent stages, although it will not appear in print that way. People progress at their own paces and in idiosyncratic ways. Not all persons will compete the tasks of young adulthood by the age of 30. Occasionally, persons will appear to be straddling two stages at once. One may observe that someone is working on tasks from each stage simultaneously. Also, it has been observed that persons who are chronically or terminally ill may be working on certain tasks of late adulthood even though they are chronologically in young adulthood. The reader is cautioned to evaluate these tasks as *normative* in the population but not as rigidly applicable to everyone. There will be specific individuals who do not fit into these stages very well. Indeed, the majority of people may not follow them precisely. However, the same admonishment would accompany developmental tasks for the years between birth and the end of adolescence. Developmental tasks have the built-in flaw that they do not seem to account for individual differences. But individual differences can be read-in by the health care professional who is using the tasks for assessment purposes. Developmental tasks are useful as guides; they are never meant to be absolute standards.

Young Adulthood

Youth or young adulthood refers to the stage in life when high school days are ended or nearly ended and the transition from adolescence to the early adult years is taking place. The approximate chronologic ages encompassed by the following developmental tasks is 18 to 30 years. The reader should keep in mind that these ages are tentative and that many persons will not fit within them well. However, over the entire society, the age range appears to be a good approximation of this developmental stage.

Developmental Tasks of Young Adulthood or Youth

The major objective here is to achieve relative independence from parental figures and a sense of responsibility (emotional, sociocultural, and economic) for one's own life.

1. Advancing self-development and the enactment of appropriate roles and positions in society
2. Initiating the development of a personal style of life
3. Adjusting to a heterosexual marital relationship or to a variant companionship style
4. Developing parenting behaviors for biologic offspring or in the broader framework of social parenting
5. Integrating personal values with career development and socioeconomic constraints

The age range in this stage is culturally determined, and the years 18 to 30 refer primarily to North America and other advanced Western nations. Since the marriage age in the United States is dropping, a person may be married and not fit well into this stage if parental independence is not being achieved. Graduation from high school seems to be a better overall indicator of the status-passage into young adulthood. However, in times of high unemployment recent high school graduates may remain in an adolescent holding pattern for awhile if they cannot find employment and cannot or do not enter a post-secondary-education program.

A physical move out of the parental home usually accompanies work on young adulthood tasks but is not a requirement. Young adults can progress and mature in the parental home if they are able to evolve more mature equalitarian role relationships with their elders and assume a greater share in the responsibilities of adult life, both in the home and in the society.

Tasks 3 and 4 are written to cover accelerating changes in our culture revolving around traditional institutions such as heterosexual partnerships, legally sanctioned marriages, and procreation. These tasks are intended to focus on personal maturation and adjustment within the chosen style of life rather than on the specific pattern of life that is chosen. It seems much too early to make judgments about whether the traditional modes of marriage and family life will prevail as the most healthy. Task 3 would include any form of single life-style. For example, it would include homosexual relationships and a variety of other companionship styles. Many young adults go through trial relationships or short-lived marriages before they find an acceptable partner. Task 4 is intended to encompass the growing complexity of parentage. In particular, Francoeur aptly showed that it is no easy matter to name just two parents for a child who is conceived, born, and lives under the mind-boggling influence of modern biologic technology. The following illustration shows how the issue of parentage and the language we have to describe it are undergoing accelerative change:

A Puerto Rican woman is married to a man of Polish ancestry. She has malfunctioning ovaries which are replaced by an ovarian transplant from a Japanese woman. A dozen of the ova from the Puerto Rican woman's new ovaries are removed for test-tube fertilization. Since her Polish husband is sterile, the ova are impregnated with sperm from his dead father who donated them ten years before. This maneuver retains the genetic line of the Polish ancestry. The Puerto Rican woman then learns that she cannot carry the child because of proneness to miscarriage. A substitute mother is found and employed to carry the pregnancy. An embryo transplant is performed and the substitute mother carries the fetus for the full term, delivers and hands the child over to the Puerto Rican/Polish couple.

Questions such as the following come. to mind—Who is the mother of the child? Are there actually several types of mothers—a genetic mother, a biological mother, and a social mother? The child also has a genetic father, a biological father who would be the biologist that inseminated the ovum and sperm in the test tube, and a social father. Such a child would have six real parents. Our concepts of parentage need revision.[29]

The phrase "social parenting" in the fourth task is meant to cover adoptions and other temporary or permanent forms of caring and to cover short- or long-term parent-surrogate efforts such as the Big Brother organization, scouting, coaching sports, and working with minority children. If the birthrate continues to decline, these types of parenting may become a primary style for a significant percentage of young adults. That is, more and more young adults may never become biologic parents themselves. They may engage in surrogate-parenting activites by helping to socialize other people's children.

Task 5 is very important in view of the significance of occupation or career in the culture. While this was once primarily a concern of men, the women's movement may significantly decrease the distinction and make this task applicable to all young adults. The increasing divorce rate also belies the old belief that a girl could circumvent concern with career development because she would soon marry and live happily ever after. The major thrust of the message in task 5 is the need for consistency between one's personal value system and the occupation or career and its expectations and rewards. Many people in our society do not concern themselves about consistency between personal values and their job in the early phases of career development. Then in their late thirties or early forties they realize that a discrepancy exists. This belated attempt at rapprochement seems problematic in view of the studies showing that depression and other symptoms of mental illness accompany the attempt to integrate career and personal values after several years have already been invested in the disparity.[30,31]

Middlescence

Middlescence or middle adulthood refers to the stages in life when the adult life-style, the occupational mode, and the family life (or single life) pattern have been chosen and the individuals involved settle down to implementing their choices. The approximate chronologic age-span encompassed in this phase is from age 30 to 70. The 40-year period is further divided on the basis of available research into two distinguishable segments: middlescence I, also called the core of the middle years, is from 30 to 50 years, and middlescence II, which is also referred to as the new middle years, covers the years from 50 to 70. As in the age-span for young adulthood, these phases are tentative. Actually, the 20 years of middlescence I will be divided into shorter phases as the knowledge about these years increases. There is already evidence that some unique challenges occur between 30 and 40 which differ from those that occur between 40 and 50.[32] Other evidence indicates that well-defined transitional crises occur between 29 and 32 and between 39 and 42.[33-35] There is enough information available to discuss each decade in some detail, and this is done in Chapter 8, but there is not enough information on each decade to set forth two sets of developmental tasks. At this early stage in the accumulation and validation of knowledge, the whole 20-year span appears to be an appropriate designation for the following tasks.

Developmental Tasks of Middlescence I, the Core of the Middle Years

The major objective is to assume responsibility for growth and development of self and of organizational enterprises. Another objective is to provide help to younger and older generations without trying to control them.

1. Developing socioeconomic consolidation
2. Evaluating one's occupation or career in light of a personal value system
3. Helping younger persons (eg, biologic offspring) to become integrated human beings
4. Enhancing or redeveloping intimacy with spouse or most significant other
5. Developing a few deep friendships
6. Helping aging persons (eg, parents or in-laws) progress through the later years of life
7. Assuming responsible positions in occupational, social, and civic activities, organizations, and communities
8. Maintaining and improving the home or other forms of property
9. Using leisure time in satisfying and creative ways
10. Adjusting to biologic or personal system changes that occur

The major objective of this phase requires some explanation. During middle adulthood one is expected, within the norms of our culture, to be his own person—to be a parent to himself, as it were. He should not depend on others to guide his life. He should know how to do that himself. But where has he learned such skills and gained such confidence? Nowhere. Consequently, middle-aged people often move into predictable maturational crises, as is discussed ·in Chapters 8 and 9.

The objective states that, in addition to personal growth, middle adults are responsible for "organizational enterprises." These two words connote that persons in this and the next phase are responsible for implementing the major institutions in the society: business and industry, government, religion, education, charitable organizations, health care, marriage, and the family. The issue here is not whether they do it well or poorly. The point is, they do it. Society expects them to do it. The very young expect them to do it perfectly. The very old expect them to do it better than their own generation did it. The responsibility is heavy and the expectations are unrealistic. Nevertheless, they do exist. These responsibilities and expectations comprise the legacy of the middle aged.

The second objective indicates that these persons are expected to provide help to younger and older generations. An earlier draft of this objective read, "to assume responsibility for growth and development of the younger and older generations." But this is an impossible responsibility. Human beings cannot have control over other human beings, so the wording of the task was changed. As it stands now, the interpretation should be that one can only provide help that others have a right to accept or reject.

"To provide help" should be distinguished from "to help," which connotes that the control lies in the helper rather than in the recipient of the help. This issue of help without control reappears in later chapters; for example, in Chapters 7, 8, and 9 the issue of control over the lives of adults who are chronically ill is discussed. By and large, Americans are a nation of controllers. We want to run other people's lives and determine how they should think and feel. In particular, American parents tend to want to give help to grown offspring in return for the right to give advice and otherwise control how those offspring will make decisions and run their lives. Such a habit is dysfunctional and produces resistance and resentment from those on whom it is used. Similarly, middle-aged offspring define an elderly parent as needing assistance, and before long they want to take control of the parent's wholeness. They justify this behavior as concern that the person is becoming too old to make decisions for himself.

Task 1 states that persons in this stage are to consolidate their progress in the areas of social life and economics. Remember that only a small minority of people in our society earn money. Infants and children do not. Even employed adolescents and young adults usually earn less than they use. The aged theoretically live on what they earned earlier in life, and for some retirees this is true. By and large, however, the actual dollars being spent by Social Security and other retirement funds comprise money from the current earnings of young and middle adults. The tax money used for welfare programs comes from the employed portion of society—the middle-aged groups. The economic supporters of the whole population are actually only about 30 percent of the population at any one time.

The first task further implies that these middle adults should be developing a pattern or style of their own, both in the social and in the economic spheres. So they do. They acquire what Bertrand calls a station in life. Station means the location of the actor in the community or society. The society defines one's station on the basis of all the positions that one holds in various groups and organizations including the family, work, civic affairs, religion, and so on.[36] From the economic standpoint it means that economic problems become crystallized and set. Those below the poverty level will tend to remain there; those who are poor but pay their own way will probably continue to do so. Those who are financially well-off will continue to be well-off until they face a potential sharp decline in late adulthood. Remember, these are descriptions of the dominant trends in our society. There are also many variants of or exceptions to the statements, but on the whole they do describe the majority.

Task 2 brings us back to the discussion of a personal value system. In order for the person to feel comfortable in the occupation, it should be compatible with his or her value orientation as summarized in Table 3. If the orientation of the occupation is predominantly in the right column and the person's values are in the middle or left column, the result is an uncomfortable mismatch.

Much of the discomfort in American society felt by people of Hispanic origin is the mismatch between people with a left-column value orientation (Don Quixote) trying to live in a society that has a predominantly right-column value orientation (Great American Dream). The same can be said for American Indians, Eskimos, and Pacific Islanders. These three groups tend to hold the orientation displayed in the middle column. Hence, the process of "growing up adult" in North American minority groups presents unique problems both for the minority group members and for those from the dominant society who assume responsibility for attempts at resocialization. Teachers, social workers, physicians, and nurses, for example, should be prepared for a tough time if they do not realize the mismatch in value orientations that they are trying to bridge. Many of the important American institutions are unthinkable for people with a left-column value orientation. Business and industry and health care, for example, are aimed primarily at conquering nature and planning for the future. These institutions are sacrilegious to people who do not believe that anyone should tamper with destiny.

During the middle years, one's value orientation goes through major changes. Americans who held strongly to the right-column orientation may begin to reevaluate and reformulate their values and move closer to the middle column. Many people in their late forties move from neutrality on the issue of God, or even from agnosticism or atheism, toward the development of a spiritually based belief system. They may develop a personal relationship with a higher power of their understanding and put trust into that relationship in a manner never experienced earlier in their lives. Some people have religious faith up through the middle forties, question or lose it, and then near 50 discover a comfortable sense of spirituality that is better than what they had earlier. Spirituality opens the way for living in the present rather than in the future. It constitutes a move toward being-in-becoming rather than doing as the activity dimension. The man–nature relationship thus moves toward harmony with nature and supernature rather than control over one or both. The shift, then, is from the Great American Dream orientation to the Live and Let Live orientation.

The third task states the major responsibility of any person toward other individuals: to promote their growth toward integrated wholeness as human beings. The example given is biologic offspring who, during this stage in the parents' lives, move from infancy, to childhood, to adolescence, and perhaps into young adulthood. Parents have many opportunities during these years to role-model their value orientation, their modes of communication and interpersonal style, and their attitudes toward self and toward the world. The success of this role-modeling determines to a great extent the kind of growth and development pattern, particularly in the cognitive and affective spheres, that the offspring will hook into. The television show "The Waltons" portrayed the influence of role-modeling a particular value orientation mode to offspring. While such shows are becoming extinct on the national networks, cable television carries endless reruns of the popular family comedies from the early 1960s.

The statement of task 3 minus the parenthetical example merits discussion. Middle-aged workers serve as mentors for younger workers. Teachers serve as mentors for students, and established professionals help to establish young colleagues. Middle adults are also in excellent positions to help each other; spouses are in an excellent position to understand and support each other through these tasks, yet spouses may be the least consciously considered object for help in mastering the developmental tasks.

A good deal of the research and writing that has emerged since the women's movement got underway indicates that middlescent women do not mature in the cognitive and affective domains unless they are in situations in which such growth is encouraged, nurtured, and role-modeled. Researchers have found that the early widowhood or postdivorce period is the time of greatest growth for women who marry in the late teens or early twenties and become housewife–mothers. Women who have found a way to keep up-to-date on their developmental task work within a marriage seem to be those who married later and made significant strides toward becoming "their own woman" prior to marriage. The type of work done outside the home appears to be a significant variable in differentiating such women. The topic of work as a significant issue in adult life is taken up in Chapter 3. In that discussion, the function of work as a maturing force is presented with specific focus on the differential function that work serves in a society that is founded on sex stereotyping.

Finally, the message in task 3 encompasses significant others in all age categories: aging parents and other family members, people with whom one works closely, friends, and other people's children. The point is that a human being cannot not communicate; a human being cannot not altercast to others in the environment. All behavior communicates. The process is continuous; it is not possible to cease communicating as long as one is alive.[37] Moreover, the altercasting has a qualitative dimension. That is, it connotes a range of attitudes toward the receiver; the communication can be growth promoting or growth stifling; it is almost never neutral. Even when the qualitative meaning is out of the conscious awareness of the receiver, the qualitative dimension is being recorded and interpreted by the deeper centers of his brain. Hence, the receiver is influenced by the message in toto.

Tasks 4, 5, and 6 have already been touched on in the discussion of task 3. The essential idea is that the relationships with spouse, offspring, or other intimates, with significant friends, and with late adult family members should all be viewed in terms of the discussion about how to interpret task 3.

Tasks 7, 8, and 9 refer to larger-system issues, beyond the immediate family, friend, and co-worker circle. Task 7 covers one of the hallmarks of this age group—they fill many of the leadership positions in the society. If one put the core of the middle years of 30 to 50 together with the new middle years of 50 to 70, the resulting cohort would probably include over 90 percent of the appointed and elected administrators in the world and certainly in the United States. Task 9 may be superfluous. It is implied in other tasks but seems somewhat useful to highlight. Again, well over 90 percent of the real estate and other forms of property is either owned, controlled, or governed by persons between 30 and 70 years old. Young people may be purchasing cars, motorcycles, or homes, but middle-aged managers of banks or savings and loan associations hold the ownership papers while the monthly payments are being made.

The last two tasks are closely allied to task 2 because they refer to responsibility to self rather than to others. Leisure may have less relevance to a highly work-oriented person in the thirties but usually takes on more significance in the forties and later. The task part lies in the terms "satisfying" and "creative." In this sense, leisure is viewed as nonneutral. Free time either relaxes and reinvigorates or bores and stagnates. A more thorough discussion of leisure is presented in Chapter 3, but it might be useful to note that concern over the creative use of leisure time is rising among social scientists. In the wake of shorter work weeks and earlier retirement policies, the opportunity to use leisure time is on the increase. The question then concerns how the population can be taught to use it in beneficial rather than stagnating ways.

The last task might be placed first in the schema of other authors. It is last here because of the basic philosophy that undergirds this book, that growth and development are more significant happenings during life than atrophy and loss or decay. Nevertheless, it is important that persons recognize physical changes that do occur in the aging process and accept them at all three levels—physical, intellectual, and emotional. It is also a form of accepting life to keep the body in shape through exercise and other physical activity so that the body as the physiology comprising the intelligence and emotions remains in good working order.

Continued acceptance of the aging self is difficult in any culture that worships the physical aspects of youth. It is far easier to accept the more mature thinking and feeling that come from the reappraisal of life-style, value orientation, and relationship to nature and supernature that occurs in these years than to accept the aging of the physical body and the approach of death. Much ambivalence and inconsistency exist in this area. The mass media and celebrities are a constant source of stimulus to hide the signs of aging and pretend that they do not exist. Honest people find this an unsatisfactory game of self-deception. Nevertheless, it is a tough game to ignore because of the societal pressures to conform and look young.

Middlesence I is the core of adulthood. It is the stage in which very slow physical and intellectual changes occur. However, major strides in emotional growth take place. Those who do not grow emotionally emerge into the new middle years and then the late adult years with retarded emotional development. Senility may be a pathologic syndrome that results from retarded emotional development in the middle years.

Middlescence II: The New Middle Years

The new years is the name given to the elongated middle of life by Anne Simon. It refers to the years of middle adult life wherein one has attained most of what one will ever attain in the work world. In this phase one is usually back to the couple stage in the marital relationship or fast approaching it. Around age 50, men become cognizant of their nurturant tendencies, and they develop more appreciation for family life. Women may show the opposite change, toward more ambition and interest in business or politics.

The age-span used in this stage is 50 to 70 years. The upper limit was chosen because of the mandatory retirement limit of 70 for even the most conservative of work situations. If persons over 70 continue to thrive and engage in new work activities, perhaps the chronologic age in this stage will be lengthened. Recently, some governmental agencies struck down their age-restricted personnel policies and went on record as saying that retirement age would no longer be used to turn down a job applicant. However, at this time, the 20-year span of time between 50 and 70 remains a justifiable designation for the tasks of the new middle years.

The percentage of this age group who actually fill high-level decision-making positions is small, but practically all of the people in these positions come from this age group. In addition, if one considers all possible decision-making positions in all the groups, organizations, and institutions in the United States, the number of incumbents in those positions is high.

The people in this stage of development who do not have the direct authority afforded by election or appointment to an official position of some kind still fulfill this major objective by providing wisdom, judgment, and restraint to the conduct of the nation's affairs. This does not mean simply the state and federal governments' affairs, but all the affairs that take place within the nation at any level. The affairs of business, industry, religion, education, and health services are directed by persons in this age group.

The general tone of the developmental tasks presented below implies that the person is refining and integrating the emotional growth that he underwent during the previous 20 or so years. In a sense this is akin to some of the integration periods of childhood and adolescence, when after a period of rapid change there was a more stable period before another spurt of rapid change.

Developmental Tasks of the New Middle Years

The major objective here is to assume primary responsibility for the continued survival and enhancement of the nation.
1. Maintaining flexible views in occupational, civic, political, religious, and social positions
2. Keeping current on relevant scientific, political, and cultural changes
3. Developing mutually supportive (interdependent) relationships with grown offspring and other members of the younger generation
4. Reevaluating and enhancing the relationship with spouse or most significant other or adjusting to their loss
5. Helping aged parents or other relatives progress through the last stage of life
6. Deriving satisfaction from increased availability of leisure time
7. Preparing for retirement and planning another career when feasible
8. Adapting self and behavior to signals of accelerated aging processes

The major goal of this stage implies that these people are given the highest positions in North American society—the presidency, positions on the cabinet, congressional seats, and comparable positions in state and local governments; presidencies and chairmanships in business enterprises; and high positions in organized religion, in social and civic organizations, and in the military. A local official may be 35, but the national chairman is much more likely to be 55. Hence, the emphasis in this stage is on the larger social systems of the society, beyond the local level of one town or a local chapter of an organization to the broader scope of regional, national, and international responsibilities.

Task 1 implies that people in this group are being confronted with accelerating changes in technology and in the social milieu created and marketed by younger persons. The task of new middle agers is to slow down too rapid acceleration by wisdom, restraint, and judgment. They may be viewed as old-fashioned or as progress reducers. However, every society requires that someone provide this service of restraint and wisdom; it is essential for the balance of the society. Otherwise the unbridled change espoused by the young could put the whole nation into shock. However, openness, flexibility, and the like are desirable characteristics, and people in this stage should strive toward them. When they do not, they lose touch with evolution and become a detriment to the society. Balance is needed between their restraining function and their responsibility to keep up with progress.

Task 2 is similar to task 1 in content focus but different in the action required. Task 1 refers to attitude, while task 2 refers to specific behaviors that follow from the attitude. By this time in life people may have moved into habituated behavior patterns that are comfortable but dysfunctional. For example, some persons may read particular types of literature but not others, or subscribe to only certain kinds of magazines and newspapers. The amount of testing, trial and error, and risk taking that they undertake may be reduced. Hence, there is increased probability that new ideas or creations will be missed. Perhaps an idea is too avante garde to appear in their favorite magazines, newspapers, or television shows.

The price that the new middle agers pay for complacency and staying in a conservative rut is that they do not get in on new trends. As new trends develop and more changes take place, these people lapse farther and farther behind the times. Eventually, they assume a defensive posture to assuage uncomfortable feelings. The defensiveness may become manifest as withholding important information needed to give a new idea a fair trial or actual sabotage of the new idea.

New middle agers who maintain openness to emerging trends and evaluate them on their own merit in a fairly objective way stand a much better chance of maintaining a positive view of life during these years. They are also more apt to be accepted by the younger generations.

Tasks 3, 4, and 5 are corollaries of tasks 4, 5, 6, and 7 in middlescence I. Task 3 signifies that the younger generation(s) now takes in a much wider range of age groups. It includes grown off-spring and grandchildren. The grown offspring are particularly in need of redefining their relationships to their parents. It is important that the relationships change from parent–child to adult–adult. Task 4 suggests that the relationship with spouse must again be reevaluated and further work done on it. If the spouse is lost through death or divorce, the stages of grief must be traversed. This would be a crisis, and such crises are discussed in Chapter 9.

During the latter part of middlescence and the major part of the new middle years, aging parents or in-laws are worrisome to many. The emphasis in task 5 is not on physical care of the aged; rather, it is on promoting their development. Again, this stems from the basic philosophy that everyone has developing to get on with, even the very old, and that their grown offspring can help or hinder them in this effort. Adult offspring can inhibit the continuing de-velopment of their own aging parents much the same as they can in-hibit the continuing development of their youths, by being overcon-trolling.

Tasks 6 and 7 are corollaries of tasks in middlescence I about work and leisure. Persons in middlescence II typically are re-lieved of some family responsibilities because their children have moved out. Things are quieter and calmer around the house. Hobbies are possible, and delicate objects will not be disturbed or broken so easily. Trips are more possible, either for vacations or to visit off-spring. Even the poor seem to take trips during this stage, usually to see relatives.

People prepare for retirement in different ways. The trend in industry and government is to develop specific adult education programs for future retirees. Many of these programs fail when they are based on a philosophy of self-gratification and meaningless re-creational pursuits. Similarly, they seem to fail when the uncomfort-able feeling of being forced into the category of has-been is not dealt with in a useful manner. The more successful preretirement pro-grams seem to be based on the philosophy of exchange: Exchange this type of work for another type suitable to you at this time in life. Exchange leisure activities for some portion of your former occupa-tional activity time. Exchange service to mankind for service in business and industry. The proportion of the work to nonwork time allotments shifts over the course of the stage. The time shifts are minimal in the early fifties and increase through the sixties. The situational crisis of retirement is explored in Chapter 3 on work and leisure and from another perspective in Chapter 9, where the maturational and situational crises of the new middle years are discussed in more detail.

Task 8 is comparable to task 10 in middlescence I and appears last for the same reason—to deemphasize it. Too many people in our society would see it as the only process going on in these years. Once again, the key idea is that, if a person is growing emotionally and spiritually, he can accept the signs of physical deterioration, which may or may not include actual symptoms of acute or chronic disease. Changes in hair and skin pigmentation, collagen loss, muscle changes, and eyesight and hearing loss are but a few of the atrophic cellular changes that are experienced. A person whose value system continues to be wrapped up with physical beauty, agility, power, and a prestigious occupational image may suffer greatly during the late fifties and sixties. A person whose value orientation has shifted from the Great American Dream value system in Table 3 to the Live and Let Live value system will be more apt to take this developmental stage in stride and reap gratifying benefits from the experience.

Late Adulthood

No prototype of the developmental tasks of late adulthood could be found in the literature. Erikson, Maslow, and Pikunas did not go beyond retirement age. They seemed to imply that human development is finished by then. Such a position seems ridiculous in view of the findings of census takers and gerontologic researchers, particularly from those studies that concentrate on the well elderly, who are still maturing. The following tasks were constructed in 1972 to illustrate that even in late adulthood people have further developing and growing to do.[38] If the length of life were to shift upward to 120 or more years, the age range for these tasks would shift upward and a new span of years in middle adulthood would need to be inserted. For the present, the years between 70 and death have been chosen. Whatever the chronologic age-span in this stage the following list appears to encompass the final list of tasks that will bring maturity to full culmination and adulthood to an end.

Developmental Tasks of Late Adulthood

The major objective is to assume responsibility for sharing the wisdom of age, reviewing life, and putting affairs in order.

1. Pursuing a second or third career, new interest, hobbies, and/or community activities that fulfill some heretofore untapped inner resource or otherwise enhance the self-image and maintain worth in society

2. Learning new skills that are well removed from prior learnings or at least do not produce cognitive dissonance with prior learnings
3. Sharing wisdom accrued from the past with individuals, groups, communities, and nations
4. Evaluating the totality of past life and putting successes and failures into perspective
5. Progressing through the stages of grief, death, and dying with significant others and with oneself

The intellectual goal in the first several stages of childhood is knowledge. The intellectual goal in the earlier adult years is integration and synthesis of knowledge. The intellectual goal of the last two stages, particularly the last one, is wisdom. What a difference exists between these two words. Unfortunately, dominant American values tied to mastery over nature in Table 3 put too much emphasis on knowledge to the devaluation of wisdom. If we valued wisdom, we would value old people.

Knowledge and Wisdom Compared. "Know" and "wise" are both Anglo-Saxon words, and in some ways their meanings overlap. But for the most part they each pertain to separate human operations and behaviors that emanate from the cognitive domain. "Know" is defined in the dictionary as, "to perceive with certainty; to understand clearly; to be convinced or satisfied regarding the truth or reality of; to be informed; to have a clear and certain perception." The term "knowledge" is defined as "the clear and certain perception of that which exists; cognizance; learning or erudition."[39] "Wise" is defined as "having the power of discerning and judging correctly; sensible; sage; judicious; possessed of discernment, judgment and discretion; prudent." "Wisdom" means "the power or faculty of forming the fittest and best judgment in any matter presented for consideration; sound judgment and sagacity; sound common sense; often opposed to folly."[40]

So the light begins to shine through on the developmental ties of these two words. The word "wise" has been used throughout history to refer to older persons or to those young persons who used the kind of sage judgment usually attributed to the seers of the society. Knowledge over wisdom has been in vogue since the beginning of the Industrial Revolution in the Western nations. The search for reality, for scientific facts, for clear understanding about the environment and about controlling nature has been dominant for many decades.

It is hoped that the current trend toward an increasing percentage of older persons in the society, together with emergent attempts on their part to organize themselves into politically and socially powerful groupings, will have an impact on the trajectory of knowledge dominance over wisdom. Our culture could certainly use more of the qualities contained in Webster's definition of wisdom. We could use more sound judgment, sagacity, and evaluation of scientific facts. We could use less folly and more common sense and prudence. Viva la difference between wisdom and knowledge.

Discussion of Specific Tasks.   The specific charge in the major-objective statement is to do three things: share one's wisdom, review one's life, and put one's affairs in order. The first activity is externally directed; it is directed toward improving human life in the immediate environment or in the larger community. Success in sharing one's wisdom is not the relevant issue, only that the attempt was made. If it falls on deaf ears, that is unfortunate for the society, but the late adult has done his part. The second activity is an internally directed activity. It is highly important to a successful culmination of life. It should not be misinterpreted by younger persons in the environment as useless reminiscence. Rather, it represents a type of inventory of the entire life-span. Accomplishments and failures can be put into perspective through the life review process. The third activity is fairly easy to understand and refers to material possessions, wills, insurance policies, and the like. It is a significant sign of maturation when a person can accept his own eventual nonexistence and have enough concern for his survivors to put his business affairs in order.

Task 1 reiterates the theme developed in the new middle years that additional careers or occupations can appropriately be pursued after retirement. Colonel Sanders of Kentucky Fried Chicken fame is a popular example. He allegedly started the Kentucky Fried Chicken business with his first pension check at the age of 65. At the age of 80 he sold the chain but stayed on as an advertising figurehead. At the age of 83 he and his wife started a new chain under her name but featuring his original secret recipe. Maggie Kuhn, the originator of the Gray Panther Movement, was a social worker until retirement age. Six years later she was the somewhat arthritic but very spirited heroine of the organization against "agism" called The Gray Panthers. Charlie Smith was the legendary ex-slave who did not retire until age 131, when the price of wholesale Coca Cola got too high for him to tolerate and he retired from his seventh career. This last career, which lasted for 20 years, was as a small-store owner. These three examples were chosen because they show different forms that the "new careers" can take. Sanders did "his thing" in business and made a fortune. Kuhn did "her thing" in a social movement in which the objectives were nationwide consciousness raising and legal action to decrease stereotypes and discrimination against the aged. Charlie Smith's efforts were generally unsuccessful throughout his life, including the several business enterprises pursued after his 100th year.[41] He was a slave, an outlaw, a bounty hunter, a factory worker, an orange picker, and finally a sodashop owner before he retired at the age of 131. The fact that he was never financially successful did not phase Charlie. He just kept on thriving.

Task 2 is very closely allied with task 1 and was originally written to take into account the large number of studies done in the 1950s and 1960s showing that older workers had great difficulty making small or subtle changes in old habit patterns. One sample of subjects had trouble using a new machine that had been changed in only subtle ways from their old machine—for example, when certain switches were reversed. However, they had no trouble with new machines or ones that had major design changes. The concept of cognitive dissonance, which refers to interference between new information and prior knowledge, has applicability here.[42]

The findings were then extended and found to hold in behavioral research studies of subtle versus major changes in socioemotional aspects of work life. For example, a worker who had been with one company for 30 years would react strongly to subtle changes in that company, but if he moved to a new company he would be more accepting of progressive changes in the latter place. The ususal interpretation of such an occurrence is that the person's self-image and personal history are tied into the first company. Therefore, he has trouble separating himself from the objective need for change. No such tie exists at the second company.

Task 2 may be based on research that would no longer hold. Only further research will tell. It has been left on the list as a tentative caution for those who are in this stage in life and for those who are involved in adult education. It would be particularly relevant in the areas of health care teaching or patient teaching about a medical regimen to be followed. If the task requires subtle changes, or is difficult to remember, or is a major change in something really significant (eg, eating habits), then long-term retraining is needed. One explanation aimed at an intellectual appeal will not be sufficient. If a person must learn a new way of cooking, it might be worthwhile to start with a new stove and new cooking utensils. Otherwise all the old habits will creep back in, some slowly, some quickly. Even the new appliance may not make enough of a difference.

Task 3 is simply the statement in task form of part of the

major objective described earlier. Task 4 is a statement of the life review task. The importance of putting successes and failures into
perspective was documented by the extensive work of Charlotte
Buhler on biographies of people in their later years. Those who
could not see that they had had significant successes in life moved
into despair. She found that such people were filled with feelings of
nonfulfillment in their existential awareness of their total past life.
Those who saw their lives as generally worthwhile moved into acceptance. They put their sorrows, disappointments, and failures into
perspective alongside their successes, achievements, and happy
times. Generally, they believed that their lives had more comfortable
than uncomfortable moments.[43,44] Butler reframed the negatively
viewed habit of older people toward reminiscence.[45] Instead of viewing such rumination over the past as an indication of senility, he
suggested that it be viewed as a necessary inventory taking, which
he called the life review. Such work is useful to older people. One
disadvantage of the label life review is that it implies orderliness,
and this apparently is not accurate. Late adults seem to go through
life reviews in sometimes orderly and sometimes disorderly fashion.
Sometimes they focus on just one part of their lives for an extended
period of time in order to get it into better perspective or to overcome
particularly strong feelings attached to it.

In the developmental sense, life review is desirable because
it allows for revision and expanded understanding of experiences
that may have been poorly understood and poorly accepted at the
time they happened. Hence, the late adult can enhance his emotional
maturity and acceptance of the past, at least in part, through a life
review.

Task 5 indicates that the loss process becomes significant
during this stage. The reader should be reminded that loss is a process encountered all through life. Children lose possessions, animals,
and grandparents. Adults lose parents, spouses, jobs, children, and
possessions. But the ultimate loss generally occurs in this phase: the
loss of personal being, of existence. Usually the person has ample
opportunity to practice the processes of grief before the occurrence
of his own death. Perhaps one of the functions of the life review is to
help the individual better prepare himself for death. Data from persons engaged in life reviews support this notion. Many of them report that they dreamed about death or dreamed that after they died
they were asked for a report on their lives. They were told in the
dream that the inventory of their lives was a prerequisite to peace
after death.

This concludes the presentation and discussion of the stages of adulthood from postadolescence to death. The developmental tasks are tentative and should be treated in that way. Much more research and evaluation will be necessary before revised forms of these tasks can be considered to be reasonably valid. Even if that happens, there will be a need to change them from time to time as man evolves into the twenty-first century. Notwithstanding such disclaimers about the developmental tasks, they can be useful in their present form to young people who are learning about their own and older generations because they present an idealized view of what the phases of life could be like. Further, they present a set of criteria or standards for assessing a person's maturation within a developmental phase. Finally, they can serve as goals that people can apply to themselves and try to achieve in their own growth process through the life cycle.

Some of the developmental tasks are more appropriate to the middle classes and may seem irrelevant to those from variant value orientations, particularly from the "man is basically evil" perspective. Such a bias no doubt exists, but no apology is made for it. The tasks were stated wherever feasible in terms that would make it possible to achieve them in a wide variety of ways. Thus, it should be possible for many different groups of people to make their way through these tasks. The concept of equifinality, which is presented in the following chapter in the discussion about open systems, encompasses the belief that living systems can achieve similar goals by very different routes. Man is a living system; therefore, man can achieve lifelong development by different routes.

References

1. *Encylopaedia Britannica*, 1968 ed., s.v. "Bronze Age," p. 275 (vol. 4).
2. Ibid., s.v. "Prehistoric Technology, The Bronze Age," p. 750A (vol. 21).
3. J. Alsop, *From the Silent Earth* (New York: Harper, 1964).
4. *Encyclopedia Americana*, 1965 ed., s.v. "Bronze Age," p. 589a (vol. 4).
5. *The Cambridge Ancient History*, 1974, 3rd ed., s.v. "Homo sapiens," p. 170.
6. H. H. Wilder, *Man's Prehistoric Past* (New York: Macmillan, 1923), p. 249.
7. *The Cambridge Ancient History*, p. 170.
8. A. W. Simon, *The New Years; A New Middle Age* (New York: Knopf, 1968).
9. P. Aries, *Centuries of Childhood*, trans. R. Bacdick (New York: Knopf, 1962).

10. United States Bureau of the Census, "1970 General Population Characteristics," Final Report, PC (1)-B1, U.S. Summary (June 1973), pp. 1–259, 1–263.
11. G. L. Maddox, ed., *The Future of Aging and the Aged* (Atlanta: SNPA Foundation Seminar Books, 1971).
12. United States Bureau of the Census, "Projections of the Population of the United States, by Age and Sex, 1970 to 2020." (Current Population Reports, 1971).
13. Metropolitan Life Insurance Company, "Centenarians," *Statistical Bulletin* 52 (November 1971): 3–4.
14. Ibid.
15. *World Health Statistics Annual* (New York: World Health Organization, 1972).
16. K. Keniston, "Drug Use and Student Values" (Paper presented at the National Association of Student Personnel Administrators Drug Education Conference, Washington, D.C., Nov. 7–8, 1966).
17. B. Neugarten, ed., *Middle Age and Aging* (Chicago: University of Chicago Press, 1968).
18. E. Kübler-Ross, ed., *Death, the Final Stage of Growth* (Englewood Cliffs, N.J.: Prentice-Hall, 1975).
19. Metropolitan Life Insurance Company, "Increase in Survivorship Since 1840," *Statistical Bulletin* 45 (August 1964): 1–3.
20. "World Population 1963," *Population Bulleting* 19 (October 1963): 137–156.
21. C. Eisdorfer, "Background and Theories of Aging," in *The Future of Aging and the Aged*, ed. G. Maddox (Atlanta: SNPA Foundation Seminar Books, 1971), p. 3.
22. S. Merrill, "The Oldest Living American at 133," *New Times*, 6 (6 February 1976): 32.
23. F. R. Kluckhohn and F. L. Strodtbeck, *Variations in Value Orientations* (Evanston, Ill.: Row, Peterson, 1961), p. 17
24. Ibid., p. 11.
25. E. H. Erikson, *Identity and the Life Cycle*, Psychological Issues, Monograph I (New York: International Universities Press, 1959).
26. A. H. Maslow, *Motivation and Personality* (New York: Harper, 1970).
27. J. Pikunas, *Psychology of Human Development* (New York: McGraw-Hill, 1961).
28. J. Pikunos, *Human Development: A Science of Growth* (New York: McGraw-Hill, 1969).
29. R. T. Francoeur, *Eve's New Rib* (New York: Harcourt, 1972).
30. H. L. Wilensky, "Orderly Careers and Social Participation," in *Middle Age and Aging*, ed. B. Neugarten (Chicago: University of Chicago Press, 1968).
31. M. E. P. Seligman, "Fall into Helplessness," *Psychology Today* (June 1973): 43–48.
32. J. Davitz and L. Davitz, *Making It from 40 to 50* (New York: Random House, 1976).
33. R. Gould, "The Phases of Adult Life: A Study in Developmental Psychology," *American Journal of Psychiatry* 129 (November 1972): 521–531.

34. G. Sheehy, "Catch 30—and Other Predictable Crises of Growing Up Adult," *New York* 7 (18 February 1974): 30–44.
35. R. Gould, "Adult Life Stages: Growth Toward Self-Tolerance," *Psychology Today* 8 (February 1975): 74–78.
36. A. Bertrand, *Social Organization: A General Systems and Role Theory Perspective* (Philadelphia: Davis, 1972), pp. 35–36.
37. P. Watzlawick, J. H. Beavin, and D. Jackson, *Pragmatics of Human Communication* (New York: Norton, 1967), 48–51.
38. J. S. Stevenson, "A New Value Orientation Toward Aging," an unpublished paper (Columbus, Ohio: Ohio State University, 1972).
39. *New Webster Enclycopedic Dictionary of the English Language,* 1971, s.v. "knowledge" (Chicago: Consolidated Book Publishers), p.473.
40. Ibid., s.v. "wise," p. 961.
41. S. Merrill, "The Oldest Living American at 133," New Times 6 (6 February 1976): 32.
42. L. Festinger, *A Theory of Cognitive Dissonance* (Stanford, Calif.: Stanford University Press, 1967).
43. C. Buhler, "The Course of Human Life as a Psychological Problem," *Human Development* 11(1968): 200.
44. C. Buhler, "Theoretical Observations About Life's Basic Tendencies," *Journal of Psycho-Therapy* 13(1959): 561–581.
45. R.N. Butler, "The Life Review: An Interpretation of Reminiscence in the Aged," in *Middle Age and Aging,* ed. B. Neugarten (Chicago: University of Chicago Press, 1968).

Suggested Readings

Anderson, R. E., and Carter, I.E.: *Human Behavior in the Social Environment: A Social Systems Approach.* Chicago: Aldine, 1974.
Cowdry, E.V. *Aging Better.* Springfield, Ill.: Thomas, 1972.
Davitz, J., and Davitz, L. *Making It from 40 to 50.* New York: Random House, 1976.
de Beauvoir, S. *The Coming of Age.* New York: Putnam, 1972.
Francoeur, R.T. *Eve's New Rib.* New York: Harcourt, 1972.
Keniston, K. *The Uncommitted.* New York: Harcourt, 1965.
——— *Young Radicals.* New York: Harcourt, 1968.
Kimmel, D.C. *Adulthood and Aging.* New York: Wiley, 1974.
Neugarten, B.L. *Middle Age and Aging.* Chicago: University of Chicago Press, 1968.
Pikunas, J. *Human Development: A Science of Growth.* New York: McGraw-Hill, 1969.
Sheehy, G. *Passages. Predictable Crises of Adult Life.* New York: Dutton, 1976.
Simon, A.W. *The New Years; A New Middle Age.* New York: Knopf, 1968.
Smith, D., and Bierman E. L. *The Biologic Ages of Man.* Philadelphia: Saunders, 1973.

2

BASIC CONCEPTUAL FRAMEWORKS

The theoretical framework underlying the content and commentary in this book emanates from a systems perspective of man and the world. Many books are available on the theoretical and conceptual underpinnings of the systems view. Nevertheless, it is appropriate to present in this chapter a brief overview and discussion of systems theory as it is used in this book. Much of this discussion centers around the definition of terms because systems theory contains many terms or concepts that can be used as analytic tools for investigating the nature of human and other phenomena.

The second section of this chapter deals with role and other pertinent terms emanating from role theory that are used in various discussions throughout the book. The section on role theory is placed in this chapter because of the specialized way in which role is used here—to refer to dyadic interpersonal relationships—which is somewhat different from the common usage of role.

SYSTEMS PERSPECTIVE

The origin of systems theory is multidisciplinary, and the purpose of systems analysis is multidisciplinary understanding. The greatest advantage of systems theory and systems language is that diverse groups of disciplinary experts can communicate with each other in one language. Engineers, architects, administrators, and social scientists, for example, find it possible to work together in something like urban redevelopment in an orderly and team-cooperative way if they all have systems language and a systems perspective as a theoretical base. They can talk to each other and reason problems out more easily because of the common approach to viewing the world.

The health professions could make equally efficient use of systems for a similar kind of team-planning or problem-solving target. The planning and implementation of a new or the reorganization of an old health care organization can be accomplished in a successful manner only when the input of all the relevant groups of professionals and managers is integrated into the plan. Otherwise change will be sabotaged or nonintegrated because splinter groups will break off to do their own changing. True integration of the parts of a complex organization like a hospital is virtually impossible if each person speaks a different language based on a different philosophical and theoretical view of the nature of health care delivery. Hence, multidisciplinary health team collaboration requires basic underlying congruence in theory and language among the participants. Systems theory and systems language provide a basis for the needed congruence while maintaining the natural heterogeneity among the different professions represented in the group. In some universities this approach is started during student days. Students from several health-related professions may work together on some kind of health care delivery project. In one such course, students from nursing, medicine, dentistry, respiratory therapy, dietetics, rural sociology, and home economics live in an Appalachian village for a quarter and, with help from a preceptor and their university instructors, try to provide comprehensive health services for the inhabitants. Such an experience requires much attention to interpersonal relationships and territorial rights of the members. But the basic framework of a systems perspective certainly makes it possible for these students to at least understand each other.

Definition of a System

In general systems theory, a system is defined as a set of units with relationships among them. Systems may be open, closed, relatively open, or relatively closed. All living systems are relatively open. An open system is one that exchanges matter, energy, and information with the environment. The word "relatively" is used before open to connote that all living systems have boundaries. Boundaries serve to limit the degree of openness of the system and thus protect it from dissolution into the environment.

Boundaries determine the outer parameter of the system and comprise the interface between systems. Boundary maintenance is the function of making the system more or less open. It is a crucial process because it determines the extent of interaction with the environment, which means the amount, extent, and frequency of exchange of matter, energy, and information that is allowed to flow in and out.

The Utility of Defining Levels

One of the most useful conceptual skills in the systems perspective is the parameter-setting function of defining levels. Systems are hierarchically arranged. The organization or group that one wants to look at or work with is defined as the target system. Everything that is larger or outside the target system is called the suprasystem, and any smaller units within the target system are called subsystems. This phenomenon of systems is called the Janus effect after the Greek god with two heads who could simultaneously look in opposite directions.[1] So it is with the systems analyst. He looks outward toward the suprasystem and inward toward the subsystems while being primarily concerned with what is happening in the target system.

A simple diagram and example may clarify the ideas presented so far. In Figure 1 the target system could be a department or unit of some health care organization. The reader might find it helpful to have a specific target system in mind, perhaps a place where there was student experience—for example, a patient unit or ward in a hospital. Look at Figure 1 and find the target system shown as the second largest circle. Name it. The suprasystem that is represented as entirely encircling the target system is the parent organization. Look at the suprasystem and name it. The subsystems would then be work groups, teams, and the like within the target system. Name a few. Examples of the suprasystem as pictured, if the target system were a hospital ward, could be the entire hospital or a portion of it such as the surgical division. Some subsystems on the ward would include the nursing teams, the patients, the medical house staff, the housekeeping staff, and so on.

Consider the boundaries of the levels defined. Think about how the suprasystem maintains its boundaries. It probably has

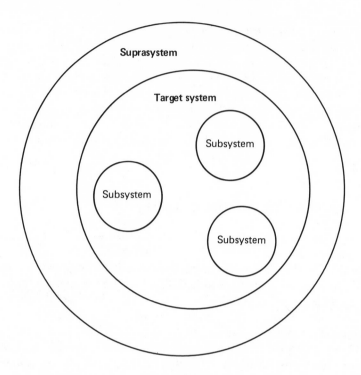

FIG. 1. Schematic representation of three system levels.

membership lists or other rosters containing the names of those who belong in the system and those who do not. There are gatekeeping mechanisms and gatekeepers hired specifically to make certain that matter, energy, and information, including people, are allowed in or out according to some predetermined criteria or rules. For example, patients must be admitted, and professional personnel must be licensed and then hired or appointed. Visitors must abide by rules about visiting hours. Information flow is attenuated by confidentiality rules. The flow of matter into the system is controlled. For example, visitors would be stopped from bringing a patient's bedroom furniture into an acute-illness hospital. The reader can continue this exercise by thinking about parallel boundary maintenance examples at the target system level and at the subsystem level. Each subsystem probably has idiosyncratic ways of managing its boundaries.

The drawing in Figure 1 is useful for taking a simplified look at any system or for taking a thorough look at a simple system like an average family. However, there are other components that are

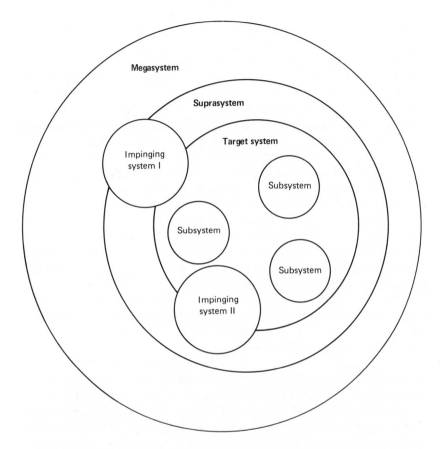

FIG. 2. Schematic representation of system levels in a complex organization.

important in a complex system, and a few of these have been added to the first drawing and are shown in Figure 2.

All of Figure 1 has been placed inside Figure 2, and the new outside circle is called a megasystem. The term "megasystem" is often used to denote the environment outside the suprasystem. This environment, which includes other organizations and the community at large, has relevance to the ongoing life of the suprasystem. However, the systems analyst decides to ignore many of these influences in the megasystem because he cannot take in and collate all that information; so usually the megasystem components are not analyzed in detail.

The other additions to the schematic drawing in Figure 2

are the circles labeled impinging system I and impinging system II. Impinging system I represents a system that operates in the target system, elsewhere in the organization (suprasystem), and outside the suprasystem in the megasystem. One example of impinging system I for a hospital ward would be the attending medical staff who impinge on the target system and have patients and other responsibilities like committee memberships elsewhere in the hospital. They also have positions in the megasystem such as appointments in other hospitals, one or more private offices, and so on. A second example would be the public health or visiting nurse agency that sees patients in the hospital to assess them for aftercare. A third example would be social service agency representatives that assess financial or other socioeconomic problems that need to be worked on. Impinging system II represents the type of system that belongs entirely within the suprasystem but only partially within the target system. Examples of impinging system II for a hospital ward would be the adjunctive services that supply all the wards with certain services or supplies: dietary department, pharmacy, or central supply; middle-level administrators and supervisors who manage several wards; nurse clinical specialists who consult on several wards; and clergy and mental-health consultants.

Defining levels is useful in that the observer is made aware of the hierarchy of influencing forces that are relevant to the target system to be analyzed. This minimizes tunnel vision. Too often it has the opposite effect and overwhelms the neophyte with complexity. This sense of mental overload will pass if the student remembers to keep a focus on one level at a time and to concentrate most of the attention on the target system.

Levels make it possible to analyze small, large, or medium-sized target systems with the same conceptual tools. In order to change the level of the target system, one simply relabels the circles in Figure 1. If the target system is to be the whole organization, the old target system becomes one of the new subsystems. Redefine the suprasystem accordingly. If the target system is to be whole hospital, the new suprasystem will probably be the community where the hospital is situated. One could just as easily move downward in system levels and designate one of the clusters or teams of people on the ward as the target system. Individuals or cliques within that cluster would become the subsystems, the whole ward would become the suprasystem, and the whole hospital would move up to the megasystem level.

Social Systems

The focus of systems in this book is man and the groups and organizations that man creates in order to live out his life as a social being. A few scattered myths about children being raised by animals notwithstanding, the essence of humanness rests in the intellectual and affective development that cannot take place in the absence of other human beings. Hence, we are primarily interested in those man-made systems that are termed social systems. The examples used in the previous section were of social systems, specifically that subset of them called social organizations. A hospital is a type of formalized social organization.

The requisites for a functioning social system according to Bredemeier are adaptation to the environment, integration of the parts, and decision making about modes used to carry out the allocation of resources.[2] If one reiterates the definition of a general system, it is easy to see how a social system fits the definition. Earlier a system was defined as a set of units with relationships among them. This definition holds for social systems as well.

A social system, for example, a family, is a set of individuals (units) with multiple forms and kinds of interpersonal relationships among them. In order to survive, families must fulfill the functions defined by Bredemeier.[3] Families adapt to the environment vis-à-vis living space, neighborhood, public laws, and the acceptance of other norms and expectations of the environing human groups. A second function is integration of the parts, in this case integration of individual members into the family. A family that cannot integrate its members runs a high risk of splitting into fragments. Often nonintegration is centered around one member, and that person may be removed from the family. Divorce, run-away children, or institutionalization of a member are examples of the effects of nonintegration. Finally, families must make decisions about how the family is to operate and about how tasks and resources are to be allocated. This function refers to all parts of family life from the development of norms, roles, and values through the allocation of chores and the distribution of money. One may observe that in many families decisions are not made; things just happen. That is another form of decision making. It could be called decision making by default. Decision

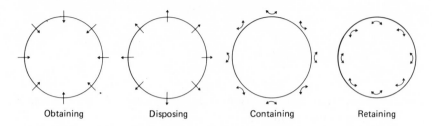

| Obtaining | Disposing | Containing | Retaining |

FIG. 3. Four essential functions of social systems.

making need not be openly discussed in order to exist. It may be observable to an outsider but unnoticed by the insider.

Bredemeier has described four processes that social systems carry out in order to help meet the requirements of adaptation, integration, and decision making.[4] These four processes are depicted in Figure 3 as circles, with each denoting the target system. The lines that form the circles represent the boundaries of the system. The arrows depict the flow of matter, energy, or information. The two circles at the top of Figure 3 show boundary *crossing*. The two circles at the bottom depict boundary *maintenance*. The obtaining function shown in the upper left circle refers to the process of bringing elements into the system from the environment. Disposing, shown in the upper right circle, refers to moving matter, energy, or information from inside the system across the boundary to the outside. Containing refers to a process of keeping some matter, energy, and information in the environment, that is, outside the system. Finally, the circle at the bottom right shows the process of retaining. It is a boundary maintenance process of keeping certain matter, energy, and information inside the system. Through a continual succession of decisionlike choices, open systems pick and choose what is to be obtained, disposed, and contained. Any living system is thus able to fulfill its requisite of *adaptation* to the environment. Further, by using decisionlike choices about how those elements that are obtained and retained are to be *integrated,* a system is able to fulfill its requisite of internal adaptation. In human systems this choice mechanism is called *decision making.*

Wholism and Steady State

Systems are influenced as wholes through their functioning in relation to adaptation, integration, and decision making. Although major actors in the system may have more power and authority relative to the three functions, the outcomes of their power moves affect all the units in the system. Living systems, and consequently social systems, are identifiable as wholes greater than the sum of their parts. Man is greater than the sum of his parts, a family is greater than the sum of its members, and a social organization is more than all the subsystems added together. The missing element in the simple summation of parts is the relationship among them. The whole includes these relationships. That is the distinction between holism (simple summation) and wholism (greater than summation).

Terms used by other systems writers to describe the matter, energy, and information flow through systems are input and output. They are akin to obtaining and disposing, with shades of a different meaning. Obtain and dispose imply an active movement, while input and output refer to the content of matter, energy, or information that is being moved across the boundary.

Designation of these terms leads naturally to the use of a third term called throughput. Throughput refers to what the system does with the matter, energy, or information between the time of obtaining it as input and the time of disposing of it as output. The system reorganizes and transforms the input so that when disposal occurs the matter, energy, or information has been processed through the system. This idea is easy to grasp at the single-person level. If a human being takes in matter, energy, or information, he naturally processes it before output occurs. Families and larger organizations also do this. Consider some ways that families, small groups, and larger organizations process the matter, energy, or information that is taken into their system.

Throughput is the processing of inputs within the system. However, the system also needs information about the acceptability of its throughput work. The system needs two kinds of information as input; the first is new information in order to begin a new cycle of throughput, and the second is information about the system output from the preceding cycle(s). Feedback is the mecahnism by which systems adjust present behavior on the basis of reports about past performance. Feedback is a powerful learning, adapting, and change tool for living systems. It is akin to evaluation. It provides a system with an outsider's view of the system's performance. Hence, the information can be used to make changes in the system's future performances.

Another important tenant of systems operation is communicated by the term "negentropy." Entropy is defined by the second law of thermodynamics for closed systems. The second law states that all naturally occurring processes or spontaneous changes in nature are accompanied by an increase in the entropy of the system. Entropy is the portion of the energy in a system that cannot be converted to work. When entropy increases in a system, there is a resulting degradation toward simplicity, homogeneity, increasing disorder, and inertness. Negentropy, or negative entropy, means approximately the opposite of entropy and refers to the phenomenon in open living systems in which either spontaneous or planned change in a system is accompanied by an increase in the portion of energy that can be converted to work. Negentropy is characterized by an increase in complexity, of hierarchical order, and of heterogeneity in living systems.[5] Negentropy makes it possible for systems to fend against deterioration and destruction for long periods of time. Perhaps it is difficult to comprehend that increasing complexity and increasing order would go together; however, they do because of hierarchical formulation. An example of negentropy is the development of the human fetus. It moves from a single cell to an increasing complexity of cells that differentiate and develop into hierarchies of molecules, cells, organs, tissues, systems, and finally the whole or a complex body. Feedback is one of the major sources of negentropic force for any system. Reports of system performance are fed back into the system as input. This serves to keep the system constantly appraised of its status and helps the system to constantly grow and improve. Growing systems move in the direction of increasing the variety and complexity of both processes and structures. Some systems authors refer to this process as morphogenesis.

A concept that is closely allied to negentropy and feedback is equifinality. In 1950 Von Bertalanffy published a rudimentary conception of this important phenomenon. Equifinality is a characteristic of systems which constitutes a powerful new principle about science and the scientific method. According to this principle, two or more living systems can achieve the same final state of functioning even though they begin with different conditions and pursue different paths.[6] Examples would include diverse cultures throughout the world that share a similar goal of disposing competent developing offspring into the environment; they accomplish this, but in different ways. Another example might be at the university level. The top-ranked universities probably do what they do very differently, yet the results, in terms of graduates and research outputs, seem relatively comparable.

The major significance of the principle of equifinality is that it has a profound implication for scientific research based on cause–effect theorizing. The cause–effect perspective is not compatible with equifinality and in truth is not compatible with the general systems perspective in toto. The implications of this fact are mind-blowing. To a great extent this implication of systems theory has served as a major deterrent to its widespread use in those disciplines in which cause–effect research is deeply entrenched. The medical–biologic sciences such as physiology, microbiology, and physiologic chemistry are examples of such sciences. Medical science itself has been based throughout its history on cause–effect relationships, between either symptoms or causative agents (germs) and diseases. The systems perspective is therefore not readily accepted in these sciences because it requires major renovation of their theories and methods of scientific inquiry.

The final system characteristic to be presented in this chapter is steady state. Katz and Kahn call this dynamic homeostasis.[7] Others call it dynamic equilibrium, and Rogers calls it dynamic homeokinesis.[8] The term "steady state" is used in this text, but one of the other words may be more acceptable to the reader.

Steady state refers to the range of flexibility possible for each of numerous components of the units in all living systems. This range of flexibility means that the system can remain stable despite changes and imbalances occurring within and between the units of the system. This range of flexibility has limits.

When the flexibility of the system is exercised beyond its limits, a stress is produced which constitutes a threat to the system. The system must then use its capacities for adaptation, integration, and decision making to reduce the stress and stabilize the system. All the pertinent mechanisms described in this chapter are brought into play. The system uses feedback to make decisions about obtaining, containing, disposing, and retaining with the goal of reentering a steady state. An example would be a family that experienced temporary or permanent unit loss (eg, run-away child, death of a member, divorce between two members). Such a system would go through a series of processes aimed at returning the family to some level of steady state. This would be accomplished through the processes described above and throughout the chapter. The availability of feedback from outside the system would provide information about the success of achieving a steady state once more.[9]

Application of Systems to Middlescence

The systems perspective is presented in this chapter because it forms the theoretical and analytic framework for the rest of the book. In the next four chapters, social system assumptions underlie the definitions and descriptions of work and leisure, marriage and the family, community, and maturation. In Chapters 7, 8, and 9, the distinctions between maturational crises and situational crises in youth and young adulthood, in the core of the middle years, and in the new middle years are systems-tied. That is, maturational crises emanate from differentiable sets of variables in the individual and his significant others. These tend to be more closely tied at the subsystem level. Situational crises emanate from other differentiable sets of variables, which tend more often to emanate from the suprasystem level. These distinctions between situational and maturational crises are oversimplified here for brevity, but the generalizations are accurate in the aggregate. The approach taken in the following chapters is to deal with the issues of growth and development of individuals through the middle decades of the life cycle by means of systems theory and systems analysis.

ROLE THEORY

Several concepts used in the subsequent parts of the book have specific sociologic meanings in this text. To some extent at least, these meanings differ from the way they are used in the vernacular or in some of the health care professional journals. These concepts emanate from role theory and fit into the overall framework of social systems theory as it is described in the first part of this chapter. These role concepts will be used to describe the location of people and their activities in the four major areas of the life space, which are work and leisure, family, community, and self.

Norm: The smallest unit of social structure. Norm is required or accepted behavior that provides both the standards for behaving and the standards for judging the behavior. Norms are translated into acts that are then judged as appropriate or inappropriate by the other person(s) in the situation. The prime mover also possesses the ability to judge the effect of his behavior. This capacity to evaluate comes from the enculturation process.

Role: The second-level unit of social structure. Role consists of any subset of grouped norms that are more or less integrated. The role is made up of similar norms, which might be considered a category. *All roles are dyadic relationships.* Power distribution in the dyad is variable. In some role relationships one person is the dominant role altercaster and the other person is the target of the altercasting. In other role relationships the altercasting attempts are roughly equal. In still other relationships, there may be a power struggle over who has the right to do the altercasting. The following example illustrates the first case with a well-defined altercaster.

Example: Consider a mother and newborn infant. The mother is the role altercaster, the infant is influenced by the mother's behavior. The infant learns his role from the altercasting behavior of the mother. At the same time the infant's behavior influences the mother's next behavior and so on. Mother and child form a role dyad. She cannot be a mother without a child, and the child cannot thrive without mothering. The mother has a set of norms about her behavior in relation to the infant and also has a set of norms about the infant's behavior in relation to her. She judges whether her actions are appropriate and whether the infant's responses are appropriate on the basis of these learned norms.

Status-position: The third-level unit of social structure. The terms "position" or "status-position" are used interchangeably to signify the locations of people in social systems. Status-positions are filled with incumbents but are not synonymous with those individual persons. The position exists regardless of the present occupant. Examples are governor of a state, minister of a church, supervisor of a plant, and father of a family. A position is made up of many roles, and any individual in society can hold several positions simultaneously. Positions are held in the areas of work, leisure, family, and community. Some positions are much more complex than others because of the numbers and complexity of the role sets that make up certain positions. For example, an administrator of a health care agency must have the position of administrator plus other positions as committee chairperson, as consultant to other agencies, as member of other allied organizations, and so on. Bertrand[10] refers to the total set of one person's status-positions within one organization as situs. He uses the word "station" to refer to the total set of one person's status-positions in the whole society. Thus, the list of terms in ascending order of complexity is as follows: norm, role, status-position, situs, and station.

The reader should understand that, in the vernacular, people tend to use the term "role" to mean many things—for example, to refer both to the tasks or activities of a position and to the interpersonal relationships of that position. Most generally, role is seen as a singular or one-sided concept, eg, the expanded role of the nurse. In this book, role always refers to a dyadic relationship; it takes two people to enact each half of the role dyad: parent–child, wife–husband, employer–employee, congressman–congressman, and lawyer–client, to name just a few examples. It is therefore meaningless to speak of an "expanded role" for health care extenders. One can speak of an expanded nurse–client relationship, of the expanded nurse–physician relationship, or of the expanded tasks carried out by the care extender.

In the chapters that follow, the terms "norm," "role," "status-position," "situs," and "station" are used as they have been defined. Norm means some small piece of expected behavior, role refers to the reciprocal relationship in a dyad, and position means one cluster of roles in a group or organization. Situs means the total of all positions held by one person in one organization, and station refers to the sum total of all positions held by one person in the various groups and organizations of which he is a member in the whole society.

Dimensions of Role

Role relationships are exceedingly important to developing human beings as they live out their lives in social systems. Haas has contributed significantly to the understanding of role relationships by describing four dimensions that are inherent in every role dyad regardless of its nature.[11] The four dimensions are task, authority, affect, and deference.

The task or activity dimension refers to the division of tasks between the members of the dyad. Each is expected to perform some subset of activities in the relationship. An example would be the specification of which marital partner is expected to initiate sexual activities or even how the whole sexual encounter is played out vis-à-vis activities enacted by one partner or the other. The task dimension of role implies that, when one partner is regularly expected to carry out a task in the relationship, that task is considered part of his role in this dyad.

The authority dimension operates the same way as the task dimension in terms of habituated expectations, but in this instance the focus is on who holds the power in the relationship. Every role contains norms about how decision making will progress. In other words, there are always norms about how much authority each partner has in relation to the other partner.

The third dimension is affect or the sentiment dimension. Dyadic relationships contain some specification about how the actors should feel toward each other. Sometimes actors are supposed to love each other or resent or hate each other. In other relationships, such as worker–worker relationships, strong affect such as love or hate is frowned on, and the sentiment expectations are closer to mutual respect.

The last dimension is deference. This refers to whose needs take precedence. In the mother–infant dyad, the mother typically defers to the infant's needs. In a professional–client dyad, the professional is expected to defer to the needs of the client.

The four dimensions of role refer to the predetermined direction in which a set of norms are to go. Knowledge of these dimensions can be extremely useful in analyzing role conflict. When people do not get along, analysis of their difficulty usually shows that there is a mismatch in one or more of the four dimensions; that is, they are not congruent. One partner may expect more sharing of authority than the other partner. One partner may expect more overt signs of affection than the other partner. Perhaps there is recurrent conflict over whose needs come first or who should perform which activity. The four dimensions cover the gamut of potential conflicts that may occur between people in work, in leisure, in family life, or in community participation.

References

1. A. Koestler, *The Ghost in the Machine* (London: Hutchinson, 1967).
2. H. C. Bredemeier, "Social Systems—Integration and Adaptation," unpublished manuscript. (New Brunswick, N.J.: Rutgers, The State University). Also in S. A. Smoyak, "Toward Understanding Nursing Situations: A Transaction Paradigm," *Nursing Research* 18(September–October 1969): 405–411.
3. Ibid.
4. Ibid.
5. L. Von Bertalanffy, "The Theory of Open Systems in Physics and Biology," *Science* 3 (13 January 1950): 23–35.
6. Ibid.
7. D. Katz and R. Kahn, *The Social Psychology of Organizations* (New York: Wiley, 1966).
8. M. Rogers, *An Introduction to the Theoretical Basis of Nursing* (Philadelphia: Davis, 1970).
9. Ibid.
10. A. Bertrand, *Social Organization: A General Systems and Role Theory Perspective* (Philadelphia: Davis, 1972).
11. J. E. Haas, *Role Conception and Group Consensus* (Columbus, Ohio: Bureau of Business Research Monograph 117, 1964).

Suggested Readings

Anderson, R.E., and Carter, I.E. *Human Behavior in the Social Environment: A Social Systems Approach.* Chicago: Aldine, 1974.

Berrien, T.K. *General and Social Systems.* New Brunswick, N.J.: Rutgers, The State University, 1968, p. 197.

Bertrand, A. *Social Organization: A General Systems and Role Theory Perspective.* Philadelphia: Davis, 1972, pp. 97–105.

Boulding, K.E. "General Systems Theory—The Skeletons of Science." *Management Science* 2 (1956):198–200.

Bredemeier, H.C., and Stephenson, R.M. *The Analysis of Social Systems.* New York: Holt, 1962.

Buckley, W. *Sociology and Modern Systems Theory.* Englewood Cliffs, N.J.: Prentice-Hall, 1967, p. 39.

Churchman, C.W. *The Systems Approach.* New York: Dell, 1968.

Katz, D., and Kahn, R.L. *The Social Psychology of Organizations.* New York: Wiley, 1966, pp. 19–26.

Koestler, A. *The Ghost in the Machine.* London: Hutchinson, 1967.

Kuhn, A. *The Logic of Systems.* San Francisco: Jossey-Bass, 1974, pp. 282–283, 390, 433–434, 437.

Miller, J.G. "Living Systems; Basic Concepts." *Behavioral Science* 10 (1965): 193.

Rogers, M.E. *An Introduction to the Theoretical Basis of Nursing.* Philadelphia: Davis, 1970, p. 51.

Smoyak, S.A. "Toward Understanding Nursing Situations: A Transaction Paradigm." *Nursing Research* 18 (September 1969): 405–411.

Von Bertalanffy, L. *General Systems Theory.* New York: Braziller, 1968.

Wiener, N. *The Human Use of Human Beings.* Garden City, N.Y.: Doubleday, 1954.

II

SIGNIFICANT ISSUES DURING THE MIDDLE YEARS

Four major areas of experience make up the adult's life space. The choice of only four is somewhat arbitrary, and other persons might wish to name different areas or may see the need to differentiate between ones that have been merged here. The four major areas of life that are discussed at length in the four chapters in Part II are (1) work and leisure; (2) the family, including the marital relationship and child-rearing functions; (3) community responsibility and participation; (4) development of personal maturity.

Work is discussed first in Chapter 3. It is an instrumental activity that many people use as a justification for their continued existence. Work is highly valued in North American culture. Leisure is considered by many to be the antithesis of work, but a truly satisfactory definition for leisure has eluded us to date, perhaps because our culture is tied up with the work ethic. The problem is that activity that is work for some is leisure for others, and so the only distinction becomes a matter of how it is defined by the actor.

In Chapter 4 on the family, marriage is discussed as an intimate, enduring sexual companionship mode that includes not only heterosexual couples married in traditional ways, but also variant styles of marriage and enduring homosexual relationships. The family is also viewed traditionally and contemporaneously. A definition of family presented which covers the traditional forms of nuclear and extended kinship networks, the variant forms of non-blood-related "families," variant familial forms created by the high divorce rate and successive remarriages, adoptions, and extralegal arrangements of children living with grandparents or other nonparental relatives, and other enduring congregate living patterns.

Chapter 5 deals with the adult's participation in community life. Community participation is presented in terms of the responsibilities of adults to direct, lead, manage, plan, and implement community life through government, business, service organizations, and the extrafamily organizations that enculturate such as education and religion.

The development of the adult self is discussed in some detail in the chapter on family; in Chapter 6, it is discussed from a more individualistic standpoint. The adult self is largely the accumulation of all prior life experiences. In addition, there are other historical and contemporary experiences that impinge on the development of maturity. Several of these, such as personal philosophy of life, spirituality, self-concept, aspirations, and personal goals in life, are discussed. The area of religion is not considered to be a fifth focus but is subsumed within this discussion of adult maturation in the context of changes in the man—nature—supernature relationship.

The concept of maturity presented here attempts to dispel the idea that maturity is a static goal to be reached. Rather, it is presented as a constantly changing process with differing criteria and standards. Maturity at 25 means that one is current in terms of the developmental tasks of that stage; maturity at 60 means that one is current in terms of the developmental tasks of that stage; and so on. A final static maturity is not reached until the process of dying is experienced, perhaps not even then.

An early section in the chapter on work contains distinctions between the sexes. The historical overview of how human begins developed into workers contains distinctions between the historical development of men's work and women's work. These distinctions are contrasted with the trends evident in the late 1970s away from the clear-cut distinctions between men's work and women's work. Some of these clear-cut sex distinctions in the area of leisure are fading as well. Similarly, the clear-cut sex-determined functions in the family and in the community are blurring. Finally; through the efforts of the women's movement and other minority movements of modern times, the formulation of adult self-concepts may be more singularly *human* in form, and variations may be independent of age, sex, or race. In the future, self-concepts should become less tied to the traditional stereotypes of age, sex, race, or religion. However, that is not to say that self-concepts will become more reality-based. That would be a worthy dream, but it is just as likley that new stereotypes based on other differences among peoples will take the place of race, sex, age, or religion.

3

WORK AND LEISURE

Work is something that nearly everyone knows something about from firsthand experience. Building a generally acceptable definition of work is difficult but it is possible to do. The term "leisure" is much more elusive, and man has generally given up trying to define it in operational terms. Instead, leisure has usually been described as the antithesis of work. This seems a shoddy way to treat such a noble concept. The Greeks venerated leisure to a high degree and saw work as drudgery not fit for learned men. Middle-class Americans seem to take an almost totally opposite view. They tend to worship work and have disdain for nonwork.

The first part of this chapter deals with the evolution of work and the division of labor between the sexes as it developed during the evolution of the human race over the past several thousand years. A modern definition of work is presented and discussed along with the views of work held by learned men throughout history.

The section on the place of work in adult development contains a discussion of the developmental tasks presented in Chapter 1 that pertain to work. The work-related tasks relevant to each phase in the adult life cycle are discussed briefly within the context of the concept of work and its meaning to modern society.

Finally, there is a discussion of leisure, including an attempt at defining what it is rather than what it is not. The brief presentation on leisure is followed by a reiteration of the developmental tasks that involve leisure together with a discussion about them and their meaning to persons in the various age groups.

WORK IN HUMAN EVOLUTION

Very little is known about how people in antiquity perceived human labor. The fragmentary evidence available from history, from the remains of Stone Age peoples, and the study of primitive tribes existing today indicate that work has had different cultural meanings in different societies at various points in their evolution. Morgan developed a model of cultural evolution based on the various modes by which man maintained his existence and obtained subsistence from nature.[1] He categorized the evolution of *Homo sapiens* into three stages. Each stage represents a substantial enhancement in the resources that man used to subsist. The three major stages of savagery, barbarism, and civilization are each further subdivided into low, middle, and high phases to communicate something about the development of labor and the inventions with each stage. Table 1 depicts these three stages and their primary forms of work.[2] In the low phase of savagery, early man depended on gathering for subsistence. Each person probably ate directly from a bush or the ground and then learned to gather small quantities of solid foodstuffs in his hands. At the same time, the original form of hunting was probably the physical hand catching of slow animals. It is not clear how division of labor between the sexes began to be crystallized, but it may have occurred through the middle stage of this age. Most authors hypothesize that both men and women gathered and hunted when this required minimal physical strength and no specialized, practiced skills or a long period away from camp. Birthing and breastfeeding of infants were jobs that could be done by women only, and some of their time and energy was taken up this way. Men probably had more free time to spend in working on ways to improve their physical skills and to spend away from the cave or camp. The invention of stone implements and weapons is generally attributed to men.

Labeling this era the Stone Age is an example of naming a culture according to the major characteristics of its inventions, which typically are inventions to help in human labor. In particular, these instruments extended the physical capabilities of the human body. Data indicate that there were two significant forms of human invention: stone weapons and containers. In their earliest form, containers were probably naturally occurring concave objects found in

TABLE 1. Overview of the Three Ages of Man

TIME LINE

	SAVAGERY			BARBARISM			CIVILIZATION		
	Low	Middle	High	Low	Middle	High	Low	Middle	High
Types of work	Nomads Hunters and gatherers			Squatters Tillers of soil			Property owners Industrialists		
Man–nature relationship	Adaptation to nature			Human intervention in nature Cultivation of land Domestication of animals			Human manipulation of nature on mass scale Commodities exceed needs Transportation and communication by technology		
Inventions	Early stone implements Gathering devices Snares, weapons Cooking of food			Instruments for animal herding and tending Gardening tools Semi-permanent dwellings Cloth processing Food processing for storage			Work by machines Simple motors to computers and space technology		

After Morgan[2]

59

the area—nests, shells, hulls, and the like. Later, containers were made by paring out the middle portion of logs or stones.

In all likelihood, men and women began to move toward division of labor in this period. Men began to specialize in hunting and in the invention of techniques and instruments to improve their hunting. Some of the literature puts hunting and fishing together as men's work, but this seems to be oversimplified. Shoreline fishing could easily have been done by women, while fishing in boats for extended periods of time, making heavy catches, or using unwieldy nets were probably done by men. Crying infants could have been detrimental to landing a good catch of fish, so this may have added to the rationale for making fishing a man's job.

Women did not shirk their responsibilities as workers simply because of their child-rearing tasks. They became specialists in the invention of techniques and instruments to improve the process of gathering or, to put it more correctly, to expand the quantity of gathering that could be done and the quantity of foodstuffs that could be carried back to the tribal headquarters. So they invented containers. Too often, authors put all the emphasis on the invention of weapons and cutting instruments but give no credit to the equally significant invention of containers and holders.[3] Whether these two types of invention really split along sex lines cannot be proved. However, the probability is high that they did because infants could be taken along on gathering parties, where they were fed on demand, but they could not be taken along on hunting parties, where their unpredictable behavior might disturb the prey or endanger the whole hunting party.[4]

By the end of the high phase of savagery, both the technology of hunting and the technology of containing were well underway.

The second stage is called barbarism and is associated with the development of settled agriculture and the large-scale domestication of animals. Like the age of savagery, the age of barbarism had low, middle, and high phases. The low phase represented the initial transition from the nomadic life of hunting, fishing, and gathering to the early dawn of agriculture. The earliest farmers did not sow grain; they simply harvested what grew wild. They did not initially breed animals, but simply collected them from the surrounding areas and domesticated them. During the later phases of barbarism, true sowing of seeds and tilling of the soil as well as breeding, tending, and herding animals became institutionalized human activities.

Specialization in the types of labor to be performed by each sex continued. Men were more mobile, did heavier work, risked greater physical dangers, and were responsible for domesticated animal care as well as attack and defense from enemies. Men were responsible for fabricating what they used—primitive fences, herding staffs, and instruments for stunning, slaughtering, skinning, and carving animals. Women concentrated on the field work with crops, the domestic work, and the child care. Women became the fabricators of clothing and household items and the processors of food. Women may have been responsible for inventing furniture, garden implements, weaving devices, and the continued elaboration of container technology. There were no specialists among these workers except on the basis of sex. All men made implements to fulfill their tasks, and all women made implements to fulfill their tasks. Even chiefs and shamans were primarily laborers who worked side by side with the other tribal members all day and acted in their specialty positions at other times.

As described in Chapter 1, the concept of childhood did not exist at this time, so there were only two age groups—infants and adults. Women did somewhat less strenuous physical work and stayed at jobs where they could nurture the infants. Infants in primitive societies continued to nurse until about 7 years of age, when they became adults and were expected to take part in the labors of the tribe.

The high phase of barbarism included the years of feudalism in Europe. The accomplishments of all these peoples brought us to what is commonly called civilization. The most noteworthy contribution that civilization made to the realm of human labor was the Industrial Revolution. The changes brought about were unprecedented in kind, scope, and speed through the prior history of mankind.

The Industrial Revolution had its beginning in Britain in the 1760s but did not really have an impact on the United States until much later. When the steam engine went into mass production nobody really gave much thought to the impact it would have on the relationship between men or on the relationship between man and work. Division of labor, specialization, and interchangeability of workers led to alienation of the worker from his work. The worker was no longer a jack-of-all-trades who did all parts of a construction and could claim ownership of the production in a personal sense. Rather, he was just a pair of hands that put a part together on an assembly line. When he looked at the finished product, he was hard put to place significance on the part that he had contributed to the whole.

The foregoing description of the negative results of industrialization are grossly oversimplified, but it does state in brief the major disadvantage most often described by the classic writers on this topic.[5-9]

Civilization brought money to people who were not born as kings, and this resulted in the creation of new monied populations: the industrialists or nouveau riche. Civilization pushed the Western world into a value orientation of human manipulation of nature—of the land, the minerals, the sky, and other men. In this way it was possible for a relatively few workers to produce food and other commodities that fulfilled the needs of most of the nonworking population. Children, the aged, and the disabled could be subsidized from what the workers produced.

The major inventions of civilization include work done in part or in whole by machines, transportation of people and commodities by mechanized transportation systems, and mass communication networks that keep widespread peoples in immediate touch with what is happening around the world and in outer space. Mankind seemed to go through several stages of development in order to catch up with the impact that the Industrial Revolution had on mankind. The world went through joyful acceptance of the mass production and new money, through tragic suffering from wars that were worldwide for the first time, through a long period of suspicion and cold war mixed with aid to underdeveloped countries in the form of food and weapons, and now apparently through detente on the world level and encounter groups at the interpersonal level. Leonard states not only that the world is about to undergo a transformation, but that some of the world is already engaged in it.[10] The rising popularity of transcendental meditation, yoga, and other Eastern forms of spiritual systems may attest to the beginning of this transformation.

The age of industrial technology and the rise of cities changed the historical view of men's work and women's work from *different but equally necessary and equally worthwhile*. There was a definite movement toward different and unequal. A distinction began to arise between paid and unpaid labor. It became a cultural belief that only activity done for pay was true work. Once a money economy was firmly established, household labor and bearing and caring for children were no longer considered work. In industrialized societies there is a firm bond between work and compensation. Many believe that one works only when money changes hands. This close connection between work and money drastically changed the differential male–female status vis-à-vis work. This occurred because the household and child-rearing forms of labor were left out of the work-for-monetary-compensation network. Under these circumstances only the male wage earner came to be called a worker. And the term "working woman" has come to signify those women who hold a job outside the home or make some commodity in their home for which money is exchanged. The position of housewife was excluded from the labor market, and the position eventually took on the amended label of "only a housewife." While the roles and functions of the position remained basically the same, the status changed drastically during the postindustrial period.

MEANING OF WORK FOR HUMAN BEINGS

Neff maintains that man is the only "working animal" and that work represents a significant qualitative distinction between human and infrahuman animals.[11] Archeologists use the presence of artifacts like stone tools as an important distinguishing factor when they are deciding whether a set of bones is human. Many animals do something akin to work for their subsistence. They build nests, build dams, make honey, obtain and store foods. However, only *Homo sapiens* plans and implements alterations in the physical environment.[12] In the preceding discussion of man in the age of savagery, man was described as a hunter. But man is poorly equipped in a physical sense to be a hunter. He cannot run fast; he is clumsy and weak compared to the animals he wishes to hunt. Man was the only animal unable to depend on his natural physical resources to capture game; hence, he began to invent prosthetic devices to extend or enhance his own body's capabilities. Man learned to dig pits, to make clubs from branches, to make snares, and to sharpen stones into spears.

Neff states that there are four basic elements in the meaning of work to man: (1) Work is an essentially human activity; (2) work is an instrumental activity; (3) work is required to maintain life, so it is self-preservative; and (4) work is an alterative activity. In Neff's definition,

work is an instrumental activity carried out by human beings, the object of which is to preserve and maintain life, which is directed at a planful alteration of certain features of man's environment.[13]

The earliest recorded ideas about the meaning of work came from the ancient Hebrews and Greeks. They saw work as punishment for evil or a curse. The Greeks developed a slave state so that the male citizens could be freed of work in order to spend time in higher pursuits in the cognitive domain. During the Dark Ages, a distinction evolved between intellectual or spiritual forms of work, which came to be called the liberal arts in medieval universities, and manual labor, which came to be called servile work.[14]

People of the Middle Ages saw work as an obligatory part of life but worked only for sustenance. They did not believe in saving or earning interest. The religious leaders of the era viewed making money without work as evil, and this belief held sway. Later, views began to change, and there was some recognition of value beyond working for the basics of life. A slow realization dawned that beyond a hand-to-mouth existence lay a better life that contained the life of contemplation. Monks and other religious contemplatives were thus able to spend their time in preserving the culture through the study of books and translating and copying written materials. Tighler reports that Luther modified the meaning of work somewhat. He ruled that all should work, even the contemplatives and intellectuals in the monasteries and universities. He saw work as the best way to serve God.[15]

Calvin allegedly made major changes in cultural attitudes toward work, and Weber views this as one of the major influences that opened the way for capitalism.[16] Calvin viewed men as intrinsically evil but mutable according to the Kluckholn–Strodtbeck paradigm in Table 3, Chapter 1. He saw work as the only means available to curb evil; that is, he saw work as a means of mutability for man. In order to serve this purpose, work must be continuous, and man must reject the fruits of it. The followers of Calvin thus invested their payments for work, and the whole notion of investment began to take root. The investment of money from work had deep religious connotations for the Calvinists. It was a rejection of money and therefore a strong proof of religious standing. Weber points out that with the practice of investment, money began to make money and the stage was set for capitalism.[17]

Leonardo da Vinci viewed work in a very different way, and his view expresses the spirit of the Renaissance. He believed that work was the act of mastering nature. By the act of work, man became less animal and more human or even godlike. The da Vinci influence spread the value of work as intrinsically worthwhile, as both a means and an end in itself.[18] Lofquist and Dawas summarize three basic meanings that work had up to the time of the Industrial Revolution: (1) Work was a curse or punishment that was painful; (2) work was an instrumental activity, a means to an end, especially a religious end; (3) work was both the means and the end. In the third view, work was considered intrinsically good because it distinguished man from subhuman forms.[19]

The Industrial Revolution brought a fourth dimension to the meaning of work: the function of work in manipulating man's self-concept. Much of the behavioral science literature on the meaning of work (post-Industrial Revolution) indicates that, in the man–machine system, man is reduced to a machine tender and the concept of work as intrinsically good is lost. Under these circumstances man becomes a slave to a nonliving form, the caretaker of machines. He feels dehumanized. Men whose self-concepts are enhanced by their work are afforded high status. Professions such as the ministry, law, medicine, and dentistry are examples of work that aggrandizes the self-concept. Supposedly this occurs because such workers are not machine tenders but are human caretakers. They provide services to other individuals that are of worth in the society.

THE PLACE OF WORK IN ADULT DEVELOPMENT

The tasks presented in Chapter 1 for the phases of adult life will be looked at in a different context. This time the issue of work and its development through the phases will be emphasized. The developmental tasks related to work during young adulthood are tasks 1 and 5. Although task 1 refers to all four areas of life, we will be concerned only with how it relates to work. Task 5 deals with the relationship between value orientation, career development, and money.

Task 1 —Advancing self-development and the enactment of appropriate roles and positions in society. This developmental task refers to the maturing processes that result from enacting responsible roles and positions in society. The underlying thesis is that the enactment of roles and positions makes us what we are. The interaction among people that is implemented through role enactment is an educative process. Man as a social animal cannot exist, and therefore cannot learn, outside society.

Task 5 —Integrating personal values with career development and socioeconomic constraints. One's beliefs about man and the nature of human life will determine to some extent how a career will be chosen and how it will be carried through.

The tasks of the core of the middle years that are work related include tasks 1 and 7.

Task 1—Developing socioeconomic consolidation. Most persons in the society produce greater monetary earnings during middle adulthood than during young adulthood. In some instances they also command more earnings during middle adulthood than they will at a later stage in life. The years between 30 and 50 represent the time when savings accounts, insurance policies, stocks and bonds, and retirement plans become important to Americans. A significant number of people purchase real estate, particularly houses. There is less spending of money on immediate gratifications and more concern with long-term goals and future needs.

Task 7—Assuming responsible positions in occupational, social, and civic activities, organizations, and communities. During these years, the people in society who seek upward mobility in their occupations and who have the wherewithal to move into higher positions will do so. Apprenticeships of all kinds are completed, and persons become full-fledged members of the occupation. This is true both in the skilled trades and in the professions. People move into whatever track is appropriate to that occupation. There they can begin to climb the career ladder.

For another segment of the working population there can be no upward mobility, or at least they can see no possibility of it. These people have several choices: (1) to become more skilled at their job, if this is possible, and gain satisfaction from their skills;* (2) to live their life outside of work and numb themselves during the periods of work;† or (3) to perhaps increase the quantity of their output in situations in which high productivity brings in more earnings.[20] The last alternative could hold for small-business owners who cannot be promoted in the bureaucratic sense because they do not work in bureaucracies.

The developmental tasks of the new middle years that pertain to work are tasks 1, 2, and 7.

Task 1—Maintaining flexible views in occupational, civic, political, religious, and social positions.

Task 2—Keeping current on relevant scientific, political, and cultural changes.

---

*The mason in Studs Terkel's book Working is a good example of this.
†The steelworker in Studs Terkel's book Working exemplifies this approach.

The thrust of the first two developmental tasks is to prevent the conflict that so often arises among workers in different stages of life. The youngest ones are most willing to take risks, to try something new, while the persons in the new middle years may be reluctant to take such chances. Certainly it seems appropriate to decrease risk taking in later life. Nevertheless, the people who avoid stagnation and senility in late adulthood are those who remain open to innovation and change in all spheres of life including the work sphere. In terms of post hoc data on the mentally incompetent elderly it seems desirable for persons in the new middle years to continue to learn, to be open to new ideas, and to keep current on matters that are relevant to their work. It is particularly important that they continue to expand their knowledge base during these years rather than operate with knowledge and attitudes gained in their own youth.

Task 7—Preparing for retirement and planning another career when feasible. Retirement has different meanings for different workers. Many people who have worked at monotonous jobs all their life see retirement as a hard-earned reward for the labor they have come to detest. They view retirement as a prize, something they have earned the right to enjoy.

Other persons view retirement with a mixture of dread and anticipation. They may be glad to end a boring, impersonal job but afraid of what retirement will mean in their lives. What they will find to do in the ensuing years is unclear and fearful.

A third group of people may view retirement in an extremely negative light. They resent forced retirement, resent turning their position over to others, and wish to continue in the job indefinitely.

A fourth group of people may see retirement as an opportunity to do what they have wanted to do but could not because of job constraints. They plan far in advance for what they will do after retirement. They may plan to travel or engage more time in a hobby, an organization, or an art form. They may return to school for more education. Military personnel who retire in their middle years are particularly prone to earn additional academic degrees after their military retirement.

The value explicated in the seventh developmental task is that each person should spend time defining what retirement will mean in his life and prepare for it. The financial preparation is very important in a time of rapid inflation, because living on a fixed income is a substantial cut from the salary that one is accustomed to receiving.

Perhaps even more important than the financial preparation is the emotional preparation. The worker must come to grips with the phenomenon in industrial societies called human obsolescence, the time when society defines that people are no longer desirable as workers. Primitive societies of nomads traditionally left their ancient members to die alone when they could not keep up with the tribe. When they could no longer climb mountains or cross rivers, they simply separated themselves from the tribe. However, this was on the basis of physical criteria rather than chronologic age. People in modern times are typically very physically capable of additional years of active participation in society. However, they are subjected to a form of discrimination that Maggie Kuhn and the Gray Panthers call "agism." While agism is a pervasive form of discrimination based on one's age rather than on sex or race or religion, the effects are similar.

Emotional preparation for retirement includes acceptance of one's life up to this point and an early form of life review. Retirement is a maturational crisis and is discussed in more detail in Chapter 9. It is important to note that the trend in American society is toward earlier retirement, and so retirees have more chance for a second career. In some cases this is a hobby of some kind that is turned into a business. In other cases the activity may be more in the line of a service to be rendered. Frequently people in the retired population have skills that younger persons do not possess. Handiwork around the house and the grounds, knowledge of gardening, and carpentry are but a few examples. In still other instances highly developed managerial skills can be put to work in charitable organizations that could not afford to pay the high salaries commanded by young or middle adults. Many retired business people can render a real service in voluntary service organizations.

A significant number of retired workers simply take to their houses after retirement. They fill their day with television or other sedentary pursuits that amount to "taking in" what others have produced. Such people may become narrow, self-centered, and rigid fairly quickly. They form a sharp contrast to outgoing retired persons who carry a date book to keep track of their commitments. People in the latter group have active, alive faces; they are alert and spirited.

The contrast is almost identical to the contrast one can see between groups of young children. One group seems dull. They have the pitiful faces of those who are unstimulated, who are overstuffed with television, who do not engage in cognitively or socially stimulating relationships with adults or other children. The contrasting group are bright-eyed, active, highly verbal and imaginative, excited, and assertive children who are regularly challenged and stimulated by people and experiences in their environment. A similar contrast is distinguishable between the elderly who are bright and alive and those who are bored and depersonalized.

The contention is that people of all ages atrophy and become less human when they remain inactive in the three domains of human existence. They become cognitively dull, emotionally numb, and physically stiff from inactivity.

Even in late adulthood there are developmental tasks that refer to work. This is in keeping with the value inherent in this book that death is the last stage of human development.

Task 1—Pursuing a second or third career, new interest, hobbies, and/or community activities that fulfill some heretofore untapped inner resource or otherwise enhance self-image and maintain worth in society. This task is similar to the one dealing with retirement in the new middle years. The value is the same—that persons in the postretirement years should remain fully human in the best sense of that word. If Neff is correct and work is actually one of the distinguishing features of human beings, they should do it until death or at least until physical incapacity occurs. We know that great segments of our work force hate their work. Therefore, they are challenged to find different pursuits that can still be categorized as work or useful activity of some kind. This activity need not fill a five-day week, as many persons can best handle two or three days of worklike activity per week. Persons is the middle eighties that are known to this author manage better on about three or four days of work per month. That is still useful in maintaining the image of self as worker and worthwhile contributor to society.

Task 2—Learning new skills that are well removed from prior learnings or at least do not produce cognitive dissonance with prior learnings. The rationale for this task was described in some detail in Chapter 1. To reiterate briefly, this task was developed to cover the results of many research studies indicating that persons form habit patterns and attitudes around phenomena that are familiar to them, for example, their preretirement occupations, which may be nonuseful to them elsewhere. Rather than attempt to modify these attitudes and habit patterns slightly, it is often easier for them to engage in something about which they have a minimal backlog of experience. In this way they can start "fresh" with learning as a neophyte in that occupation. Although this task is based on research findings, there is plenty of room for doubt about its necessity and its feasibility. Most of the work that older persons find to do is "people oriented." In one way or another the services that they can best perform involve offering some kind of service to people. Hence, their previous interpersonal relationship patterns come into play, and in those cases in which interpersonal skills and attitudes about people are negative they have trouble unless they are willing to change in a positive direction. Managerial skills, mathematical skills, as well as interpersonal skills all transfer well to new situations. Even when these situations appear to be different in significant ways, basic skills such as those listed above can usually be transferred well.

LEISURE

Any discussion of leisure seems to begin with the confession that defining leisure is an elusive goal. Most people do not know what it is, and others who claim that they do disagree with each other. Many descriptions of leisure tell one what it is not. For example, Sebastian de Grazia says it is "freedom from the necessity of being occupied."[21] This type of description gives us minimal information because it focuses on what leisure is not. This statement does not tell us what the phenomenon is, but rather that it is freedom from something else. Aristotle discussed leisure at length in Politics, and in truly Greek fashion concluded that it was "a state of being in which activity is performed for its own sake or its own end." He finally listed only two activities worthy of the term "leisure:"[22] music and contemplation. Artistotle and de Grazia are very careful to distinguish between leisure and recreation. Recreation is more like play, a frivolous kind of activity that is not so much an end in itself but gives the variety and the relaxation of mind and body that one needs in order to return to work and be productive once more. The "rest and recreation" that military personnel were given in tourist areas outside Vietnam is an example of positively sanctioned recreation that employers believe to be necessary at designated periods in the working year.

The distinction between recreation and leisure is sharp and clear for some people such as Aristotle. But Friedmann seems to equate the two and speaks about all manner of hobbies engaged in by the English, French, and North Americans as "active leisure time pursuits." He defines a true leisure activity as something freely chosen and pursued at the time and in the manner desired by the actor, who expects from it satisfaction and even a certain inner growth.[23]

Besides occupation, recreation, and leisure there are other activities that should also be mentioned and put into some category. A person must see to his own hygienic and physical needs and attend to housework and repair work routinely. Even if hired persons take care of cleaning, fixing, and gardening they must be interviewed and their work supervised. The vast majority of American workers carry out their own domestic chores in whole or in part. Examples are weekend lawn mowing, leaf raking in the fall, and maintenance of the house and other buildings. Inside the house there are myriad jobs to be performed daily or at least weekly which must be done by or for all people regardless of their occupation. These activities might be classified as maintenance activities. They are neither chosen nor particularly desirable to do, and so they cannot be called leisure or recreation pursuits. Nor are they work in the sense of the major occupational pursuit. In the case of the "traditional housewife" such activities do constitute the major work in life, at least for some period of years. But this phenomenon is rapidly decreasing since many women now work outside the home or do something inside the home that goes beyond family maintenance and actually adds to the income. In these instances the housework still must be done frequently at night and on weekends. Division of the maintenance chores among all family members regardless of sex is becoming more common.

Another difficulty with finding a clear definition of leisure and being able to distinguish between work, leisure, and recreation is that many times an activity can be any of the three depending on the intent or the function that the actor has in mind. For example, painting can be leisure if it is an art form engaged in for its own sake. If a commercialized painting kit that allows no free expression is used, it might be considered recreation. In this context, paint by number might be closer to recreation than to leisure. For the commercial artist, painting is work. In this instance selling the paintings is the goal. One can take other activities through such a test and discover that many of them by nature are not solely work or recreation or leisure. Consider tennis, golf, football; consider singing or playing musical instruments; consider reading. Even watching movies is work for the movie critic and personnel in the motion picture industry. Hence, defining certain activities as work and others as leisure or recreation is not a useful approach.

There are some elements of leisure as it was practiced in ancient Greece and in the ruling classes throughout history that might help us capture the elusive spirit of leisure. Although only the ruling classes were able to enjoy leisure in past centuries, more like a majority of persons in the Western industrial nations have the wherewithal to engage in leisure today.

The elements of leisure are the following:[24]

1. Invokes pleasant anticipation and recollection
2. Is accompanied by a perception of personal freedom
3. Relates closely to values of the culture
4. Has minimal involuntary social position obligations
5. Is antithetical to work as an economic pursuit
6. Covers the range from inconsequential to important impact on society

These elements do seem to capture some of the proper sense of leisure. The anticipation of leisure is pleasant, and its recollection is sweet. Before, during, and after leisure, one has the sense that it was done out of freedom rather than responsibility or obligation. In order to be so pleasurable and free, leisure logically would consist of behaviors that are not negatively sanctioned by the culture. If it did, pangs of guilt or fear would accompany the actions and they would not qualify as leisure. Leisure does have at its core a minimum of obligation and hence a minimum of the status-position sense that one has in work. Leisure is done for its own sake and not for monetary compensation. Finally, the outcomes of leisure may be totally insignificant to the larger society, or they may have a heavy impact. However, by its nature, leisure cannot be goal directed toward societal impact or it becomes work. If there is to be societal impact, it must be accidental.

Another way of pursuing the elusive nature of leisure would be to compare it with work. Table 2 shows the outcome of an attempt to use this approach. The dimensions in Table 2 probably are not exhaustive, but several useful ones are included, and it would be fairly easy to add additional ones as appropriate. Work is designated as more externally controlled than leisure. The external refers to outside the individual. There is more spatial freedom with leisure; that is, leisure is less confined by predetermined spatial boundaries. It is

TABLE 2. Comparison between Work and Leisure

DIMENSION	WORK	LEISURE
Decision-making control	Relatively more external	Relatively more internal
Spatial parameter	Continuity of space	Freedom of space
Time parameter	Structured time	Nonstructured time
Social structure	Permanence of structure	Transiency of structure
Activity	Defined activity	Emerged activity

likewise less bounded by time factors; there are no clocks to punch. The world of work consists of more or less stable and enduring organizational structures; the world of leisure consists of more transient social structures. The activities of work may be complex and varied, but they are nonetheless relatively well defined compared to the activities of leisure, which may be simple or complex but are characterized by spontaneity.

The Place of Leisure in Adult Development

The developmental tasks relating to leisure presented in Chapter 1 will be examined in light of the foregoing discussion about what leisure is and how it differs from work and other categories of human activity.

The second task in the young adulthood phase implies leisure but does not specify it directly.

Task 2—Initiating the development of a personal style of life. This task covers the gamut of behavior patterns that are becoming habits during the young adult period. Among the behavior patterns that are emerging is either a repertoire of habits of leisure or the absence of leisure. There is a tendency to exclude leisure on the part of some highly career-oriented youth. However, most persons crystallize their favorite forms of leisure during the young adult years, and these will probably remain fairly consistent for years to come. Adults go through a variety of changes in their adult years, and some forms of leisure may be added and others discarded. Nonetheless, the underlying likes and dislikes will most likely remain pretty much the same.

Task 9 of the core of the middle years relates to leisure.

Task 9—Using leisure time in satisfying and creative ways. As stated, this task places requirements on the use of leisure time. The exhortation is that leisure time be used in doing something that is personally satisfying. This part of the task is consistent with the elements of leisure discussed earlier in this chapter. For example, one element is that leisure invokes pleasant anticipation and recollection; another is that leisure is accompanied by a perception of personal freedom. Both of these elements logically lead to a personal sense of satisfaction if they are fulfilled.

The second exhortation is that the leisure time be used creatively. The dimensions of leisure compared to work are more apropos to the belief that leisure time ought to have an element of creativity. Recall that leisure is relatively more internal or intrinsic, that it is freer in time and space, and that it is an emergent activity. All these descriptions are simultaneously descriptions of creative activity.

In the new middle years there is one developmental task dealing with leisure.

Task 6 —Deriving satisfaction from increased availability of leisure time.   The term "satisfaction" is used in this task for much the same reason that it is used in the task about leisure in the core of the middle years. The satisfaction element seems most important to designate the activity or inactivity as leisure rather than boredom, loneliness, idleness, or some other description word with a negative connotation. Neugarten found in her studies that persons fit into several varied groupings depending on how they used the additional time available to them as they grew older. Some used it feverishly, much as they had all their lives. Others used it calmly. Some used the rocking chair approach to leisure, while others used the activity approach. Just about all of those interviewed considered their way to be suitable for them. Nearly all reported satisfaction with the freedom to do more of what they wanted to do if and when they wished rather than under the social or occupational pressures they had experienced in the past. As is required for true leisure, these people did not concern themselves with the products of their leisure-time pursuits.[25]

We come to the close of the discussion on leisure and it is still elusive, although some of its elements and dimensions have been elucidated. The paradox remains that the only comprehensible way to describe leisure is to say what it is not. All efforts lead only to a disappointing definition of leisure as participation in some type of activity, either vigorous or relatively passive, that is not required by daily necessities.

References

1. L. H. Morgan, *Ancient Society* (Chicago: Charles H. Kerr, 1887).
2. Ibid.
3. E. Morgan, *The Descent of Woman* (New York: Stein and Day, 1972).
4. O. T. Mason, *Woman's Share in Primitive Culture* (New York: P. Appleton, 1895).
5. E. Durkheim, *The Division of Labor in Society* (New York: Macmillan, 1933).
6. M. Weber, *The Protestant Ethic and the Spirit of Capitalism* (New York: Scribner, 1930).

7. R. Blauner, *Alienation and Freedom: The Factory Worker and His Industry* (Chicago: University of Chicago Press, 1964).
8. E. Mayo, *The Human Problems of an Industrial Civilization* (New York: Macmillan, 1933).
9. D. Riesman, *The Lonely Crowd* (New Haven: Yale University Press, 1953).
10. G. B. Leonard, *The Transformation* (New York: Delacorte Press, 1972).
11. W. S. Neff, *Work and Human Behavior* (New York: Atherton, 1968).
12. Ibid.
13. Ibid., p. 78.
14. L. H. Lofquist and R. V. Dawas, *Adjustment to Work* (New York: Appleton, 1969).
15. A. Tilgher, *Work: What It Has Meant to Men Throughout the Ages* (New York: Harcourt, 1930).
16. Weber, *Protestant Ethic and Spirit of Capitalism.*
17. Ibid.
18. Ibid.
19. Lofquist and Dawas, *Adjustment to Work.*
20. S. Terkel, *Working* (New York: Avon Books, 1974).
21. S. de Grazia, *Of Time, Work, and Leisure* (Garden City, N.Y.: Anchor Books, 1962).
22. Aristotle, *Politics*, trans. Benjamin Jowett (Oxford: Clarendon Press, 1905).
23. G. Friedmann, *The Anatomy of Work, Labor and Leisure, and the Implication of Automation* (New York: Free Press, 1961).
24. M. Kaplan, "The Uses of Leisure," in *Handbook of Social Gerontology*, ed. C. Tibbits (Chicago: University of Chicago Press, 1960).
25. B. L. Neugarten, "Grow Old Along with Me! The Best Is Yet To Be," *Psychology Today* 5(1975):45–81.

Suggested Readings

de Grazia, S. *Of Time, Work, and Leisure.* Garden City, N.Y.: Doubleday, 1964.

Friedmann, G. *The Anatomy of Work, Labor and Leisure, and the Implication of Automation,* New York: Free Press, 1961.

Havighurst, R.J., and Feigenbaum, K. "Leisure and Life-Style." In *Middle Age and Aging.* Edited by B. L. Neugarten. Chicago: University of Chicago Press, 1968.

Kaplan, M. *Technology, Human Values and Leisure.* Nashville: Abingdon Press, 1971.

Lofquist, L.H., and Dawas, R.V. *Adjustment to Work.* New York: Appleton, 1969.

Neff, W.S. *Work and Human Behavior.* New York: Atherton Press, 1968.

Schaw, L.C. *The Bonds of Work: Work in Mind, Time and Tradition.* San Francisco: Jossey-Bass, 1968.

Terkel, S. *Working.* New York: Avon Books, 1974.

4

THE FAMILY

A social systems framework will be used to present pertinent ideas about the family as a social institution of major importance during adult life. Many discussions about the family refer only to a specific kind, the legally sanctioned man–woman marriage contract, which produces a relatively independent nuclear family. Exemplifying this approach are such writers as Bell and Vogel, who say that "the family is a structural unit composed, as an ideal type, of a man and woman joined in a socially recognized union and their children."[1] This "ideal type" definition lacks utility for health care professionals who are preparing to care for a myriad of variant rather than ideal types. Murdock includes a few more helpful criteria in his definition:

> The family is a social group characterized by common residence, economic cooperation and reproduction. It includes adults of both sexes, at least two of whom maintain a socially approved sexual relationship, and one or more children, own or adopted, of the sexually cohabiting adults.[2]

The major difficulty posed by the Murdock definition is the restriction of sexual cohabitation by adults of each sex. The majority of American families may still fit this requirement, but the number of variant forms is so large that to pretend that none of them lives in families seems ridiculous.

A definition of family that would suit the needs of professional health care workers must be more inclusive. A cohabiting group composed of multigeneration adult females and their children is a family in terms of the manner in which they interact and influence each other as a primary social system. It seems more appropriate to construct a process definition of family than a structural definition. A process definition would emphasize the functions served by the cohabitation and other interactions of the group, while a structural definition would emphasize the rules for composition of the family. Bell and Vogel's definition is structural in large part with a traditionally accepted process tag of "socially recognized union."[3] Murdock's definition contains functional aspects, such as common residence, economic cooperation, and reproduction, but is restricted by the addition of structural criteria, such as "adults of both sexes" and "children, own or adopted, of the sexually cohabiting adults."[4] Many families in the lower socioeconomic brackets raise children who are neither their own nor adopted. They may be foster children, grandchildren, nieces, nephews, or cousins of the primary adults in the household. Their biologic parents may be dead, deserted, divorced, remarried, imprisoned, incarcerated, inhabitants of other cities or states, or simply unable to see themselves fulfilling the status-position of parent.

PROCESS DEFINITION

The following definition is an adaptation of one developed by graduate students in nursing[5] to communicate a concept of family that has utility for professional health care workers:

> Family is a culturally produced social system composed of two or more people who thus comprise a type of primary group. The persons in this group are (1) related by blood, marriage, adoption, or mutual consent; (2) interact with each other through designated or assumed familial status-positions and roles; (3) create and maintain a common subculture. Functions performed by the family include at least two of the following:
> 1. Maintenance of a common household
> 2. Rearing of children
> 3. Companionship and mutual support among members
> 4. Sexual relationship between one or more pairs of adults
> 5. Financial cooperation
> 6. Enculturation of members

The utilitarian feature of this definition is that the emphasis is on the *functions* performed by the social system rather than on delineation of specific blood ties, legal sanctioning of the sexual relationships, or designation of the sex mixture or the developmental stage of the adult family member(s). Application of the criteria in this definition makes it possible to differentiate between a primary group of people who are or who are not functioning as a family system. Examples of primary groups that could fulfill the criteria include: traditional nuclear family units; several cohabiting adults of one generation, as in some communes; several adults of one sex, as in some religious groups; one adult and one or more children; heterosexually or homosexually cohabiting couples; two or more generations in an enduring congregate living pattern. In system terms, any of these variants could *function* in ways that are familial and thus serve as primary or secondary socializers for all the developing human beings who comprise their membership.

The definition must also be checked to see if it excludes those group relationships that should not be defined as a family. One example is sharing of living space by college roommates. Such a situation does not fulfill the second criterion, which is "interact with each other through designated or assumed familial status-positions and roles." Nor does the college roommate relationship "create and maintain a common subculture" to any significant degree. The primary purpose of the common household, financial cooperation, and mutual support among roommates is for each to fulfill individual educational goals and further the personal career. The relationship between the roommates is viewed as situation limited from its inception. Furthur, the roommate relationship only fulfills one function: the maintenance of a common household. Other examples of close, interpersonal relationships can be tested against the definition of family presented in this chapter to see if the definition covers those that it should cover and excludes those that it should exclude.

STAGES OF FAMILY LIFE

Since the family is a small-group type of social system it engages in development. Families grow, mature, re-create themselves, and eventually die off. Duvall puts major emphasis on the early stages of family development, just as human development experts have tended to put major emphasis on the developmental stages of children and adolescents. Duvall[6] defined eight stages of the family life cycle as follows:

Stage I: Beginning family—married couple with no children
Stage II: Childbearing family—oldest child birth to 30 months
Stage III: Family with preschool children—oldest child 2½ to 6 years
Stage IV: Family with school-age children—oldest child 6 to 13 years
Stage V: Family with teenagers—oldest child 13 to 20 years
Stage VI: Family as launching centers—first to last child departure
Stage VII: Family in the middle years—empty nest to retirement
Stage VIII: Aging family—Retirement to death of one or both spouses

The two major difficulties with Duvall's model are that it is primarily child focused and it names five stages that account for approximately 25 years of the family life cycle but only two postchildren stages, which now last approximately 40 years. Notice that the stages of family life are totally child focused until stage VII, and then the nature of the stages changes to emphasis on the adult members. For the purposes of this book, it seems worthwhile to redefine all the stages of family life in terms of the adult members' development rather than the child members' development. Doing this about-face might seem iconoclastic because we are a child-oriented nation, but, in truth, children would have a better chance of healthy development if adults in the culture were given more guidance and role-modeling in maturation processes through the adult years. Family life is certainly one important focus for work in adult development.

Consider the following alternative form of the stages of family life with a focus on the development of the adults in the family constellation rather than on the children:

Stage I: Emerging family—first 7 to 10 years of cohabitation
Stage II: Crystallizing family—10 to 25 years of cohabitation
Stage III: Integrating family—25 to 40 years of cohabitation
Stage IV: Actualizing family—40 to 60+ years of cohabitation

Stage I

The emerging family is the name given to the first seven to ten years after the initiation of a family system. A significant percentage of American families disintegrate during the emerging phase. Both traditional male–female marriages and a large segment of the variant family forms do not last ten years. The reason for the breakup of families in the emerging phase can be found through data collection and analysis of the family as a system that has status-positions to be filled and functions to perform. When important functions are not being performed within the family system, or when crucial role relationships are not enacted, the family becomes dysfunctional and will disintegrate into two or more parts unless something reparative is done. A more detailed discussion of analyzing family systems is presented later in this chapter.

The emerging family is fraught with stressful situations and the necessity of making rapid changes of major proportions over and over again. Any two or more people who come to live together for the first time to enact familial roles and positions must discover individual mismatches between their expectations about each other. The challenge is to negotiate mutually agreeable compromises so that the rules of the new life together can be developed in an acceptable form.

In families in which childbearing and/or child rearing take place, this process starts during the emerging phase. It might be noted that even in those instances in which the family has been organized for more than ten years, the entrance of a new child puts such demands for change and compromise on the family system that even an older family takes on many of the functional characteristics of an emerging family.

Emerging families typically must deal with the parallel stage of emerging work life of the adult breadwinners. The variance on this issue is wide. In some families, the 20-year-old adults are already well settled in their positions as unskilled or semiskilled laborers; in others, the adults are still in school or in training, and financial support comes from the extended family or from one adult in the emerging family. Stress occurs in relationships because of the simultaneity of rapid change and adjustment required among family members compounded by rapid change and growth that may be required in the career.

By the end of the first seven to ten years of family development, most of the rules for family life will have been set up and turned into habit patterns. Family members will have well-defined roles, which they enact in relation to each other. If these roles are tolerable and have some rewards for enactment, they will be continued. If most necessary functions of family life are being fulfilled to some extent, at least marginally, the family will stay together and move into the second stage, which is labeled the crystallizing family.

Stage II

In the crystallization stage of family life, the adults and children go through a quieter, more comfortable period of slower change and less familial turmoil and stress. At least this is true for the years when children are in middle childhood. The emergence of adolescence in the children puts many stresses on the family because new rules must be created for how the family will operate under these new conditions. Eventually the stress subsides, and younger children tend to experience less turmoil in the family when they become adolescent than was true for the firstborn. Despite the teenage turmoil this period may be more comfortable than stage I. Everyone is surer of his place in the family, and the payoff can be seen in the relationships. Growth and change must continue to take place throughout this period or stagnation will result.

Family development during the stage of crystallization includes tasks such as broadening independence of children, adult self-development, continued work on the relationships between and among the adults of the family, and finally work on the relationship between the adults and their larger social systems. Home becomes the departure and return point for ventures into the larger social systems beyond. All family members still depend heavily on each other for primary social contact, but the dependence is much less than it was during the emerging stage. Families with no children go through many of the same processes of both independent and relational growth and development, or the family breaks up during this stage for lack of growth.

Stage III

At the end of the crystallizing stage, most offspring will have been launched and the middle-aged adults will be approaching the start of the new middle years. The family, now composed primarily of young, middle, and perhaps aged adults moves into stage III, which has been labeled the integrating family. Integrating families, in the lower classes particularly, often absorb small children into the family even at this stage. In this case, some elements of emerging family life recur, and the stress of that must be dealt with. More typically, young children are in the extended family network outside the integrating family's boundaries. They may be loved, cherished, cared for, and played with, but responsibility for their rearing belongs to others.

An important task of the integrating family is the reevaluation and enhancement of the quality of the relationships among the adults who initially created the family. In the traditional family, this would be the middle-aged husband and wife. In the matriarchal family comprised of several generations of women, a new head of the family may be designated to replace an aging matriarch. When this occurs status-positions, role relationships, and functions will undergo reshuffling and reintegration.

The relationship of the family members to work and leisure is as important in this stage as it was in the emerging stage, except that the emphasis is switched. Typically, both men and women are in the work force during the integration stage. However, the importance of work and the Great American Dream of control over nature frequently dwindles about this time. Leisure takes on an importance that it may never have had before. There is nearly always more time for leisure. Only those persons who are compulsive or neurotic about filling their time with work or climbing still higher on the career ladder before forced retirement ignore the availability of increased leisure time.

The major change that occurs in the integrating family over time is the shift in value orientation as seen on the Kluckhohn—Strodtbeck value orientation paradigm presented in Table 3, Chapter 1. Continuously maturing adults come to realize over the decades that mastery over nature is futile and eventually brings environmental disaster. They come to realize that persistent living in the future is ridiculous and wastes the only time that one really has in which to enjoy life and live it fully—the 24-hour period happening right now. The shift away from mastery over nature also implies a shift away from mastery over other people. Hence, the high motivation for doing may gradually be replaced by motivation for being-in-becoming. Finally, the emphasis on individualism that characterizes North Americans in their earlier years grows into an appreciation that one person is not human alone; humanness exists only through one's relationships with other human beings as a part of the social order. For many persons, their most significant other human being takes on new importance. Hence, the spouse or other closest adult becomes even closer during this stage.

Many people see the movement in value orientation described above as a movement toward spirituality. It need have nothing to do with organized religions, although some people find or enact their emerging search for spirituality through organized religious practice. For most people, it is simply attending to the relationship between man and nature. Perhaps it is deciding to accept this relationship as it was never accepted in younger days—in harmony.

Stage IV

The final stage of family life is called the actualizing family to reflect the relationship between the ideal ending of the family system with the ideal culmination or peak of life as described by Abraham Maslow.[7]

For the continually maturing familial adults in an old family, ie, a family that has existed for over 40 years, movement through this stage can be dyadic. They can do it together, and the familial relationship can be enhanced through the growth process. In the event that one adult drops out, through death or through mental–emotional deterioration, the other adult must choose between growing on alone or deteriorating.

Many late adults, women in particular, have to make familial transitions in the late adult period. They may choose to live alone and enhance their extended kinship and friendship network in order to make up for the loss of family functioning. They may move into the family of grown offspring and attempt to grow through the actualizing stage as individuals while the rest of the family is growing through stage II or stage III. Transplanting a late adult into a well-settled family precipitates some recurrence of emerging-family stresses, which must be handled. Reorganization of rules and habit patterns must take place.

In the event that the late adult goes into an illness-maintaining system the likelihood of achieving actualization is practically nil. An illness-maintaining system is one that stifles growth and promotes dependence and rigidity by its rules and behavior patterns. Sometimes the home of grown offspring turns out to be this way, but most frequently this situation is found in organizations that specialize in care of the elderly ill. Establishments that have a biased view of late adults as senile old people cannot simultaneously view them as growing human beings who have developmental tasks to be performed in their last years.

The fortunate families who do live through the actualizing stage of family life together are in good positions to discover the meaning of life and to put their lives into perspective as individuals and as family units through the process of inventorying their successes and failures. They will continue to count on a few friendships, particularly the friendship with each other. Finally, the family members will help each other go through the process of grief and loss when one of them is dying. The person who remains can then continue to grow through the remaining years of his life as long as he can strike a balance between his needs for dependence and independence. Too much taking over by others will stifle the aged person, but too much independence could result in accidents or other undesirable outcomes. Finding a good balance is one of the greatest challenges facing the aged and their middle-aged offspring during this stage.

THE PROCESSES OF FAMILY LIFE

Virginia Satir presents a simple, but powerfully effective framework for the analysis of family process. There are four aspects of family life: communication patterns, rules about how people should feel and act, self-worth of the individuals in the family, and the family's links to society.[8] These four aspects of family life exist in every family system, and the gathering of data about each of them can provide much useful information for developing hypotheses about how illness in the family is handled, or how the plan of care for a chronic disease is likely to be implemented, ignored, or altered in the family, or how health teaching will be put to use.

Communication Patterns

The way that family members send messages to each other is important. Six modes of communication cover the range of ways that family members communicate with each other. They are placating, blaming, computing, distracting, leveling, and confronting. The first four modes are generally more dysfunctional and the last two are generally considered more functional communication modes. The following brief discussion of each mode may be enough to help the reader recognize situations in which he has experienced each specific mode. Further reading, discussion, role playing, and supervised practice of the modes are encouraged if the reader would like the ability to detect habitual use of the first four modes in families, to confront them about their dysfunctional communication patterns, and to help develop new habits of communicating honestly and clearly.

The mode of placating is characterized by ingratiating, syrupy speech, for example, frequent descriptions of other people as "sweet," "so nice," "such a lovely person," and the like. Placaters try always to please and to be liked. Placaters believe that they cannot not be liked since they give in to the desires of other people so often. They are always willing to be of service, and the last thing they can deal with is someone asking for their opinion or preference about something. Because they so seldom make decisions, they can never be held responsible for poor decisions or mistakes. They see themselves as having no rights in the relationship. In truth, they see themselves as having no responsibilities in the relationship either.

Blaming is close to being the opposite of placating in some respects and very similar to placating in other respects. Blamers usually feel superior, and their voices are tough, tight, authoritarian, and loud. The other members of the family are frequently accused of errors or inadequacies. Blamers convey the message that the world would be fine if only the stupid, inadequate people in it would stop making so many mistakes. Blamers avoid responsibility in much the same way that placaters do, by putting responsibility for how they feel and how situations turn out on other people. If a blamer is angry, frustrated, scared, or resentful, it is somebody else's fault. He puts responsibility for his feelings and his situation onto others' shoulders.

Computing, the third communication mode, is less easy to accept as a dysfunctional mode because it is so highly valued in the larger society outside the family—in work, politics, mass media, and other larger-system institutions. Computing refers to a communication pattern that is ultrareasonable, devoid of feelings, objective, calculating and factual, and superior in an intellectual way The observer can sense that the computer's intellect and feelings are disassociated.[9] While the computer is being calm, cool, and collected, the others in the family are feeling more and more uncomfortable. They may begin to act in more emotional ways to show their frustration and sense of inadequacy. This enhances the computer's game and strengthens his act of being absolutely accurate on all points.

Distracters use irrelevant tangents, words, stories, or allegories in their conversations. Frequently they pepper sentences with nonspecific referents and other vague words that leave the listener with no idea about the meaning of what was said. Distracters are known to go off on lengthy tangents that seem to have no relevance to the topic at hand. Frequently they trail off in the middle of sentences and expect the listener to fill in the rest from imagination. Some distracters appear to mesmerize themselves during a soliloquy and do not even seem to be listening to themselves. Others in the family evidence frustration because the distracter cannot be counted

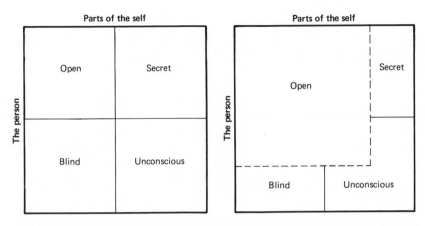

FIG. 1. *Left.* The Johari window. *Right.* Expanded-pane Johari window. (From Luft, *Group Processes. An Introduction to Group Dynamics,* 1963. Courtesy of the Mayfield Publishing Company. Copyright © 1963, 1970 by Joseph Luft).

on to enter into discussions or decision-making processes usefully, only in a futile, time-consuming way that produces dysfunction for the family.

Before going on to the two growth-producing modes of communication, it is useful to fully discuss the Johari window (Fig. 1) and then to use it as a point of departure for the discussion of leveling and confronting.[10] The Johari window shows four parts of a person's self-system. The area marked "open" is a freely shared area that the person talks about in interactions without reticence. The pane labeled "secret" is a hidden area that is known to the self but unknown to others. It contains suppressed feelings and needs and attitudes about self and others that the person is uncomfortable in sharing.

The "blind" pane represents the side of the self that is known to others but unknown to the self. Features contained in the "blind" are mannerisms, traits, nonverbal communications, and metaverbals such as voice tone, speed, and pitch. People are frequently blind to matches or mismatches between their verbal and their nonverbal behaviors, such as a mismatch between speech and facial expression or hand movements.[11,12] People are also blind to other features about themselves when they are moving and interacting un-self-consciously. People who show distress and shock while watching themselves on video tape are responding to exposure of some portion of their blind side.

Human beings are blind to themselves in part because of anatomy. The eyes are situated on the front of the face. We cannot see ourselves from a distance in perspective because our eyes are attached to the body. Our vision loses detail when we focus on distant things. Mirrors are not much help in revealing our blind side because they are two-dimensional and because they do not show us how we operate during interactions.

The "unconscious" pane represents the side that is unknown either to the self or to others. There are memories, abilities, and talents that are present but unknown to anyone. Occasionally an insight from the unconscious will burst forth, but it is not a daily occurrence.

Growth of the family system can be enhanced if each person can become free to share part of the secret side and if persons share with each other what they observe as the blind side. The term given to sharing part of one's secret side is leveling. This means telling others frankly about yourself, how you feel, and what you want or need. When persons level, they show a little of their secret sides. The other process, that is, sharing a part of one's blind side, is called confronting. One can confront with feelings one has with reference to the other, with data about the other's behaviors, or with hunches about what the other is feeling.

The Johari window can be redrawn to show a shift in the relative size of the window panes when leveling and confronting are modes of communication that are used appropriately among family members (Fig. 1). Notice that the open pane has expanded because some of the secret and some of the blind areas have been converted to open. The bonus from such family process is that tiny parts of the unconscious become available to persons in moments of revelation during or after times of leveling and confronting.

The outcome for family life of moving from dysfunctional to functional communication patterns is growth for the individuals and increased strength and resiliency for the family system. Use of leveling and confronting increases intimacy and enhances the quality of the subculture that exists within the family.

Rules

Every family lives by a set of rules. Rules are essential guides to conduct if two or more people are to live together for any length of time without chaos. Rules are the blueprint for family behavior. This blueprint comprises the norms of the subculture that exists in each family. Easy rules for most families to list include those about household chores, money and bill paying, scheduling of activities, and dealing with infractions. Less obvious rules are those about deference, socioemotional acting out, special privileges, emergencies, privacy, sex, communication networks, territoriality, power, and authority. The second set of items are perhaps collectively more significant than the first, but they are less frequently overt and understood by all family members. That is unfortunate.

Frequently family members, particularly the adults, indicate that rules are known and understood by all. Yet careful questioning reveals the converse. Rules are misunderstood, and different members have different definitions of the rules. Rules are often grossly out-of-date. Some rules that were created to deal with elementary schoolers may be operating in a family with teenage children. Keeping rules up-to-date is an important component of growth-producing family life. Rules go along with leveling and confronting; they should be honest, open, and current.

Rules in a growth-producing family are determined on the basis of input from everyone. Sometimes it is inappropriate to be democratic because only the adults can make the kind of judgment required. But as the family moves through the emerging stage and into the crystallizing stage, more and more of the rules should be jointly set. In this way, young people develop a sense of interdependence, self-reliance, and responsibility.

Self-worth

Self-esteem or self-worth of the individuals who make up the family system must be considered in any discussion of the family process. Self-esteem is created and either nurtured or diminished for children in that system. Adult members' self-esteem already will have become partially set in their family of origin. But self-esteem is never static; it can continue to grow in a nurturing family system, or it can depreciate consistently over the course of family life. People who fall into despair or depression or have a "nervous breakdown" have probably reached their personal "bottom." That is the bottom of their ever-lowering self-esteem.

High self-esteem is the most basic of all ingredients for

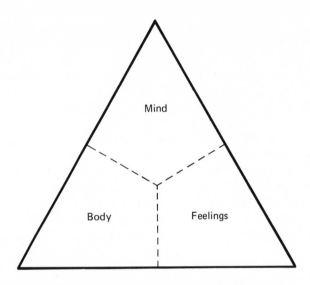

FIG. 2. Triangle of the self-system.

lifelong development and emotional growth. The family system is the first and most significant setting for the determination of how self-esteem will develop. The self-system can be diagrammed as a triangle composed of three equally vital parts (Fig. 2): the body, the mind, and the feelings. These three are inseparable in reality but distinct in the abstract since each can be discussed by itself.

One part is the body. Size, sex, beauty, and athletic ability are a few of the physical components of that part of the self-system called the body image. Body images are culturally and parentally influenced, depending on what is valued by the significant others in the environment. The match between the expectations of the infant's caretakers and the reality of the infant's body condition in early life determines in large part how the infant will be judged. Each infant begins life under the shadow of some evaluation by adults. The infant may be defined as big, good, happy or scrawny, hyperactive, and so on. This evaluation helps to shape what he will develop as a self-image.

The body image undergoes revision all during childhood because the physical body changes visibly and new people in the environment bring various expectations which help to make up a composite picture of the self that the growing human being absorbs and mirrors to himself. The physical fitness, health education, and athletic programs of formal education and numerous organizations around the United States are a strong testimony to the high value placed on sound bodies and physical prowess.

The mind is nurtured and highly valued in North American society. Only a small minority of persons with variant value orientations do not put major emphasis on intellectual development. The public school system with its 12-year program attests to the value placed on the mind. Most North American youths also attend college or vocational training beyond the 12 years. Families spend a good deal of time, effort, and money attending to the needs of the younger generation in their intellectually related pursuits.

The North American culture strongly supports the development of mind and body. But what about the third part of the triangle? In Figure 3 it is equal in size to the other two. It certainly is biologically equal in importance to mind and body. Unfortunately, the school systems and other organizations that serve as enculturators of the young do not deal with development of the segment of the self called the emotional self—the psyche. There is no institution set up to enhance this area of human life. Religion used to help but has generally gone intellectual. The only groups of people trained to deal with feelings are set up to deal with diseased feelings, eg, psychiatrists, clinical psychologists, psychiatric nurses, and social workers.

Natural enhancement of feeling development has never had the aggrandizement that enhancement of the intellect and the physical body enjoys. Consequently, neither children nor grown-ups have learned how to fully attend to their feeling needs. Most do not even know how to identify feelings or how to constructively dissipate uncomfortable ones. How to fulfill their emotional needs in honest, straightforward ways is a mystery to many. North Americans are taught to bury and never express certain feelings. They are taught to constantly express other feelings whether or not they are genuine. People believe that feelings come in bads and goods. Such teaching is a major error in the development of young people. Further, the teaching comes from the conventional wisdom of relatives and friends rather than from trained professionals; hence, it is informal and covert rather than formal and overt.

Feelings do not come in bads and goods. They are chemical reactions that take place in human body systems. Each person is born with a set of "recipes" or chemical formulas for the range of feelings carried in the genetic code.[13] To judge certain feelings as "unacceptable" and therefore to pretend that they were not felt is to deny reality. When a chemical reaction has occurred, it has occurred. It is a reality. Feelings are not under direct control of the higher intellectual centers of the brain. Hence, it is useless to attempt to *will* feelings into existence or out of existence.

Feelings dissipate only when they are fully felt, acknowledged, and attended to by the feeler. When feelings are denied and suppressed, the self-system becomes distorted. Self-esteem is difficult to develop in a self-system that has been taught that it ought to be capable of controlling a certain set of chemical reactions within itself. Over the course of years of denying the existence of real feelings and trying to create other "culturally desirable" feelings, both the intellect and the body become destructively affected. Both begin to malfunction in some way. The person is a whole and must nurture all the components. If he spends all the time and energy at his disposal on only two components, namely, intellect and body, neglect of the third will cause him grave difficulty.

Satir calls the feelings component "pot" and uses the terms "high pot" and "low pot," respectively, to refer to feelings that are comfortable and feelings that are uncomfortable.[14] The most important issue about "pot" is that nurturing families should encourage members to fully feel and express their feelings regardless of what they may be. All feelings are legitimate and, if they can be expressed verbally, danger from violent outbursts or acting out behavior is negligible. Keeping up-to-date on feelings is the single most important function of the modern American family. Other institutions are geared to the development of the mind and body. Almost nobody is geared to the development of the human being's knowledge about and awareness of his internal milieu, his feelings.

Many Americans cannot easily speak about feelings. They have never learned to converse in feeling language, only in mind language. People get "I think" and "I feel" all mixed up. It is common to hear a sentence such as "I feel that we should consider these plans more thoroughly before making our decision." That sentence contains no expression of feelings. It is a thought sentence and should begin with "I think. . . ." Very likely the person is also experiencing a feeling, but that is not what he expressed. If we could guess at his feeling, it might be one of the following: frustration, fear, or anxiety, if he is uncomfortable; hope, confidence, concern, or warmth, if he is comfortable.[15]

A definite connection can be hypothesized between types of dysfunctional communication patterns and inadequacy of feeling expression. One can hypothesize, for example, that the computer and the blamer are covering feelings of inadequacy by taking the offensive. Or one might guess that placaters and distracters are covering feelings of loneliness or fear of abandonment with their behavioral habits. None of these hypotheses has been tested by research. They are simply conjectures. However, it is logical that definite connections do exist between feeling states and communication styles.

Probably the major utility of Satir's term "pot" is that it can be used with families to help them begin to acknowledge and deal with the third component of the triangle shown in Figure 3, their feelings or psyche. Members of the family who are introduced to the meaning of high pot, low pot, dragging pot, and so on can use this term to signal others about their feeling states. This activity can grow into leveling on the part of the originator and confronting about the blind side on the part of the other. Such communication exchanges lead toward healthy relationships and continued development of each self in the family system.

A wide variety of training groups, feeling groups, and the like have come into vogue in recent years to help Americans begin to develop the neglected dimension of their self-systems. To the extent that family members avail themselves of the experiences in such groups, family life can be improved. Such experiences help family members to move from ignorance about a significant part of the self to some level of sophistication. In a small way such learning bolsters the family's capacity to act as the institution that teaches the rules about feeling states.

Choosing a reputable group is difficult because the group cult has fostered the emergence of many unprepared group leaders. Regulation and certification of group leaders are fast approaching so that the citizenry can have a modicum of trust in the competence of the group leader they choose.

Societal Linkages

Every family is linked to the larger society of which it is a part. Families are linked to one or more organizations at the local level that are part of the major institutions in the society: government, business and industry, education, religion, work and recreation, and civic and charitable associations. Every local geographic entity has social organizations that represent the specific embodiment of these institutions. The local environment has specific businesses, specific religions, specific organizations, a specific form of government, and so on. Families are linked to other families through these organizational avenues, as well as through extended family networks and neighborhood contacts.

We are told that every family is linked to society, but the interesting questions to be asked are: How? What are the results? The four system processes discussed in Chapter 2 are relevant in this situation. Families *obtain* energy, matter, and information as *input* through their links to society. A relatively open family system will relate to a wide variety of outside influences and then pick and choose among them for what will be used for *throughput* in the family process. A relatively closed family will have predetermined, rigid rules about which societal links are permissible and which are not. One reflection of a family's relative degree of openness or closedness is their overt and covert rules about the links to society.

Families dispose energy, matter, and information to the society as *output*. How free are the family members to do this? Some families dispose much of their time, energy, and information into the larger social system—work, recreation, church, and civic or charitable associations. Other families do not give of themselves but give of their possessions; matter is disposed. Still others keep disposal to a minimum; they remain relatively self-contained and do not exchange easily with society.

What are the results of relatively closed or relatively open exchanges with the environment? Relatively closed family systems usually are characterized by suspicion, hostility, and fear. Such family systems view the resources in the society as negative and requiring close scrutiny and screening to filter out all possible toxic elements. These families *contain* and *retain* with rigid boundary maintenance. Relatively open families may be characterized as hopeful, trusting, and curious. They want to see what society has that they can use. They try new ideas on for fit. They experiment with alternatives to their way of doing things. They make decisions based on the reality of the facts rather than by default or predetermined edict. They are open to change and to growth. The boundaries are more permeable.

The results of relatively closed, compared to relatively open, families are clear. Open families change in small ways constantly over time. They are flexible and can withstand a great deal of stress because of their resiliency and flexibility. Relatively closed families resist small or incremental changes from the environment. They remain fixed and rigid. Hence, their need for change becomes overdue, and eventually a major crisis will ensue as a symptom of the out-of-date character of the family life. Crisis can take many forms: A member gets into drug abuse or other legal problems; someone is diagnosed as chronically ill; someone dies or is injured severly. Crises of this nature are often symptoms of accumulated missed opportunities for growth and incremental change in the family system.

Roles and Positions in Family Life

The names given to the status-positions in the family differ among straightforward nuclear families and the variant forms of family life prevalent in North America today. However, the norms, tasks, and role relationships generally do not differ. In a matriarchal family, the grandmother may fulfill many of the norms attached to the father position in a nuclear family. Hence, it is difficult to use the traditional labels like father, mother, male child, and female child, for these may be construed to mean that the principles are not relevant to variant forms of family life. That is not true. The same functions are performed, and comparable relationships are enacted. Only the labels given to status-positions, the partitioning of roles to status-positions, and the sex of the incumbents may differ.

Society requires that each household designate somebody as its head for identification by governmental, religious, or educational organizations. The social organizations that conduct relationships with the family need to have a designated family head for their use in relating to the family.

In every family, a person or persons in the family system must either work or receive subsistence because of inability to work. In either instance the status-position of primary adult must be filled. The sex of the primary adult is traditionally male but need not be. More and more females are filling this status-position.

Someone else usually fills a status-position of the second adult. This person or may not have near equal headship functions. Traditionally the major function of the second status-position was to serve as coordinator and socioemotional leader of the family system. In the single-sex family the official worker head of the family may be a middle-aged woman. The socioemotional coordinator position may be filled by a late adult, such as the middle-aged woman's mother or aunt.

The four dimensions of role relationships described in Chapter 2 are applicable to family life. Many norms of family life deal with the task dimension, such as norms regarding cooking, cleaning, washing, ironing, mowing grass, repair work, painting, and so on. The second element is the authority dimension, which includes the norms about how decisions are to be made in the relationship and how much authority each actor is to have in relation to each other actor. The third element is deference. Deference refers to whose needs come first. In some families deference is shown to the elders, in others to the adult males or the adult females, or in others to the children. In the mother–infant relationship, the mother shows deference to the infant's needs much of the time. Finally, there is the affective or sentiment dimension. Every role carries expectations about how the actors ought to feel toward each other. In families this affective dimension contains expectations such as respect, love, and concern that members hold toward one another.

The fabric of life within the family system, the throughput, is processed via the enactment of roles and status-positions by the family members. Many times the norms held for members of the family are unacceptable or burdensome. Role conflicts can arise. Such conflicts can be resolved with clear communicative interaction that is comprised of leveling and confronting techniques followed by compromising or other forms of conflict resolution. However, the more prevalent modes of communication in families are the growth-impeding modes of placating, blaming, distracting, and computing. When the latter modes are used either singly or in combination, role-conflicts are aggrandized rather than diminished, and further stress and strain result within the family system.

A persistent buildup of such stress and strain in family relationships over the course of several years can result in many undesirable outcomes. Dissolution or fragmentation of the family, mental or physical illness of one or more members, and violence to self or others are a few of the possibilities. In Part III illustrations are given which focus on illness-induced changes in the roles, positions, and general functioning of the family system during different stages of adult, and hence of family, development. It is well to bear in mind that a probability exists that dysfunctional modes of family functioning predated the acute or chronic illness. Indeed, many theorists contend that just such a persistent stress on the individual family member can cause the pathophysiology to occur that results in either chronic illness or recurrent patterns of acute illnesses.[16,17]

THE PLACE OF FAMILY IN ADULT DEVELOPMENT

The tasks presented in Chapter 1 for the phases of adult development will be discussed from a different point of view. This time the development of the individual as a family member through the adult life phases will be emphasized. The developmental tasks related to family during young adulthood are tasks 3 and 4.

Task 3.—Adjusting to a heterosexual marital relationship or to a variant companionship style. This task refers to the compromises that must be made by the developing young adult when he begins living with a heterosexual or a homosexual partner in an intimate relationship Each person comes to the relationship from a separate family background, and it is highly unlikely that there will not be mismatches in the expectations that they hold for each other's behavior based on the role models in their past. Stubbornness and selfishness are the terms frequently applied to one partner by the other, but more often the fact is that both partners are refusing to compromise on their expectations of the other even though these expectations may be mismatched to their life-style. The process of working through these mismatches results in growth for each partner as a person and for the family as a social system.

Task 4—Developing parenting behaviors for biologic offspring or in the broader framework of social parenting. The young adult has minimal sense of self as parent when an offspring is born. Previous experiences with baby-sitting or other short-term responsibilities for children do help one to gain experience in child care, but they do not do much toward the development of a self-image as parent. Hence, the early phases of child development are paralleled by emerging phases of parent development. Some young adults re-create the parenting behaviors of their parents. Others consciously try to do the opposite of everything their parents did. Still others try to use books and experts as their guide for child rearing. However, at a more personal level, each parent is struggling with the position of mother or father and all the dimensions of role that the position entails. Each parent eventually comes to some assessment within himself about his sentiments toward the child, about the task and deference dimensions, and about the authority dimension. The woman in particular may have to struggle with the deference dimension vis-à-vis the child and the marital partner; she must decide whose needs come first. Marital conflicts are common over the issue of deference. The authority dimension may also become problematic as the child begins to grow and there are struggles over who holds the power in the relationship. Much of the struggle with 2- and 3-year-olds revolves around the authority dimension between parent and child.

The tasks of the core of the middle years that relate to personal development within the family system are tasks 3, 4, and 6.

Task 3 —Helping younger persons (eg, biologic offspring) to become integrated human beings.   Persons enter this stage from young adulthood, where they have become somewhat comfortable with a sense of self as parent and with the roles attached to the status-position of parent. In middle adulthood the parent is still developing parallel to the child's development. The expectation for the adult is that he will be a growth-enhancing force in the child's milieu rather than a growth-impeding force. Parents who are themselves maturing along the lines of middlescent developmental tasks are much more likely to serve as a role-model of growth and hence will be a help to the younger generation in their developmental processes. Truly neurotic parents can be so only if they are not developing human beings. The concept of neurosis implies the need for a steady state. In that sense it is the antithesis to adult development. However, neuroticlike behaviors are often seen during developmental crises of adult life. Thus, in the latter sense, temporary neurotic behaviors may be indicative of a transition that is approaching in the adult's life. Children then cannot expect consistent stability from parents anymore than parents can expect consistency from children. Both generations are moving along separate cycles of crisis, growth, stability, transition, crisis, growth, and so on.

Task 4—Enchancing or redeveloping intimacy with spouse or most significant other.   This task is stated rather awkwardly in order to encompass several alternatives that occur in the population. Persons who have had fairly continuous marital success would be expected to further enhance their relationship. Those who have grown apart during the latter years of young adulthood and early middle age would take a hard look at the cooled relationship and make some decision about it. Perhaps the couple would reestablish intimacy; perhaps they would separate or divorce. If the relationship dissolved, this task implies that a new significant other would be found and that intimacy would be established in the new relationship. In order to simplify the discussion, only the case of enhancing an already existing relationship will be presented. The reader can easily make the extrapolation to other cases.

As the maturing person moves through middle age there is a reassessment of priorities in life. Most often this review shows that career, children, and community activities have taken precedence over the marital relationship. Such an insight now results in a mutual decision by each partner that the priorities need to be reordered so that more time and effort are devoted to enhancing the marital relationship. Timing of the reassessment frequently coincides with the time when children are old enough to be more involved with school and friends, when the career or careers of the marital partners have reached a period of stability.

Task 6 —*Helping aging persons (eg, parents or in-laws) progress through the later years of life.*   The parents of middle adults may be independent throughout the whole 20-year period. There may be minimal evidence of change in the relationship between the two generations. More often there is a gradual transition in the relationship, with the middle adult showing more concern for the welfare of the older adult. Retirement is one event that may get the attention of the middle generation because it is a concrete milestone attesting to the advancing age of the older adult(s). The middle generation begins to think about the future and responsibilities that may be upcoming toward the older family members. Old conflicts may resurrect themselves from earlier parent–child days. The mixed feelings of guilt and dread may begin to settle in. Persons in this age group may be faced with their first experience of having responsibility for planning a funeral or for dealing with the estate of a dead relative. If it is a parent's death, the process of grief must be worked through.

The task, as stated, suggests that middle adults are in a position to help the older generation progress through the later stages. This means that the middle adult becomes familiar with the developmental tasks of later life and, in a way similar to that pursued with children, acts as a growth-enhancing force rather than a growth-impeding force in the older adult's life. Too many middle-aged offspring attempt to control the lives of their elders with authoritarian tactics that promote hostility or dependence.

The family-related tasks of the new middle years are tasks 3, 4, and 5.

Task 3 —*Developing mutually supportive (interdependent) relationships with grown offspring and other members of the younger generation.* The nature of the parent–child relationship must change continuously as each generation matures. However, there are events that require major modifications in the parent–

offspring role relationships. Marriage of grown offspring is an example of such an event. Just as the young marital couple must work out compromises between them, the middle generation is equally responsible for changing their relationship with the grown offspring to acknowledge the new status-position in the new family system.

Task 4—*Reevaluating and enhancing the relationship with spouse or most significant other or adjusting to their loss.* Even though there may have been a successful evaluation of the marital relationship in the early middle years, a new examination is often called for when all the grown children have moved out and the parents are experiencing the empty-nest syndrome. There are no buffers left, only the couple. They can choose to enhance their relationship with each other or not. Many times a reexamination of the marriage shows that they would be better off apart, and divorces do occur in this age group. Death of a spouse requires working through the grief process, and this too is seen as a growth-producing process. Most marital couples, however, report that they become more intimate and value each other more during the new middle years.

Task 5—Helping aged parents or other relatives progress through the last stage of life. Many persons in the new middle years spend much of their time dealing with the needs, illnesses, deaths, funerals, and sorrows of the late adults in the extended family network. The death of one aged spouse leaves the other aged spouse in need of emotional support, financial advice, and more. The death of a parent is a multifaceted crisis because it requires a great deal of logical decision making about arrangements at the same time that there is a strong emotional shock.

The core theme of this task is that aged persons have work to do during the last stage of life. They have life review work to do; they should put their life into perspective in preparation for its termination. They have grief work to do; if not grief work about the death of a spouse or other relatives, then certainly about their own impending death. The charge to persons in the new middle years is to facilitate rather than impede the late adult's progress through the last stage of development.

This concludes the discussion of the family through the 50 or more years of middle life. Family life is not static; it changes a great deal over the course of its five or six decades. Concomitantly, the adults that head the family change and grow a great deal during the several decades of adult life.

References

1. N. W. Bell and E. F. Vogel, "Toward a Framework for Functional Analysis of Family Behavior," in *A Modern Introduction to the Family*, eds. N. W. Bell and E. F. Vogel (New York: The Free Press, 1960).
2. G. P. Murdock, "The Universality of the Nuclear Family," in *Social Structure*, ed. G. P. Murdoch (New York: Macmillan, 1949).
3. Bell and Vogel, "Framework for Functional Analysis."
4. Murdock, "Universality of the Nuclear Family."
5. Class discussion, Nursing of Adults: Course No. 806.04 (Columbus: The Ohio State University School of Nursing, February 1973).
6. E. M. Duvall, *Family Development*, 3rd ed. (Philadelphia: Lippincott, 1967).
7. A. H. Maslow, *Motivation and Personality* (New York: Harper, 1954).
8. V. Satir, *Peoplemaking* (Palo Alto, Calif.: Science and Behavior Books, 1972).
9. N. Branden, *The Disowned Self* (New York: Bantam, 1973).
10. J. Luft, *Group Processes. An Introduction to Group Dynamics* (Palo Alto, Calif.: Mayfield, 1963).
11. J. Fast, *Body Language* (New York: Evans, 1970).
12. E. T. Hall, *The Hidden Dimension* (Garden City, N.Y.: Doubleday, 1966).
13. A. C. Guyton, *Textbook of Medical Physiology*, 5th ed. (Philadelphia: Saunders, 1976): 758–759; 988–991.
14. Satir, *Peoplemaking*.
15. V. E. Johnson, *I'll Quit Tomorrow* (New York: Harper 1973), Appendix 6.
16. D. L. Dodge and W. T. Martin, *Social Stress and Chronic Illness* (Notre Dame, Ind.: Notre Dame University Press, 1970).
17. G. E. Moss, *Illness, Immunity and Social Interaction* (New York: Wiley, 1973).

Suggested Readings

Cavan, R.S. *The American Family*. 4th ed. New York: Crowell, 1969.

Hall, J. E., and Weaver, B.R., eds. *Nursing of Families in Crisis*. Philadelphia: Lippincott, 1974.

Handel, G., ed. *The Psychosocial Interior of the Family: A Sourcebook for the Study of Whole Families*. Chicago: Aldine, 1967.

O'Neil, N., and O'Neil, G., *Open Marriage*. New York: Evans, 1972.

Rodman, H., ed. *Marriage, Family and Society: A Reader*. New York: Random House, 1965.

Satir, V. *Peoplemaking*. Palo Alto, Calif.: Science and Behavior Books, 1972.

Skolnick, A.S., and Skolnick, J.H. *Family in Transition: Rethinking Marriage, Sexuality, Child Rearing, and Family Organization*. Boston, Little, Brown, 1971.

Sussman, M.B. "Adaptive, Directive and Integrative Behavior of Today's Family." In *Family Process*. Edited by N. W. Ackerman. New York: Basic Books, 1970.

5

COMMUNITY PARTICIPATION

Adults are the major overt participants in community life. Children do participate but only in a few institutions and largely on a sliding scale of low to high participation as they move toward adulthood. Community and the even larger social system of society are the suprasystems of smaller entities such as social organizations, small groups, families, and individuals. In this chapter, we will focus on adult participation in larger social systems with specific focus on community as a large-system prototype. Large systems are important to adults for two reasons: first, because adults depend on large systems constantly vis-à-vis their occupation, their family, their welfare, and their personal well-being; and second, because successful adult coping depends heavily on the sophistication with which one negotiates larger systems and thus benefits from them. Further, the Janus effect operates here because these larger systems would not exist in their current form without adults in all the decision-making positions.

CONCEPTIONS OF COMMUNITY

Warren presents important information about community but succumbs to the fallacy of presenting only an outdated definition of it. He defines it as a geographically designated area with identifiable land boundaries.[1] This geographic approach apparently worked well when the direction of wagon wheel tracks coming from each farm could be used as the distinguishing feature of where one community stopped and another started. It also worked when each geographic area was relatively independent and provided its citizens with most of the goods and services they used. However, in the more complex interdependent life-style of present-day America this technique is too simplistic.

Bertrand indicates that community can better be conceived as occupying social space, that it, is more usefully defined as a social system composed of role relationships rather than a geographic location composed of residents occupying physical space.[2] Klein approaches the problem by using the word "domain," which can refer to both a physical place and a socioemotional place that is phenomenologically real but not geographically real.[3] For example, members of a profession belong to a community of interest rather than to a geographic community.

Another error frequently perpetrated in the literature on community is what might be called the personality fallacy. This conception of community is based on an individualistic approach; it is the belief that a community is composed of certain groups of individuals or personalities and is idiosyncratic because this group of personalities happened to come together in space and time.[4] Within the social systems framework presented throughout this book, the personality mix thesis would be rejected. A community that is in existence will persist through time regardless of the initiating personalities. The significant structural units of community, as of all social systems, are norms, roles, positions, situs, and station. These five levels of social life can be fulfilled even though individual incumbents come and go. Hence, in the systems context, role theory would replace personality theory as an explanation of community development and stability over time.

Community as a social system is comprised of the same basic social components such as norms, roles, and positions. Communities also must adapt to their environment, and so they, too, carry out the functions of obtaining, containing, retaining, and disposing, which are described in Chapter 2. Community is a higher level of social system designated according to size and complexity. The distinguishing feature attributed to the concept of community is that it is the smallest level of social system that can maintain life for its self and its members. Interdependence with other communities and the total society not withstanding, most authors tend to agree on this stipulation in the definition of community. Import of goods and services does not negate this criterion because much of this importation is by choice. A true community contains all the social structures or institutions required to fulfill the needs of its members. It is frequently useful for students to partition communities into geographically tied communities and communities of interest. Geographically located communities import goods and services but could probably subsist on their own resources if they chose to; it would be a simpler life-style, but they could be self-sufficient. Communities of interest do not exist alone; persons within them have physical and other needs met through their individual geographic community. Communities of interest refer to a social structure with a focus limited in scope to the defined common interest. Within the parameters of this interest, the community contains all the social structures required to fulfill the needs of the members relative to their special interest.

Bertrand's definition of community is presented here primarily because it fits the systems framework used in this book:

> A community is a social system that encompasses a sufficient number of institutionalized social structures for individuals, groups and organizations to satisfy their needs through the formation (and maintenance) of symbolic role relationships that cut across the total system structure. It is the smallest of unit social structure which can maintain itself.[5]

Klein defines community in a similar way except that he emphasizes process to a greater extent. He views community as patterned interactions among a domain of individuals.[6] He specifies that their purposes for engaging in these patterned interactions are to achieve security and safety, for support in stress, and to gain a sense of self-worth and significance.

In general, the authors tend to agree that persons come together for purposes of mutual support, protection, and meeting of basic human needs including socialization needs. When such interactions are not sporadic but frequent and repetitious, the interactions become patterned. The persons involved accept altercasted expectations and engage in habituated role relationships. They begin to occupy specialized positions in the emerging social fabric. Later these positions become institutionalized so that, when the original incumbent vacates the position, it is subsequently filled by another person. The next incumbent then must enact the same sets of functions and role relationships as his predecessor. He can be different within some specified range of idiosyncratic permissiveness, but if he is too different he will be called incompetent and may be forced out of the position in overt or covert ways. Over the course of many generations of incumbents, the norms of the position may take on more tolerance for variance, but more often it becomes more rigidly specified over time.

A community in which a large percentage of the positions are rigidly specified will be more traditional and conservative about change than a community in which there is more internal variability or flexibility at the level of status-positions and role relationships. Time is probably an important variable. A community that has endured for several generations will tend to have the positions and stations more rigidly fixed. A relatively new, emergent community may be more flexible about positions and stations because trial and error and testing are taking place.

COMMUNITY FUNCTIONS

The major functions of a geographic community include such things as the following:[7]

1. Space allocation: providing and distributing living space, working space, leisure space, and education space. In an emerging community this could be exemplified by a collective decision about the placement of a new school. In a formalized community it could be exemplified by the use of zoning laws to decide which kinds of buildings could be built on certain land parcels.
2. Distribution of goods and services: providing the means for production, importation, and distribution of necessary goods and services. The governing body does not typically do this. Usually businesses emerge that engage in production, transportation, sales, and delivery of goods and services to the citizenry.
3. Safety and order: providing mechanisms for the maintenance of safety and order and for the resolution of conflicts among individuals or groups. Each community, by virtue of its definition, must be able to maintain itself. This requirement implies that it can provide protection, make order out of the complex of social interactions, and arbitrate disputes in some fashion.
4. Education and enculturation: providing mechanisms for the education of children and for the enculturation of both children and outsiders who have migrated into the community. In addition to formal education this function encompasses religious training and inculcation of the major value orientation of the culture as a whole.
5. Information flow: providing means by which information, beliefs, values, and ideas can be exchanged among the community membership.

These five functions cover the major needs of groups of human beings living together in a social system that is relatively independent from other such social systems. They also imply the existence of the major social institutions in the community, namely, marriage and the family, economics, education, religion, government, work, and leisure.

The four basic processes by which any community, whether geographic or functional, operates have been designated by Klein as communication, boundary maintenance, decision making, and systemic linkages.[8] These are almost identical to the processes defined by Satir for the family as a system, which are described in Chapter 4.[9]

Just as individuals cannot not communicate, so it is with communities. Any transferral of information among individuals or groups of people is communication. Communities also have formal communication systems such as newspapers, television and radio stations, and mail delivery networks. One can gain a good deal of information about a community by analyzing its communications and looking for patterns in the content and by analyzing the values portrayed through its media. For example, do the newspapers, radio, and television focus mainly on national and international happenings? Is the televised national news relegated to 30 minutes per day from the network, or do local persons discuss such matters as well? Is the reporting from primary data or the national news services? Is there any analysis of the news? Is it consistently biased in one direction? Does the community communicate primarily positive and hopeful types of information or primarily negative, crisis, or disaster types of information? Such analyses of easily obtained data are useful in gaining understanding of a community.

Boundary maintenance is another of the basic processes of community life. The geographic community must maintain its geographic boundaries in order to keep itself distinct from the outside environment. Formal methods of extending or contracting boundaries can be found in cases of land annexation or land loss between communities.

Communities of interest also must concern themselves with boundary maintenance. In this instance, membership is one primary target for boundary maintenance activities. Criteria for membership, induction mechanisms, initiations, and the like are methods by which communities of interest maintain their boundaries and keep unwanted members contained in the environment.

The third basic process is decision making. Most aspects of community life occur as a result of decision making or lack of decision making. Exceptions include natural disasters, uncontrollable events caused by weather conditions, or decisions made at higher levels such as the national level. Otherwise community life is in large part qualitatively dependent on the types of decisions made and the timing of these decisions. The thesis taken here about decision making is synonymous with the one taken regarding communication. That is, one cannot not decide because paradoxically that is a decision. The consequences of the decision to not decide will follow suit, and persons will have to live with these consequences. Thus, whether one decides to act, decides not to act, or decides not to decide, he has made a decision in each instance.

Decision-making processes are a major source of trouble for communities because decisions are being made constantly by individuals and groups at all levels of community life. Many of these decisions are in direct conflict with each other; many others deal with small fragments of community life and thus burn up resources in an inefficient and costly manner. Community decision making is rarely integrated. Rather, it appears to occur totally by chance, in a chaotic, random type of progression over time. Community leaders seem to be endlessly faced with the need to repair errors made because of nonintegrated decision-making processes. The alternative, however, is some form of authoritarian decision-making mechanism, and that approach is unacceptable in a democracy.

The fourth basic process of community life is systemic linkages. All discrete communities, whether geographic or communities of interest, must exchange information and energy with the larger society beyond their own parameters. Communities can do this in very open, positive ways or in relatively closed, paranoid ways. Between these two extremes are many shades of difference in the systemic linkage styles of communities. Sometimes a community is open to a strong linkage with some parts of the environment but equally inclined to close the boundary to other parts of the environment.

ADULT PARTICIPATION IN COMMUNITY LIFE

In Chapter 2 the five levels of individual participation in social systems are presented and discussed as norms, roles, status-positions, situs, and station. Situs, you recall, is the sum total of all the status-positions one actor holds in a complex organization such as a large corporation or university. In this discussion of community it is appropriate to discuss the highest level of individual participation in social systems, which is called station. Station refers to the sum total of all the status-positions held by one actor. It includes family positions, work and leisure positions, as well as those related to the other major institutions such as religion, government, and civic concerns. An example of one person's status-positions would be wife, mother, daughter-in-law, aunt, niece, and cousin in the family; company supervisor, committee member, committee chairperson, and liaison officer between departments on the job; union member and bargaining representative of the work-related union; athletic team member, team manager, and partner in recreation activities; organist, choir member, and discussion group leader in a church; lobbyist and office holder in civic organizations. The combination of all these status-positions would comprise the station of this single individual in the community.

The services provided within, for, and by communities meet the basic needs of the members largely to the extent that the needs are presented and sought by a large segment of the membership. Desires such as a good school system, adequate police, fire, sanitation, and other services, business and employment opportunities, efficient and honest local government, and religious freedom are attainable only to the extent that a higher percentage of the population is committed to these desires. When practically all the community membership is apathetic and only a few persons are left to make and implement decisions, efficiency increases temporarily. However, in a short time, the small group of decision makers begin to make errors because they lose touch with the needs of the majority. Eventually, the community membership finds itself in the position of having to react to these errors as they come to light, usually haphazardly. The ascribed leaders are then caught in the bind of resenting the former apathy of the citizenry and needing to defend themselves against negative reactions to their decisions.

The most attractive and possibly the most stable type of community is one in which a fair-sized segment of the population participates in decision making in different areas of community life. A community run by one man, one family, or a clique is less desirable to members than an egalitarian community, even though the latter may deal with decision making less efficiently.

Probably the major tool needed by adults in order to contribute as active participants in community life is a good conceptual grounding in the structure and operation of the levels of social systems. A community participant should know about simple and complex groups, about simple and complex organizations, and about the community as a whole in a very general way. Satir's delineation of the components of family life can be usefully extrapolated to community life: Visualize that every group of persons, regardless of the number or complexity of their organizations, will have rules, communication patterns, and societal linkages on both horizontal and vertical levels and that the individual members will have self-images.[10]

A significant part of adult learning during the post-formal-education years is the experiential learning obtained through participation in the groups, committees, and organizations of community life. Such experience is easy to obtain. One need only begin to attend meetings or gatherings and make a few comments or suggestions. In a short time, perhaps after only one meeting, inquiry will usually be made as to the availability of the newcomer for some kind of enduring involvement. This does not apply to relatively closed groups, of course, but there are many more open than closed groups. Actually, participation in open groups can sometimes lead to invitation or election into more closed groups.

Adult participation in community life can be roughly divided into four categories: influentials, effecters, activists, and marginals.[11] Influentials are the powerful persons who are usually behind the scene and may be hidden from the view of all but the most astute community observers. Such persons wield their power by acting as hidden manipulators of the next group, which are the effecters.

Effecters include top managment of large businesses, the technical and educational specialists who have the specific jobs of ascribed community leadership. Some of these persons have both the ascribed and achieved power to act on their own. More typically, effecters take orders or advice from influentials.

Activists include leaders of certain types of organizations in the community that have specific interests. Activists typically exert influence within the community in the specific area of the activist's special interest. Activists are generally outside the mainstream of general community decision-making processes and nearly always outside the economic system of the community.

Marginals include persons who do not actively participate in or influence the decision-making processes in community life. Such persons could be characterized as having to live with the consequences of decisions in which they had no part. The very young, the poor, the aged, and certain other minority groups most often comprise the marginals in the community.

Examples of active community participation through the phases of the adult years might be useful. Remember that these are only examples of a few patterns; the possible variations are almost infinite. Consider that a particular person joins the PTA when the first child enters school, is elected to several positions within the PTA, and eventually runs for and is elected to the school board. Because of an interest in youth, the disadvantaged, or the arts, a person may become involved in any number of civic organizations and may accept more responsible positions in that line. Still another alternative would be to get involved in government and occupy increasingly responsible levels of office, or get involved in church organizations and be appointed or elected to positions in that area.

Such participation by adults has a two-pronged effect. It enhances their own development and is therefore personally rewarding. Further, it contributes to the community in which they have membership and therefore is extrinsically useful. Such reciprocal give and take between an individual and his community is responsible for dynamic equilibrium between the personal system level of developing individuals and the larger social system requirements of participation by the membership. It is useful to recall often Klein's admonition that community is not man's habitat. On the contrary, community is man *in* habitat.[12]

THE PLACE OF COMMUNITY PARTICIPATION IN ADULT DEVELOPMENT

The tasks presented in Chapter 1 for the phases of adult development will be discussed from the standpoint of growth and differentiation in community participation through the adult life phases. The developmental task related to community in young adulthood is task 1.

Task 1—Advancing self-development and the enactment of appropriate roles and positions in society.   This task implies more than community participation, but the discussion will be limited to that aspect of the task. Young adults typically get into community life on a small scale at the local level. They engage in activities in the neighborhood, in political groups, in the PTA, and the like. Most of their energy is directed toward career and family development so that there is less time or energy left for participation in larger system levels.

The task of middle adulthood which includes community participation is task 7.

Task 7 —Assuming responsible positions in occupational, social, and civic activities, organizations, and communities. This task covers the two different concepts of community: the concept of community as a geographic locale containing the social structures necessary to sustain social life and the concept of community as a community of interest among people who are not spatially related. Persons during the middle years become more involved in extrafamily activities. They shift some of their time and energies toward the larger social system surrounding them and begin to take on leadership functions. They participate in the geographic community through its institutions and the local social organizations that are the embodiment of each institution. They may join communities of interest that are national or international in scope. Politically motivated middle adults begin to run for office, first at a local level and then at more widely inclusive and highly divergent levels. Many persons do not fit the picture drawn here, but the entire cohort of middle adults does. There is a progressive enlarging of their scope of community participation.

There is no specific developmental task devoted to community participation in the new middle years. The overall objective of this stage in life is primarily devoted to larger-system responsibility.

Major Objective. To assume major responsibility for the continued survival and enhancement of the nation. Persons in the new middle years are, generally speaking, the leaders of the world. In every country, the majority of the leaders of the major social institutions are in their late middle years.

Even at the local community level, persons in the new middle years hold the majority of the major decision-making positions. Hence, the community depends on them for making appropriate choices among alternatives, for insightful planning, and for decision making.

The whole process of community participation from young adulthood through late adulthood might be seen as ever enlarging, either in scope, in complexity, in numbers of memberships, or in the level of responsibility. Figure 1 shows this process as a series of enlarging circles to depict involvement at larger-system levels over the phases of adult life. The circles in young adulthood are small, and there is progressive enlargement through middlescence I and middlescence II. The size of the circle in late adulthood may vary from very small to medium sized depending on the level of activity of the late adults. Persons past retirement age may continue to participate at the national or international level as long as others let

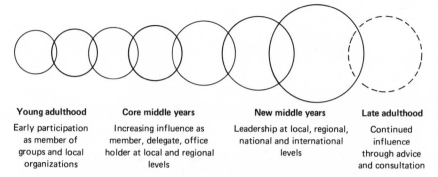

Young adulthood	Core middle years	New middle years	Late adulthood
Early participation as member of groups and local organizations	Increasing influence as member, delegate, office holder at local and regional levels	Leadership at local, regional, national and international levels	Continued influence through advice and consultation

FIG. 1. Progressive broadening of community participation during the adult years.

them and their health does not fail. However, it is more typical that such persons will decrease the scope of their participation progressively during the postretirement years. The ideas presented in Figure 1 will be taken up again in subsequent chapters and discussed in some detail in each adult stage through the new middle years. The caution is given here and repeated later that the geographically tied progression in scope depicted in Figure 1 is for illustrative purposes only. Persons can increase the scope of their community participation in many other ways.

References

1. R. L. Warren, *The Community in America*, 2nd ed. (Chicago: Rand McNally, 1972).
2. A. L. Bertrand, *Social Organization: A General Systems and Role Theory Perspective* (Philadelphia: Davis, 1972).
3. D. C. Klein, *Community Dynamics and Mental Health.* (New York: Wiley, 1968).
4. Warren, *The Community in America.*
5. Bertrand, *Social Organization.*
6. Klein, Community Dynamics.
7. Ibid.
8. Ibid.
9. V. Satir, *Peoplemaking* (Palo Alto, Calif.: Science and Behavior Books, 1972).
10. Ibid.
11. Klein, *Community Dynamics.*
12. Ibid.

Suggested Readings

Bertrand, A. *Social Organization: A General Systems and Role Theory Perspective.* Philadelphia: Davis, 1972, pp. 35–36.

Keyes, R. *We, the Lonely People Searching for Community.* New York: Harper, 1973.

Klein, D.C. *Community Dynamics and Mental Health.* New York: Wiley, 1968.

Olsen, M.E. *The Process of Social Organization.* New York: Holt, 1968.

Warren, R.L. *The Community in America.* 2nd ed. Chicago: Rand McNally, 1972.

6

DEVELOPMENT OF MATURITY

The process of maturation throughout life refers to the development of abilities in the psychomotor, intellectual, and affective domains. Maturity is reached when there is integration and synthesis of these three domains. The mature person has a reservoir of abilities, skills, knowledge, and feelings that can be used to express self, fulfill needs, and accomplish goals.

In an empirical study of adults, Heath found that people are constantly integrating changes into their self-system; integration in small bits serves to maintain a relatively stable structure.[1] Becker related to the same ideas when he discussed basic consistency in the person over time even though the person is constantly encountering new situations and is changing in the face of these situations.[2] There is a paradox of change and sameness. Each person grows but has basic patterns that remain consistent over time. A person's behavior traits are usually recognizable to old acquaintances, even when they have not seen each other for many years. It is common for reunited friends to comment that each behaves in ways consistent with the behavior of their youth.

CRITERIA FOR MATURITY

Health care workers who are dealing with families will want, in some instances, to assess the relative maturity levels of the individual members. Since this appraisal will be for diagnostic and treatment purposes rather than research purposes, the tools need to be simple and easy to use. Researchers interested in maturity have devised a number of paper and pencil instruments and interview and projective techniques to get at the multiple variables necessary for a measurement of maturity. However, it seems more pragmatic for practitioners to appraise the level of maturity by means of some generalized criteria. The criteria presented in this chapter are based on findings from research, but further research is necessary to test their validity. Nevertheless, they are offered here as a guide to the practitioner with the caution that it is easy to slip into a perfectionist attitude in applying these criteria. No one should be expected to achieve perfect adherence to them. What matters is that the individuals under scrutiny are *growing* along the lines described in the criteria.

The criteria described by Becker,[3] Pikunas,[4] Carl Rogers,[5] H. A. Overstreet,[6] and others have been taken into account. Redundancies in the qualities of maturity were removed to some extent, although not completely. If all redundancies were removed, the list would collapse to one criterion—the last one. The criteria can be listed as commitment, interdependence, self-esteem, concern for others, and serenity.

Commitment was chosen over the term "responsibility," which appears in some of the literature. Commitment seems a better choice because its connotation is deeper and more self-initiated. Commitment conveys that the responsibilities were taken on from within the person's being. Responsibility seems to imply taking on what the culture expects from a sense of duty or of guilt. It implies more externally imposed motivation. Commitment does not deny the reality of cultural influences, but it does carry the implication that the person becomes internally motivated toward accepting the responsibilities.

The extent to which an adult has commitment can be assessed by careful review of his statements about and behaviors toward work, leisure, family, and community life. Some persons simply drift through their responsibilities in life, fulfilling some, evading others, but with no real sense of commitment. Committed persons, on the other hand, are characterized by seeking realistic goals for themselves with a fairly systematic record of achieving either those goals or acceptable alternatives.

Interdependence comes when the person finds a balance between dependence on significant others and independence from control by others. Autonomy and a sense of competency characterize such persons even while they are fully cognizant of their dependence on forces outside themselves. They find ways to live in harmony with nature and to maintain synchrony in their interpersonal relationships in the family, at work, and in the community. This concept of interpersonal synchrony is comparable to the term "collaterality" found in the Kluckhohn–Strodtbeck paradigm in Table 3, Chapter 1. It also fits closely with the discussion in Chapter 2 of role congruency and role conflict. Recall the discussion about potential areas of role conflict in relation to task, authority, affect, and deference.

Self-esteem is not specifically discussed in Chapter 4 on the family, although there is a discussion of the concept of self-worth. For our purposes, these two terms might be considered synonymous. One of the clearest descriptions of high self-esteem or "okayness" was written by Virginia Satir,[7] and we are indebted to her for permission to reprint the description here:

MY DECLARATION OF SELF-ESTEEM

I am me.

In all the world, there is no one else exactly like me. There are persons who have some parts like me, but no one adds up exactly like me. Therefore, everything that comes out of me is authentically mine because I alone chose it.

I own everything about me—my body, including everything it does; my mind, including all its thoughts and ideas; my eyes, including the images of all they behold; my feelings, whatever they may be—anger, joy, frustration, love, disappointment, excitement; my mouth, and all the words that come out of it, polite, sweet or rough, correct or incorrect; my voice, loud or soft; and all my actions, whether they be to others or to myself.

I own my fantasies, my dreams, my hopes, my fears.

I own all my triumphs and successes, all my failures and mistakes.

Because I own all of me, I can become intimately acquainted with me. By so doing I can love me and be friendly with me in all my parts. I can then make it possible for all of me to work in my best interests.

I know there are aspects about myself that puzzle me, and other aspects that I do not know. But as long as I am friendly and loving to myself, I can courageously and hopefully look for the solutions to the puzzles and for ways to find out more about me.

However I look and sound, whatever I say and do, and whatever I think and feel at a given moment in time is me. This is authentic and represents where I am at that moment in time.

When I review later how I looked and sounded, what I said and did, and how I thought and felt, some parts may turn out to be unfitting. I can discard that which is unfitting, and keep that which proved fitting, and invent something new for that which I discarded.

I can see, hear, feel, think, say, and do. I have the tools to survive, to be

close to others, to be productive, and to make sense and order out of the
world of people and things outside of me.
   I own me, and therefore I can engineer me.
   I am me and I am okay.*

Several of the criteria for maturity mentioned by Pikunas
and others are included in Satir's description of self-esteem. Criteria
mentioned by other authors, such as the ability to deal constructively with frustration, the capacity for self-control, and a sense of
self-reliance become unnecessary as separate criteria. In addition,
qualifications about sensitivity to other people and to the environment or the capacity to communicate experiences in an open, honest
manner are all contained in the notion of self-esteem so vividly described by Satir.

Concern for others can be called many things: sensitivity to
others' needs, brotherhood in the Christian sense, or even sisterhood
in the women's movement sense. It would be useful to find one word
to express the concept rather than three words, but an acceptable
single word did not emerge from the literature reviewed. Nurturing
is a term sometimes used, although it has a vaguely negative connotation. This comes from a sense that too much nurturing can lead to
stifling of independence—for example, the idea of smothering rather
than mothering of children. Mature persons are characterized by
their interest in the welfare of others. This concern includes their
offspring, spouse, parents, significant other adults, acquaintances,
mankind in general, and other living things in the universe. It was
mentioned earlier that the criteria for maturity overlap, and that is
certainly true in this case. Concern for others is implied in the ideas
of commitment and interdependence. Perhaps it could be eliminated
as a separate criterion. It has been kept in this book for emphasis because, as the population density of the earth increases, the necessity
for mutual concern and caring about the needs of others is accentuated. At the same time, population density infringes on territorial
safety zones of individuals, and the pathologic reaction is an increase in interpersonal aggression and harm.

Serenity implies that the person has developed a "unifying
philosophy of life," which is Allport's rough translation for the Ger-
man concept of Weltanschauung.[8] The serene person has moved
from dependence on human beings and attempts at independently
controlling his own destiny to surrender to the will of a power

*Reprinted by permission of the author. From Satir, Peoplemaking, 1972, pp. 27–29.
Courtesy of Science and Behavior Books.*

higher than either his own, his parents', or his peers'—a higher power in some transcendental sense. This act of surrendering to a transcendental higher power results from the development of a faith that such a power exists and then the development and nurturance of faith in this higher power until surrender becomes possible. Once the person has surrendered his will and his life to a power greater than himself, the anxieties of his earlier days leave him. He feels in tune with natural law, and much of the struggle to control other people and the environment drifts away.

Development of a value system of living in tune with nature and trusting in a higher power is consistent with a change in value orientation on the Kluckhohn–Strodtbeck paradigm in Table 3, Chapter 1, from either the left or right column to the middle column. A more detailed discussion of this value orientation change over the course of adulthood appears in Chapter 9. In brief, the person changes from concentrating on mastery over nature to living in harmony with nature. The time orientation moves from concentrating on the future to living in the now. The activity orientation moves from doing to being-in-becoming, which fits very well with Satir's description of self-esteem. Finally, there is a move from valuing individualism or independence to valuing collaterality. Recall that collaterality was presented as a near synonym to the term "interdependence" in the discussion earlier in this chapter about man–man, man–environment relationships.

Serenity requires a great deal of groundwork, and the health care practitioner can easily differentiate those persons who have achieved a modicum of serenity from those who have not. Serene persons can distinguish between problems over which they have control and those over which they are powerless.[9] They do not waste time or feel anxious about the latter and they have confidence about finding solutions to the former, because of the harmony they have achieved in the man–nature–supernature dimension.

DEFINING THE MATURE PERSON

Maturity can be viewed in two ways: (1) as a relative phenomenon with criteria changing over time—ie, a person at 21 may be relatively mature for his age, a 41-year-old may also be relatively mature for his age, and an 81-year-old may be relatively mature for his age; or (2) as an ultimate goal that once achieved can be maintained until the decline occurring a few months prior to death in old age. Neither of these alternatives seems to be sufficient and yet putting them together seems contradictory at first glance. Nevertheless, putting them together is just what appears to be needed.

Maturity can be age related, and the developmental tasks presented in Chapter 1 can be used as a means of designating adults as mature or immature for their particular developmental stage. Persons can be appraised on the basis of numerous developmental task sets deemed appropriate for specific age ranges. This approach gives a measure of age-related or relative maturity. Maturity can also be appraised in a more absolute sense, using the criteria defined above as commitment, interdependence, self-esteem, concern for others, and serenity. This concept of maturity is primarily applicable to persons in middlescence II and late adulthood. In many ways this notion of maturity is similar to the concept of self-actualization described by Abraham Maslow.[10]

A person who has attained a high level of absolute maturity, then, is one who has carried out the developmental tasks for the first several stages of the life-span, has lived enough years to be mature physiologically, intellectually, and socioemotionally, and has melded these three domains into an integrated, harmonious whole. Finally, such a person lives in his environment, composed of other people and of nature, in an integrated, harmonious manner.

COMPONENTS OF ADULT MATURATION

Reference is made several times in this book to the triad of physical, intellectual, and emotional components of the human being. In the definition of maturity just presented, this triad appears again. It seems appropriate to discuss the relative rates of growth of each component over the life-span. Figure 1 shows an attempt to graph the three types of growth separately.

First is physical (P) maturation. Although this form is generally called aging in the adult years, it is nevertheless a true form of maturation that extends from the time of conception to death.

Second is intellectual (I) maturation. According to much of the early research on intellectual growth it supposedly progresses sharply to about age 30, remains stable for a few years, and then declines in the middle and later years. The longitudinal studies of intelligence done in recent years at Duke University and elsewhere refute the earlier findings.[11] In general, intelligence does not decline until very shortly before death. Indeed, a sharp decline in measures

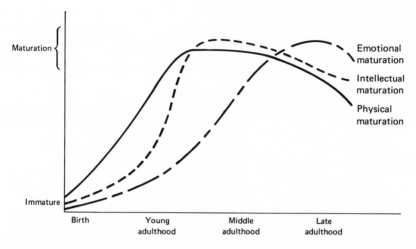

FIG. 1. Comparison of three types of human growth: physical, intellectual, and emotional (PIE).

of intelligence in the elderly can often be used as a predictor that the person will die in two years or less.[12]

Third is emotional (E) maturation, which progresses consistently over the life-span for normal people. Consistent progression does not mean that emotional growth rises in a straight line. Crises of many kinds may produce temporary stops, regressions, and the like in emotional maturation. Even mental illness may be perceived as a prolonged lack of development in the emotional sphere. Many persons who experience mental illnesses but recover go on to develop higher levels of emotional maturity, not only during but also after therapy.

Figure 1 seems to imply that emotional growth reaches a higher level than the other two. Such a judgment is not intended; rather, the curves were drawn this way to keep them separated for easy viewing. The bracket near the word maturation on the X axis indicates that the entire space within the bracket is equally a space called maturity.

A second figure was developed to attempt to integrate the three parts of individual maturation into a composite picture. Figure 2 shows one curve depicting the combined growth in all three areas simultaneously. Note that the curve in this graph begins in young adulthood rather than at birth. Dips were put in the curve to show that maturational and situational crises occur from time to time and result in temporary declines in growth processes. If the crisis is re-

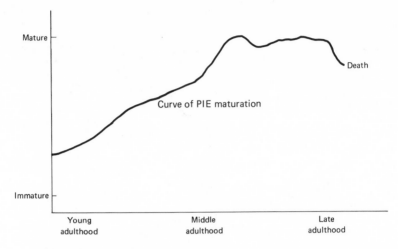

FIG. 2. Combined curve of maturation in physical, intellectual, and emotional spheres.

solved successfully a growth spurt may occur, and this is depicted on the curve by a higher level of growth following the dip. The sharp decline in the last years of late adulthood is intended to show that physical parameters such as heart rate, pulmonary functioning, and renal functioning decline, that intellectual functioning as measured by intelligence tests declines sharply in the last years of life, and that there is often an accompanying emotional decline characterized by decreased affect and lack of concern toward others. This emotional detachment from the world and human relationships may actually be a growth spurt toward acceptance of imminent death. It is exceedingly difficult to remain bias free in determining whether the final years of life are a decline, as shown on the graph, or whether one must reconceptualize growth at this point. If one does reframe the last years of life as preparation for death, then perhaps the detachment process is indicative of growth rather than decline. Perhaps the curve should continue to rise in the last years of life.

LONGEVITY

Much can be learned about maturity by studying the elite members of the population who live well beyond their peers. One such study was done by Gallup and Hill in the 1950s.[13] They used the Gallup Poll sampling technique to obtain various types of information from a representative sample of persons 95 years of age or older. The U.S. census was used as the basis for sampling. In addition, a small sample of persons were visited and interviewed at length. The interviewers were primarily interested in finding similarities among the sample. They were interested in developing a composite picture of this group if it proved to be homogeneous on some set of parameters. The investigators used both interviewing and unobtrusive techniques to search for possible cause–effect relationships between life-style variables and longevity. Five simple similarities among the subjects emerged. The first is beyond individual control, but the other four are up to the individual to control or try to control: (1) heredity—longevity of ancestors; (2) minimal interest in food—all had been thin during their lifetime; none had gourmet palates; they ate simply cooked meats and vegetables with no sauces or exotic spices; (3) belief in and attunement of their life with nature or a specific higher power; (4) hard physical labor or extensive outdoor exercise routines—the professionals among them were walkers; they had always walked outside in the fresh air; and (5) no compulsions—no excessive drinking or smoking, no excessive compulsions about work or being highly successful; at the same time many of them had been successful in the career and financial sense. The general characterization of these people fell easily into the middle column on the Kluckhohn–Strodtbeck value orientation paradigm (Table 3, Chapter 1). They saw man as a mutable mixture of good and evil, saw themselves as becoming, and lived one day at a time; they believed in living in harmony with nature, and their relationship with other human beings was collateral.

CHANGES IN MATURITY NEAR DEATH

In recent years researchers have become interested in studying changes in the self-system of very old persons who have a high probability of dying within three to five years. The research method usually involves testing the subjects quarterly or semiannually on the parameters of interest for two, three, or more years. It has repeatedly been noted that persons of advanced age tend to have decreased sensitivity or concern for others, show decreased commitment and interdependence, and evidence less self-esteem.

The time-series studies described above have shed considerable light on the alleged countermaturity trends of old age. Leiberman is one researcher who has done a number of these semilongitudinal studies.[14] The findings have shown rather consistently that persons nearing death show declining performance on various psychologic and intellectual tests, while persons who are not near death improve as a factor of test effect from repeated trials. The analysis is done three to five years later so that subjects can be divided into groups depending on whether they died during or shortly after the study or whether they were survivors.

It is hypothesized that the imminence of death is characterized by a generalized decline and detachment or withdrawal of energy from the outside (ie, from interpersonal relationships and interest in the environment) and projection to the inside in order to better cope with the inner experiences of the dying process. The general conclusion has been made that distance from death rather than chronologic age is the significant variable that parallels the decline in social and psychologic functioning of old age.[15–17]

Thus, we are faced with a paradox: At the end of life, true maturity is the antithesis of what maturity is earlier. Maturity at the end is commitment to dying rather than to living; it is detachment from, rather than concern for, others; it is transcendence rather than interdependence. However, the one criterion of maturity that does not seem to change is serenity. In the studies of Lieberman and Coplan, those who were near death seemed to be stable, serene, and coping adequately.[18]

References

1. D. H. Heath, *Explorations of Maturity* (New York: Appleton, 1965).
2. H. S. Becker, "Personal Change in Adult Life," in *Middle Age and Aging*, ed. B. L. Neugarten (Chicago: University of Chicago Press, 1968).
3. Ibid.
4. J. Pikunas, *Human Development: A Science of Growth* (New York: McGraw-Hill, 1969), pp. 314–327.
5. C. R. Rogers, "Toward a Modern Approach to Values: The Valuing Process in the Mature Person, *Journal of Abnormal Social Psychology* 68 (1964):160–167.
6. H. A. Overstreet, *The Mature Mind* (New York: Norton, 1949).
7. V. Satir, *Peoplemaking* (Palo Alto, Calif.: Science and Behavior Books, 1972), pp. 27–29.
8. G. W. Allport, *Pattern and Growth in Personality* (New York: Holt, 1961), Chap. 15.

9. L. F. Presnall, *The Search for Serenity* (Salt Lake City: U.A.F., 1959).
10. A. Maslow, "Self Actualizing People: A Study of Psychological Health," in *Personality Symposium No. 1*, ed. W. Wolff (New York: Grune, 1950).
11. L. F. Jarvik, C. Eisdorfer, and J. E. Blum, eds., *Intellectual Functioning in Adults* (New York: Springer, 1973).
12. Ibid.
13. G. Gallup and E. Hill, *Secrets of Long Life* (New York: Bernard Geis Associates, 1960).
14. M. A. Lieberman, "Psychological Correlates of Impending Death: Some Preliminary Observations," in *Middle Age and Aging*, ed. B. L. Neugarten (Chicago: University of Chicago Press, 1968).
15. M. A. Lieberman, "Observations on Death and Dying," *Gerontologist* 6(1966): 70–73.
16. M. A. Lieberman and A. S. Coplan, "Distance from Death as a Variable in the Study of Aging," *Developmental Psychology* 2(1969): 71–84.
17. C. Eisdorfer and F. Wilkie, "Intellectual Changes with Advancing Age," in *Intellectual Functioning in Adults*, eds. L. F. Jarvik, C. Eisdorfer, and J. E. Blum (New York: Springer, 1973).
18. Lieberman and Coplan, "Distance from Death," p. 82.

Suggested Readings

Kimmel, D.C. *Adulthood and Aging*. New York: Wiley, 1974.
Kübler-Ross, E., ed. *Death: The Final Stage of Growth*. Englewood Cliffs, N.J.: Prentice-Hall, 1975.
Neugarten, B.L., ed. *Middle Age and Aging*. Chicago: University of Chicago Press, 1968.
Pikunas, J. *Human Development: A Science of Growth*. New York: McGraw-Hill, 1969.

III

THE CRISES OF ADULT LIFE PHASES INCLUDING THE IMPACT OF ILLNESS

The chapters included in Part III present in-depth discussions of the three adult life phases that are the major foci in this book. These chapters are predicated on the belief that there is an order to the process of adult life and that each phase has certain identifiable discomforting forces that emanate within the person and push toward further maturity. The emergence of these forces for growth are frequently evidenced by symptoms of distress in the individual called maturational crises. Such crises are desirable, although painful experiences.

In each person's life pattern there are periods of time when a particular life structure is forming; later, that life structure will begin to break up and new formulations will emerge. There are also periods between the formulations and the breakdowns when one experiences relative stability even though subtle changes are taking place in preparation for the next transition period. Hence, the whole maturation phenomenon can be viewed as cyclic: buildup period, stable period, breakdown period, transitional period, next buildup period, and so on.

The terms "maturational crisis" and

"situational crisis" are used to differentiate between two important kinds of stress. Maturational
crisis refers to the developmental transition stresses that recur about every seven to ten years
through the adult life cycle. Situational crisis refers to extraordinary events that occur only in certain individuals, not in the total age group. Illness
or severe accidents are examples of situational variables that are of major interest in this text. Many
scientists have shown that other situational crises,
such as economic difficulty, divorce, or death of a
spouse are often followed by a health-related
crisis, and so the two types of crisis are intimately
linked. However, a thorough explication of these
phenomena is beyond the scope of this book. The
focus here is simply on situational crises of illness
or injury without regard to predisposing factors.

Chapter 7 concentrates on the situational and maturational issues that are relevant to
young adults between the approximate ages of 18
and 30. The uprooting transition between 18 and
22 years is dealt with briefly, followed by a presentation of the period called provisional adulthood,
which lasts from about 22 to 29 years of age. During the years from 18 to 30, young adults initiate
the work trajectory. Some do it later than others,
depending on the extent of post-high-school education they pursue. Specific discussion centers
around the situational and maturational stresses
involved in moving from the educational environment to the marketplace.

Next, the initial development of a new
family system is discussed from the perspective of
the conflicts and coping mechanisms used to
bring about adaptation. The issues surrounding
extended kinship networks are closely tied to the
marriage and early family stresses. During these
years there is much fluctuation and blurring of al-
legiances to the newly developed nuclear family
contrasted with the family of origin. Development
and maintenance of a separate dwelling site are an
important step in the process of moving allegiance

and dependence from the family of origin to the new nuclear family. Young married couples who live with one set of parents may experience some retardation in their development as an independent family unit and develop less functional roles and rules during their early life together. Young adults who experiment with one or more trial cohabitation relationships generally carry out these experiments in a housing situation away from the parental dwelling. However, these persons still may have many ties to their parental dwelling and their family of procreation. This is particularly evident in those who do not disclose their cohabitation status to their parents.

Community participation is perhaps the least evident phenomenon during the young adult years. However, a section on community participation is included in Chapter 7 because this area of living becomes very important in the subsequnt phases of adult life. Logically, the beginning development of community participation skills and style occurs during youth. Hence, a short discussion of how young adults participate in community life is included.

Health-related crises are discussed as the major situational stresses of interest in this book. Acute illness and its impact on the individual and young family are discussed and illustrations of cases are presented. Examples of the impact of chronic illness and disability are presented in somewhat more depth, along with illustrative case materials. Since disability from accidents is much more common in this age group than chronic illness, major emphasis in the discussion and case illustrations is given to permanent long-term disability conditions resulting from accidents.

Chapter 8 deals with middlescence I (the core of the middle years), or roughly the years between 30 and 50. There are several definable growth and integration periods in this 20-year span. On the basis of knowledge available to date, several of these are treated individually in the discussion. Gayle Sheehy's term "Catch 30" transition is used for the period between the years of 20 and 32, and the rooting period is her descriptive label for the years between 32 and 39. The fourth decade is a tumultuous one in which a great deal of stress and much change occur. The leap from 39 to 40 is culturally defined as a negative milestone. The transition from the third to the fourth decade is not easily made, and an adjustment by the individual occurs only after the middle forties. There appears to be a highly volatile, troubled period in the middle forties that is reminiscent of the adolescent years from age 13 to age 15. The environment is not really producing new or unusually severe pressures or problems for the person; rather, the person is internally troubled and restless but unwittingly uses denial and lays the blame on external affairs or other people. Descriptions of the behavior of 45-year-olds, and their own stories, conjure up a picture of a smoldering and frequently erupting blaze of uncomfortable feelings. Hence, the term I have coined for this period is the "mid-40s inferno." The core adult restabilization period occurs between 48 and 50 years. Many spouses and offspring report that there is an unbelievably sharp contrast between the behavior of family members at age 50 and their behavior during the middle forties.

The maturational issue surrounding work in this period is the experience of major career responsibility. In the traditional family it is the time when children depart, and in the nontraditional family it may be a time when the persons involved move on to new relationships. Changes occur slowly and insidiously but constantly during these years, even though relative financial stability, career stability, and household stability exist for a majority of persons in this age group.

Female menopause starts during the latter years of this phase and, depending on the severity of its symptoms, may put significant stress on the family system in general and the marital dyad in particular. Separation, divorce, and remarriage are relatively frequent changes made during the middle years, particularly when children have reached some level of independence from the nuclear family of procreation and the middle-aged marital couple do not reconstruct an acceptable relationship with them.

Persons in this age group come to see themselves as the generation in the middle. They have children who are moving toward eventual independence, and they are beginning to face the realities of responsibility for aging parents. One of the parents may die during this period, and the experiences of arranging a funeral, dealing with one's own grief, and comforting the remaining grief-stricken and lonely parent occur all at once.

The health-related situational stresses of middlescence include acute illnesses, chronic illnesses, and disabilities of self, spouse, offspring, or parents. Crises of this nature result in disruption of the family system, no matter which generation the sick person is in. However, major emphasis in the discussion is directed toward illness occurring in the middlescent. Acute illnesses in these years less frequently result from accidents than in young adulthood. More often they are either acute infections, exacerbations of chronic disease, or conditions amenable to surgical removal of the affected organ(s). Chronic diseases affect only a small percentage of the persons in this age group, but such conditions when present have a major impact on the person and on family functioning because the person from 30 to 50 is so central to the family system. Case examples of both an acute and chronic nature are discussed.

In Chapter 9, the focus is on middlescence II (the new middle years), approximately the years between 50 and 70. It is difficult to put an ending age on this phase because it seems to depend more on health, vitality, and mental alertness than on chronologic age. The age of 70 was chosen as the end because it is the age when even the most conservative employment situations usually require retirement.

Stresses dealt with during these years include impending retirement, changes in living arrangements, dealing with the ramifications of cellular aging processes, and, for both men and women, the final phases of the climacteric. The climacteric starts in the forties, and the mid-40s inferno probably is closely tied to abnormal fluctuations. The visible signs of the climacteric, especially in women, usually occur later, but by the new middle years the discomfort phase has passed for the majority of both sexes. Concurrent with several of these changes is the urge to look over one's life and to put successes and failures into perspective. No doubt this urge is also tied to physiology since the 50-year-old has a more stable hormonal milieu and is thus much more emotionally stable than ever before.

Health-related crises during these years are again discussed under the headings of acute and chronic illness, and examples of patient situations are presented. Death and dying are discussed from the standpoint of experiencing grief during and after the dying process of others, as well as from the anticipatory grief standpoint of one's own impending death in the next phase of development. Since this is a book about middlescence, the final stage of late adulthood is not covered here.

Chapter 10, which is an epilogue, is dedicated to answering the questions, So what? What specific changes ought to be made in our society in order to better promote life-span development? How should these changes be implemented? Which social institution would be the best first target for change? Recommendations are made in Chapter 10 to the following: education—from nursery school to adult education programs;

health care professions—directed primarily toward professional socialization of practitioners with a life-span developmental framework; and media—with particular emphasis on television programming and the advertising industry. Finally, there is a short discussion of the implications of a life-span developmental approach for future generations.

7

YOUNG ADULTHOOD

Many psychologists still cling to the outdated belief that mental development stops shortly after the end of adolescence. The peak is recognized as age 26. After that, slow decline supposedly sets in, both physically and mentally. The Duke University longitudinal studies, research by Roger Gould at the University of California, Los Angeles, and the data of other researchers interested in middle and late adult development attest to the fallacy of such "facts" about adult life. We are, however, many years and much research away from an understanding of adult development comparable to what has been learned over the past several decades about children and adolescents.

Emphasis in this chapter is placed on the earliest years of adult development—what might be called youth or young adulthood. Gould reports that the dominant theme for 16- to 18-year-olds is escape from parental dominance.[1] When adolescents move into young adulthood (18 to 22 years old), they already have substituted friends for family, but stress is evident in their attempts to increase independence from parents. The dominant fear is reported to be not knowing if they are good enough to make it without their parents. Yet they do not want continued parental dependence. Their ambivalence shows in the way they come and go from the parental dwelling. Between the ages of 22 and 28, self-reliance increases and substituting friends for family is less dominant. After age 28 the self-reliance declines into what Sheehy calls the "Catch 30" period, when some anxiety and depression may occur.[2] The young adult period is characterized by high energy and attempts to become competent in the environment. The major maturational goals or maturational crises of this phase are (1) initiation of the work trajectory, (2) development of a traditional or nontraditional family unit, (3) learning to live within some form of modified extended kinship network, (4) beginning accumulation of property, and (5) development of a beginning sense of community. The latter section of this chapter deals with situational crises of youth that are related to illness and disability. Acute illness is dealt with briefly because it is a transient phenomenon. More emphasis is put on chronic illness or disability during youth because permanent illness or disability often affects negatively the developmental processes.

THE UPROOTING TRANSITION

The transition years between 18 and 22 might be called the uprooting years, the period when the push–pull between family and life on one's own gains real momentum. The recurrent cycles of leaving home and returning for a while are institutionalized in American culture. Examples of temporary trials away from home are going away to college, joining the military service, and going on extended trips. Eventually the youth gets a place of his or her own and, even then, the frequency with which a youth comes home for a meal or a weekend may be high.

Researchers report that people in this transition phase find that the single most important task is adjusting to being on one's own, adjusting to the realization that one must stop depending on one's family and that one cannot depend on high school friends because they have dispersed. Many interviewees report that getting married during this period was probably their way of handling the loneliness they felt.

By the end of this transition phase, the forces pulling these youths away from the family far outweigh the forces pushing them toward the parental family. By age 22, most live away from home either in an apartment or in school, work part time or full time, pay rent, own a car or motorcycle, are married or cohabiting, and so on. Interviewed youths report feeling not quite adult, but they see full adulthood as just around the corner. They feel partially autonomous but still in partial jeopardy of being pulled back into their family of origin. To some extent they miss the soothing functions that the family did perform. However, they are loathe to ask for soothing within the parental family system because they see it as childish and not appropriate to their newfound independence. Many fear that they would be pulled back into the parental family system if they divulged this weakness to their parents. Hence, many put on a false bravado, attested to in their interview sessions.

PROVISIONAL ADULTHOOD

Gould reported a considerable shift in the dynamics of 22- to 29-year olds.[3] They were established in their autonomy from the family of origin and had begun to feel like adults. His subjects felt that they were engaged in the right course of life, and they spent little time or energy analyzing their commitments to see if these were right for them. Provisional adults rely on their peers less than during adolescence or the uprooting transition period, but peers are still important. However, peer criticism does not produce the personal devastation that it did earlier because there is more personal identity and self-confidence. The move toward inner-directed goal seeking has begun to take place, so reliance on peers for outer-directed goal seeking and criterion measures of worthwhileness diminishes.

The 22- to 29-year-olds spend their time mastering what they are supposed to be. The professional athlete is a highly visible example of this phenomenon of mastery. These athletes may have been good in college, but they become stabilized masters in their sport during the period between 22 and 29 years of age.

Sheehy reports that people in this age group do best if they can find a mentor, someone outside the family who will serve as a role-model either in their career or all-around and who will give various kinds of support and guidance through the subsequent years up to age 40.[4]. Mentors are important to both men and women, although they have traditionally been available only to men. A mentor is a middle-aged adult who is seen as more proficient and learned than the youth. Such a person must be willing to serve as mentor, which means teaching the youth in an informal manner and helping with contacts and experiences that will be useful.[5] In order to be effective, mentors must be nonparental role-models. Such middle adults help youth to overcome youth–parent conflicts and move on with further personal development.

INITIATING THE WORK TRAJECTORY

The work trajectory starts for most people at age 18. Some may start earlier with vocational training during the high school years, but there is a cultural expectation that every person will begin at graduation from high school. In the context of this discussion, enrollment in college is considered movement along the work trajectory even though actual employment may be several years in the future. A considerable number of young people are not ready to become young adults when they graduate from high school. Their emotional development and chronologic age may not be in synchrony with readiness to move into the real world of long-term career commitment. Resolutions for this maturational lag are many. For example, some persons work it out in college by staying uncommitted to a major or by switching majors several times. Some do it by taking a job with no future as a means of putting off decision making about their plan of life. Others get married and take any available job to avoid facing systematic planning. Some join the military, some girls get pregnant, and some turn to drugs or to crime or join the deviant fringes that frequently exist in large cities or near university campuses. These behaviors appear to be delaying tactics, modes of putting off facing the cultural expectations laid for post-high-school years.

The expectation that work of some kind will begin after age 18 is a heavy norm in North American culture. For pre-women's-liberation females, housewifery fell into this category, so that by the single act of marriage the female moved into status-positions of family and work simultaneously. Having one's major status-positions of family member and worker in the same system has both advantages and disadvantages. It is a simplified life-style in so far as there are fewer positions to fill; one does not get into the complex forms of role relationships that exist in complex social organizations. However, the simplicity has a negative aspect in so far as the total status depends on how well these few positions are enacted. On is a success or a failure on the basis of how well one does as a wife, homemaker, mother, and daughter-in-law.

This puts a great deal of importance on a narrow range of roles and does not allow a person to be highly competent in some positions and not so competent in other positions. Such heavy emphasis on a few family-related positions does not occur for men. Men consider career as an entity separate from marriage. For women it has been all one institution—marriage, family, work, and leisure bound together with overlapping norms, roles, and positions.

For purposes of simplicity, the remainder of this section deals with occupational development of both men and women, excluding homemaking. This plan is appropriate because homemaking is different in significant ways: It does not have a seniority or promotion-in-rank system, it is evaluated by those served rather than by any actual designated supervisor, and it is outside the business and bureaucratic institutions typically discussed in relation to occupations and careers. It could, but does not, receive direct monetary compensation.

Moving from the dubious shelter of the school into the world of work is a stressful transition for almost everyone. The hours are more stringent, the requirements about what one will or will not do are more clearly defined, and there is a general overall reduction in freedom. The compensation for some is money; for others, it is a longer-term goal like success. For many young people, the emerging and developing world of work is all-consuming. They have little time to direct their energies toward leisure, family, or community. For others, the world of work is already a bummer at this early age, and they see their real life as existing during nonworking hours.

The following vignettes illustrate some of the variety that is possible during these years. One can note the basic similarity in these examples, despite the diversity of work styles in them.

> John is 23 years old. He graduated from a prestigious eastern university, worked one year, and then decided that he had had enough of the conservative 9 A.M. to 5 P.M. life. He packed up his motorcycle and set off to see the world. After two years on the road he returned.

The next episode in this story could go several ways, but the two most common ways are that he either decides to develop a commitment to some form of settled life-style or becomes a permanent transient. In either case he commits himself to a stable life system. Chances are good that John may reconsider his choices when he is going through the transition from ages 29 to 32. However, for the time being, John will stabilize with his choice and will undergo many small, barely perceptible changes for the remaining years of young adulthood.

An illustration of dedication to work is presented by the example of Mike.

> Mike is 23 and was convinced from an early age that he wanted to be a photographer. He pursued this desire avidly through his childhood, through high school, and into post-high-school educational experiences. He is dedicated to photography. It is both his work and his leisure. The only distinction that he makes between work and leisure revolves around the kind of photography involved and the circumstances of payment that surround it. If he has a contract to photograph something, then it is work; if he is photographing as an art form, then it is leisure.

Mike may also have second thoughts about the worthwhileness of his dedication to photography during his transition into the thirties. However, for the time being, he is content to become a master at his trade. He exemplifies a segment of the young adult population who concentrate a major portion of their energies on becoming competent at their chosen occupation.

FAMILIAZATION

Erikson's key concept for the stage of young adulthood is intimacy.[6] This assumes that a strong sense of identity was formed in the previous stage of adolescence. Intimacy is something one develops in relation to a significant other, eg, a mate, children, or other important persons. It is not the intimacy of sexual or other short-lived encounters that are intimate in the physical sense only. It probably is not the short-lived intimacy experienced by members of an encounter or other short-term group in which facades are broken quickly and honest talk is the order of the day. Erikson's type of intimacy refers to enduring intimate relationships with one or a few truly significant other human beings in a mutually nurturing relationship that endures over a prolonged period of time. The word familiazation was coined to indicate the development of long-term intimate relationships that would fit the definition of family presented in Chapter 4. It includes both traditional marital relationships and long-term cohabitation relationships. Many young adults experiment with both kinds of familiazation. Cohabitation may be tried first, with the future marital partner or a different partner; marriage may come later. The converse is also common. An early marriage breaks up; one or both marital partners do not wish to try marriage again, so a subsequent experience with familiazation is without legal or religious sanctions. The sexually cohabiting partners may be of different or the same sex. It is also becoming more evident that some persons previously married to a member of the opposite sex will choose homosexual cohabitation the next time. Variation is prevalent, but many of the same basic rules of family life must be worked out regardless of the form or style the family takes.

Marriage and Initiation of Nuclear Family Unit

The familiazation process is an exceedingly important maturational phenomenon that is frequently fraught with pain, disappointments, and other negative experiences. Grace studied traditional weddings of young adults and found that one of the early instances of crisis and discomfort between a young couple revolves around the planning of their wedding. Unfortunately, neither young couples nor their parents seem to comprehend that the wedding is not just an event. It is a trial run of management, decision making, and compromise between the future spouses. How they plan the wedding is an important precedent for how their rules, communication, and decision making will go during their married life. Some couples in Grace's study formed coalitions against one or both sets of parents and made their own wedding plans. Quite often the bride and her mother formed a coalition, and the groom, his family, and the bride's father were essentially excluded from the planning. All manner of coalitions were found; for example, a coalition formed by the two mothers occurred on rare occasions. All in all, the allegedly joyous event of the wedding was very often fraught with conflict due to the formation of such dysfunctional alliances. Most of the couples in the sample indicated that the planning of the wedding was a major hurdle in their relationship. In subsequent interviews, Grace found that couples who did not collaborate with each other, but either let others plan the wedding or formed cross-generational coalitions such as the bride—mother coalition, subsequently found it difficult to make important family decisions in mutually agreeable ways.[7] The predictions based on this finding are those that one would make on the basis of the discussion of the family as a system in Chapter 4.

Developing separate identification within the newly formed family is an easier process for some young people than for others. Parents of the young couple help or hinder this process depending on whether they encourage or discourage independence from the family of procreation. Many young couples are in the position of having to deal with (1) naturally occurring mismatches between their fantasies and the realities of married life, (2) conflicts in expectations about the rights and responsibilities of each partner in relation to the other; (3) the external world of school or occupation, and (4) the enlarged kinship network of in-laws, who might be attempting to manipulate one or both of them in stress-producing ways. The following example illustrates how some of these issues would operate in a new family system:

> A young married couple named Janice and William are learning to live within their extended kinship network. In particular, the parents of each are presenting challenges to both of them as a family system and to each of them as individuals.
> The issue of separateness has always been a problem for William's mother. She has tended to view her children as extensions of herself and has not fostered their separateness, distinctness, and independence. William greatly desires separateness from his mother but does not comprehend that separateness is a process that is learned slowly from birth to adulthood. He has not accepted the fact that a single incident like marriage will not bring about all the growth processes inherent in the development of separateness. He has yet to realize that he must eventually face up to a need for remedial work on developing separateness from his mother if he is actually to achieve it on the emotional as well as physical level.
> Janice also has some residual immaturities from her adolescence. One of her parents was a silent controller, and the other was an excessively verbal distracter. Janice realizes that her family background was problematic and is determined to work hard on her own marriage so that it does not fall into the same kind of unhappy rut.
> The couple swings back and forth between independence from the two sets of parents and dependence on them. Both parents give expensive presents such as appliances, furniture, or clothes. The couple realizes that each present comes with a price tag of certain kinds of behavior expected in return. Janice and William sometimes voice their desire to return the gift rather than feel beholden, but they never return the gift. They realize that the repercussions of such an insult would be too great.

Janice and William may make the mistake of believing that a child will solve their problems. Unfortunately, a child will most likely add to their unresolved difficulties. Individual and familial maturation is what they lack.

Biosocial Complexities of Adult Sexuality

The adolescent has many sex-related growing pains, but sex-related stresses certainly do not cease at the end of adolescence. Biological development problems and hormonal imbalances diminish in young adulthood, but the biosocial complexities of sexuality certainly take on a major focus. Young adults comprise the majority of persons coming to grips with such things as contraception, pregnancy, childbirth, postpartum sexual abstinence, infertility, veneral disease, abortion, and adoption. Discussion of so many intermeshed issues is beyond the scope of this text. The reader is encouraged to pursue these important topics through the many current sources available.

It is next to impossible to summarize the topic of sexuality in this phase because the life-styles of young adults are so varied. Furthermore, changes occur in sexual behavior between 18 and 30. A person who at 22 had many sexual partners could be a satisfied spouse with one sexual partner at 28. The converse also occurs. The young adult years are a time of searching for a satisfying, long-term, interpersonal relationship with a significant other. Some youths spend a long time searching and "run through" many would-be partners in this search. Others choose a partner that is readily available without risking a search process. Those who search and test may find a match, or they may turn the process of searching and testing into a life-style. Those who choose a partner too quickly may outgrow the partnership and begin searching and testing processes later in young adulthood or during middlescence. Some reported reasons for choosing a particular partner during young adulthood include approval, safety, or practicality; to fill a void in the self, to control something, or to avoid aloneness. The process of maturation leads toward a change in such motives over time. Later chapters contain information about the changes that occur during middle adulthood in which the direction of change flows from an individualistic orientation, which is self-centered, to a collateral orientation, which is interdependent.

Community Participation

Early movement into community participation may take the form of membership in college or university groups or in student professional organizations. A small percentage of students run for office or join various campus organizations that are more or less contributory to the shared community life. Other young adults join the junior forms of civic organizations, church groups, and the like. Still others belong to athletic clubs, teams, the YMCA, the YWCA, or other organizations that have components of civic or charitable activities combined with leisure for the members. Some young adults take on leadership responsibilities in such things as the scouts, 4-H, the Big Brothers organization, and other child-oriented groups. Still others volunteer in hospitals, nursing homes, and other places that house the ill or dependent. Military service, the Youth Corps, the Peace Corps, church work, political campaign work, and other services to the larger society fit into this category of community participation.

Although the above list of community-oriented activities is fairly diverse, a note of caution should be injected lest the reader believe that the implication here is that the majority of young adults become involved in some form of community participation. In reality, the percentage of young adults with the energy to participate in community life in addition to their responsibilities in the work/ career development area, familiazation processes, and personal trials and tribulations with situational and maturational crises is probably not large. It actually depends on how one defines community participation. In a large sample of persons in the age group, it is likely that most have participated in some community-oriented function at one time or another. However, it is unlikely that a large percentage are able to maintain consistent or sustained participation during young adulthood.

Those persons who do become involved in community service work in a consistent manner at an early age tend to maintain such activities through the rest of their active lives. The form of their organizational involvement will doubtless change over time, and the participation may change from a very small local allegiance to participation on a citywide, county, state, or national level. In other cases, the participation may move from one organization to another through the years depending on changes in career, social status, goals, interests, and perceptions by others of one's capabilities and potential. The more typical trend appears to be movement from narrow, local pursuits to broader-level planning or decision-making groups that are concerned with more general interests/problems of even wider populations or groupings. One example would be a young adult who joins the PTA when the oldest child enters kindergarten, eventually becomes president of the PTA, and wins election to the school board by the time the kindergarten child is in high school. Community participation seen in the light of ever-enlarging circles, as shown in Figure 1, would suggest that this area of life, like the occupational area, also has a trajectory. It is true that the percentage of people who get on this trajectory and stay on it is small, but, for those who do, the normative pattern appears to be movement

from small, simple, local interests to larger, more complex, dissemi-
nated interests. The example shown in Figure 1 is modeled after a
multilevel organization, ie, with local, state, regional, national, and
perhaps international levels. Note that this is only an example. The
concept is equally applicable to individuals who simply increase the
number of local organizations in which they actively participate or
increase the time commitment to one local community component
through the years.

Figure 1 shows the young adult as a member of a local chapter of an organization or in some way engaged at the level of grass
roots membership. The next larger circle shows him as an officeholder in that organization. This exemplifies an increase of responsibility in community participation. From holding a local office, he
moves on to serving as a delegate from the local constituency. In the
next stage of development he can move on to higher level participation. Specifics of movement beyond young adulthood are discussed
in later chapters.

The following vignette is illustrative of how young adults
may become engaged in community work:

Billie Jean, at 23, is off to a successful start in a promising
career. She has an active social life but is becoming bored with just job and
leisure. She decides to look around for something useful that she can do of
a civic or charitable nature. After talking to several people and looking
through the newspapers, Yellow Pages, and directories of service agencies
in town, she decides to visit a few of the places that sound appealing. After
some trial and error, Billie Jean finds an interest in a particular type of

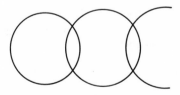

Young adulthood

Member,	Office	Initiate,
local level	holder,	next level
	local level	entry

FIG. 1. Initiation of community participation style during young adulthood.
This example can be related to a professional organization, an honorary society, a
service organization, or to the political arena. Simply name a target system and
follow through from left to right.

community service and begins to spend some of her spare time in this way. Because of her finely developed intelligence, she creates an impact in the group, and her opinion becomes a valuable component in their decision-making processes. Billie Jean begins to sense her importance in this situation and realizes that she made a good choice of putting her time in this direction, because she is providing a valuable service and as a quid pro quo is adding something valuable to her self-concept.

HEALTH-RELATED SITUATIONAL CRISES

Many types of situational crises occur during the young adult years. Health-related crises are actually quite rare in comparison to legal, financial, school- or job-related, and interpersonal crises involving significant friends or intimates. Nevertheless, because of the focus in this text, only crises that involve acute or chronic health problems will be given attention.

Acute Illness

Accidents are the major source of all illnesses during the young adult years. Short-term types of injuries can put a strain on the youth even when one knows that the disability is short term. Impatience is a significant characteristic, and when the accident is a natural consequence of an action taken by the injured person, the impatience is mixed with guilt and anger at self. The easy way to deal with these feelings is to express frustration and anger at family, friends, and health care staff.

Tom was a 20-year-old student who had hopes of becoming a professional athlete. He was currently in the hospital with a broken arm and leg sustained in competition. His mood had become a problem for the hospital staff and several of his friends had taken verbal beatings from him during his three-day stay in the hospital.

Nursing intervention consisted of gathering information from Tom about the meaning of this injury to him, of assessing his behavior in relation to a conceptual frameword such as loss or grief (in this case the stage of anger probably occurs faster than in a catastrophic illness), and of presenting some of these observations to him for his consideration with an option to openly share his feelings with a neutral professional and be guided to work on these feelings so that he could come to deal with what was really at the bottom of the uncomfortable feelings. Tom considered this offer for 24 hours and agreed to three short sessions with the nurse to work on what the accident meant to him.

He saw it as a threat to his chances of becoming a professional athlete. At the bottom of his anger was fear: fear of being passed over, fear of rejection, fear of having to find some other career. Even though he had been told that his chances of a good repair on both the arm and leg were excellent, this reassurance was not a guarantee that everything would not be ruined.

The major stumbling block to Tom's acceptance of his feelings was that he could blame no one else for his fall. It was the natural consequence of his own actions during the competition. He was faced with having to accept responsbility for the outcomes, whatever they might be, of this accident. Most awkward of all, he would have to forgive himself if the accident really did cause a change in his life plans. By the end of the third session, on the day of discharge, Tom had made some strides toward claiming ownership of his feelings about the injury and had developed a partial comprehension of the bind he had placed himself in with only one alternative for a career. With or without an injury, such an inflexible career trajectory can be very problematic.

Chronic Illness

Chronic illnesses or disabilities are not common during young adulthood, but they do occur. Disabilities caused by accidents are the most common forms, but young adults have diabetes, rheumatoid arthritis, and cancer, to name a few. Dependency is difficult for any adult at any phase of development, but for the young adult dependency caused by illness or accidents comes at a time when all the developmental tasks of this phase are aimed at movement toward independence. Young adults who are faced with chronic health problems of a severe nature often become emotionally underdeveloped in terms of the developmental tasks of young adulthood. In the following illustration, both members of the marital dyad were immature even though the husband had the chronic disability:

Andy, aged 20½, was injured in a motorcycle accident two years ago. He is a paraplegic who is currently enrolled as a full-time student in architecture. His career ambition is to specialize in designing barrier-free buildings and houses for handicapped persons. He married a shy college student named Marie during her freshman year and they have a 3-month-old baby. They live in a university apartment complex for married students. The family was referred to the nurse by the student health center because of Marie's repeated, minor complaints of stomach pains and headaches over the past few months.

Family system assessment interviews indicate that Andy is ambivalent about his family responsibilities. He wishes that he could have more quiet time to work on his studies and that Marie would spend less time complaining about her minor aches and pains. After all, there is no comparison between her minor symptoms and what he has overcome with his disability.

Marie indicates that she, too, is ambivalent about what she let herself in for with this marriage and motherhood. She saw the marriage as a way out of worrying about getting dates every weekend. The pregnancy was unplanned but did serve the purpose of getting Marie out of school, and she was not really motivated to pursue a degree. Although the marriage and baby removed her from these problems, she is now in a situation where the solution has taken on the character of becoming an even more difficult set of problems. She indicates that she loves Andy and the baby, Jamie, but has mixed feelings of self-pity, resentment, anger, and even hate much of the time. She indicates that Andy does not help her with the baby or the apartment. He is totally absorbed with his studies, his group of paraplegic buddies, and his physical hygiene regimen, which takes up considerable time in the morning and evening.

The infant is normally developed for 3 months. Marie considers him a good baby and expresses some guilt at taking out her frustrations toward Andy and her anger with herself on the baby by ignoring his cries for prolonged periods of time.

This vignette of young family life is not atypical. The two people have moved into one household to fulfill various personal needs. Some of these are fulfilled, but others are not, and a price of new inconveniences and responsibilities is added to their old way of life. Many of their expectations of each other have never been voiced aloud. They expect each other to just "know" or read the other's mind. Hence, no problem solving or compromising has ever been attempted. Andy stays away from the apartment more and more, and Marie develops physical symptoms. These are outlets for the distress each is experiencing.

Intervention started immediately with the assessment interview because each one heard things from the other that had not ever been voiced aloud. The nurse explained some of the basic mechanisms of communication barriers, principles of good communication, and processes of negotiation between married couples. Marie was more responsive than Andy, who considered the whole process unnecessary and seemed closed to working in the family sessions. Finally, the nurse found something that Andy wanted from Marie, and a negotiation session was successfully culminated. After that, the outcomes of subsequent sessions varied, but overall showed more success than resistance because family life between sessions was improving. Andy was getting more quiet time and freedom to be out with his friends without nagging and other guilt-projecting tactics from Marie. Marie had negotiated several things for herself: free time to take an assertiveness training course at the counseling center, one evening per week when she and Andy would go out alone together, and at least 15 minutes of time each day when she could have his attention to share her feelings, thoughts, and problems. Andy was reticent to take advantage of his 15-minute period to share his feelings, thoughts, and problems with Marie but eventually made some attempts that apparently were rewarding to him.

The relationship with the nurse was terminated after the predetermined ten sessions with considerable improvement in the day-to-day family pattern of life. There were, of course, clues that each of the young adults had old habits and areas of emotional dysfunction that might continue to be problematic. However, they were stable at present, and so termination was appropriate.

Note that Marie's alleged problems of stomach pains and headaches were not the focus of work in this illustration. These complaints were simply viewed as signals of system distress within the family. The goal of the nurse's initial plan was to determine the state of the family system, to see where the mismatches between expectations and reality existed. The conceptual frameworks underlying this approach included family as a social system, systems theory, role theory, communication theory, decision-making theory, and change theory. Major credit for success must go to Andy and Marie, who were willing to take risks in the family sessions by verbalizing their thoughts, wishes, and desires so that the diagnosis of family system dysfunction could be made. These risks led to the construction of therapy plans for the family that were acceptable to them and viewed as worth both the effort and the additional risks that would be involved in changing old habits.

The following case illustrates several things. The sick person, Elaine, shows how a young adult can go through some of the stages of late adulthood during the terminal stages of illness. Her husband Jack illustrates that sometimes grave adversity serves as a maturing force such that a tragedy produces some ultimate good.

A 23-year-old woman named Elaine was in the terminal stages of metastatic carcinoma. She and her husband had been married for four years, and most of that time she had been in and out of hospitals for surgery or some other form of cancer therapy. They had never had the chance to have any children because her diagnosis was made on the basis of routine testing during a physical examination shortly after their first wedding anniversary.

Jack, the 25-year-old husband, was angry and frustrated about the mess their lives were in. He was also fearful about the future and whether he could fulfill Elaine's needs during the downhill months that lay ahead. Finally, he felt guilty because of his anger and frustration, which he had no one to express to, except Elaine. He knew that she had not caused her illness, yet she was the embodiment of their ruined hopes and dreams. It was her body that had failed them.

Elaine had moved through some of the stages of grief to a greater extent than Jack. She was angry much less often. She was more often depressed and sometimes fell into a period of nontalkativeness that was disconcerting to Jack because he was afraid she might commit suicide.

Elaine's behavior began to change as she progressed through the terminal stages of her illness. She acted out many of the same kinds of behavior that are seen in the very old, such as life review and attempts at putting the successes and failures of her life into perspective. While Jack was directing his attention to the continual debilitation, the increased pain, and his increasing responsibilities in both the physical and economic sense, Elaine was more concerned with preparing for her death by reviewing her past life. They did not understand each other, and the gap between them grew as the weeks passed.

Jack became more angry because Elaine seemed more and more distant as her dependency needs increased. Elaine seemed barely aware of his existence and not at all concerned with what was happening in the environment around her.

The couple was referred to a nurse specialist in cancer care and family work. The nurse's first objective was to assess the family dynamics and determine how the system functioned. After she discovered the problematic mismatches between Elaine's behavior and Jack's expectations, she decided to concentrate more effort toward working with Jack and his progress through the stages of loss. Elaine seemed to be doing well on her own and apparently only wished to be supported rather than impeded in her progress.

In a few weeks, Elaine was admitted to the hospital and died. Jack still had much grief work left to do, but he had surprised himself with how well he had held up during the last few days, and he said that he realized that most of his worries and concerns had been for himself and his own foggy future rather than for Elaine. He said that this had been "a beastly way to have to grow up," but he had grown up a lot in the past year.

The thrust of this chapter has been to present a deeper look at young adulthood and some of the particularly significant issues that make up this phase of adult life. The examples are not exhaustive of the varieties of ways that young adults progress through the years from 18 to 30. The variety of ways is infinite. They differ according to sex, race, religion, socioeconomic group, and rural—urban location. At the same time, there are basic similarities in the ways that young adults move from adolescence to middlescence. If there were not basic underlying similarities there would be no sense to the delineation of developmental tasks for them.

References

1. R. Gould, "Adult Life Stages: Growth Toward Self-Tolerance," *Psychology Today* (February 1975), vol. 8, no. 9, pp. 74–78.
2. G. Sheehy, "Catch 30—and Other Predictable Crises of Growing Up Adult," *New York* 7 (18 February, 1974): 30–44.
3. Gould, "Adult Life Stages."
4. Sheehy, "Catch 30," p. 40.
5. Ibid., p. 35.
6. E.H. Erikson, *Identity and the Life Cycle.* Psychological Issues, Monograph I, New York: (International Universities Press, 1959).
7. H.K. Grace, "Socialization into Adult Family Roles," (Research paper presented at ANA Council of Nurse Researchers Meeting, Hollywood, Fla., August 21, 1975).

Suggested Readings

Gould, R. "The Phases of Adult Life: A Study in Developmental Psychology." *American Journal of Psychiatry* 129 (1972): 521–531.
———. "Adult Life Stages: Growth Toward Self-Tolerance." *Psychology Today* 8 (1976): 74–78.
Pikunas, J. *Human Development: A Science of Growth.* New York: McGraw-Hill, 1969.
Sheehy, G. "Catch 30—And Other Predictable Crises of Growing Up Adult." *New York* 7 (1974): 30–44.
———. "The Sexual Diamond: Facing the Facts of the Human Sexual Life Cycles." *New York* 9 (1976): 28–39.
———. *Passages. Predictable Crises of Adult Life.* New York: Dutton, 1976.

8

MIDDLESCENCE I: THE CORE OF THE MIDDLE YEARS

Until recently, adulthood was viewed as a lengthy, undifferentiated, stable, and amorphous plateau. One student summed it up well by saying that her perception of adulthood was that it was a state one achieved and then maintained until old age. Adult development was unthinkable. How could an adult be developing? One "arrived" at adulthood and should remain there.

The big, undifferentiated middle of the life-span exists most vividly for children and adolescents. Generally, they view all the years from youth to the onset of old age as unchanging. An analogy of a rock seems appropriate here. Children and adolescents see their parents and other adults as being rocks that are stable and unchanging. Perhaps this is because the children are changing in relatively obvious, concrete ways, while the parents or other adults are changing in more subtle, internal ways.

DIFFERENTIATION INTO ADULT PHASES

The undifferentiated concept of adulthood is contrary to fact. Both research and conventional knowledge belie the utility of viewing adulthood as one big amorphous hunk of life. Young adulthood generally has been accepted as a separable segment of adult life by much of the American population. This acceptance has been spawned by the period of extended education and prolonged beginning of independent living experienced by the young adult segment of the total adult population.

Many scientists have found evidence that each decade of adult life has unique features, problems, and processes. This chapter summarizes some of this research and discusses major problems and processes as they are currently viewed in the behavioral sciences. Since this chapter deals with two decades, discussion centers on both the transitional years between each decade and the interior years within each decade.

The first transition occurs toward the end of the twenties, roughly between the ages of 29 and 32. The interior period of 32 to 39 has been labeled the rooting period, and it is followed by another transition that occurs approximately between the ages of 39 and 42. The final set of years discussed in this chapter are the interior years of 42 to 49. In addition to these discussions, the important topics of work and leisure, family life, and community participation are examined within these important core adult years. Several terms such as middlescence I, the core of the middle years, the core adult years, and middle adulthood are used interchangeably in this chapter to refer to the period of life between 30 and 50 years.

"Catch 30" Transition

A dominant characteristic of each transition stage in adult life is that it is an uncomfortable time when change is necessary and imminent. The person who must go through the changes feels discomfort. In the "Catch 30" transition, persons begin to question what they are doing and why they are doing this and not that; they do some serious soul searching about their priorities for the future.[1]

The suffering seems to come from a need for each person to answer this question for himself: "What do I want my life to be from now on?" Unmarried people may reconsider the decision they made earlier and seek a mate; childless couples may revise their decision and have children of their own or adopt a child; unhappily married couples may divorce; divorced persons may seek new mates.

Many people make job changes during these transition years. Some get out of companies that have become complacent about them. Others leave situations toward which they have developed apathetic or negative feelings. A 30-year-old who has been with one job for five years has learned the ropes and might command a higher position by a move than could be obtained by the intraorganizational promotion or seniority mode. When too many higher positions are filled and stable in the organization, there is no place for the ambitious to go except elsewhere.

Sheehy stated that the desire to understand oneself is important to persons making the "Catch 30" transition. They see the need to find realistic goals and let go of the fantasized visions of what they have the capacity to become. They do some internal searching to determine who they really are, what they really want in life, and what they must do to get it.[2]

Taking Root

Sheehy calls the years between 32 and 39 the rooting period.[3] This is the time when North Americans begin to settle down in the sense of stabilizing a life-style. Commitments are defined and patterns of behavior cannot be overlooked or ignored as merely transient. Behavior patterns have now become habits and need to be accepted as part of the personal system or worked on diligently to effect a change.

This is a time of high career ascendancy and hence of high energy and time allocation to work matters. Those who have dead-end jobs with little chance for improvement may direct their excess time and energy to recreational pursuits. Time demands toward family development and child rearing are heavy during this period. Some people meet the demands and spend time and energy in the family. Others ignore or allocate meeting these demands to surrogates because they are so engrossed in something else, such as career development or their own personal system anxieties. Still others develop a workable balance.

The 35-year-old begins to experience the time squeeze. It is now paramount that the bid for success be made soon. There is no eternal future out there anymore. One cannot go on being a promising young man or woman forever. One must start becoming the senior member of the group or becoming recognized as an expert in something. Mentors may have been very important during the twenties, but by the late thirties most people begin to become disillusioned with mentors and by the age of 40 are ready to discard mentors and become a model for some young people themselves.

At the age of 30, it is difficult to know just how successful one will become, but by 40 it is fairly apparent what the pattern is likely to be. There are exceptions, of course. Some people are already famous long before 30, and some do not achieve true success until well after 40. But for the vast majority, the foregoing remarks hold fairly well. The successful 40-year-old faces the need to continue to expand and change to some degree so that stagnation in the success is avoided. The unsuccessful 40-year-old has self-acceptance to deal with. In some cases, a desire for success was present but not achieved, and the grief and loss process must be worked through. In other instances, career success was never an issue, but other issues such as youthful beauty, sexual prowess, and the like may begin to fade and present similar self-image problems that lead one to the grief and loss process.

"Catch 40" Transition

The ages between 39 and 42 are viewed as the midlife transition. According to the findings of Sheehy[4] and Gould,[5] this is a period of acute discomfort, a time when the gap between youthful fantasies and the raw realities of actual fulfillment must be faced. These transition years are stressful for many people, but, if the research to date provides an accurate picture, matters get even worse in the middle forties and then get much better in the late forties. The entire fourth decade appears to be a major transition phase, somewhat like adolescence was earlier in life.

One simple fact hangs like a black cloud during the 39 to 42 transition period: "I have stopped growing up and have begun growing old." This is the paradox of simultaneously entering the period of greatest fulfillment and being stunned by the unavoidable reality of impending nonexistence. Some people react to this awareness with one last attempt to capture the success that has eluded them thus far. They may divorce, change jobs, change occupations, change geographic settings, or change their life-styles in some other ways. Others may turn to finding a deeper meaning in life and eventually change their value orientation. Still others will feel the crisis of this period deeply and in an unmanageable way such that they show symptoms of the crisis through psychiatric or somatic difficulties. Seligman describes the phenomenon of learned helplessness or reactive depression, which occurs in some persons when they come to believe in their own helplessness but do not trust in any power greater than themselves.[6] Such persons become acutely aware of the inevitability of their own demise coupled with lack of or loss of control over their own destiny in life. Since they believe that the only source of such control is themselves, they are caught in the hopeless situation of despair. The sense of despair need not be this dramatic, but it frequently lies at the bottom of middle-aged turbulence.

A different kind of depression described by Seligman is success depression, which can also operate in the transition years between the late thirties and the early forties.[7] Success depression occurs when one has achieved a high degree of success and the concomitant accolades. Positive reinforcements of money and prestige are no longer contingent on day-to-day efforts. It seems that no matter what one does, the attention is directed from the outside at what one did in the past. Reinforcements come because of who one is rather than what one is currently doing.[8] This phenomenon is simply the mirror image of the former one; both exemplify a reaction to powerlessness or lack of control in the here and now. Both have at the base a belief in oneself as the ultimate source of control. When the realization dawns that the all-important thing, one's own life-span, cannot be controlled, shock or even panic may result. Restabilization eventually occurs, but very little research has been done about how the dilemma is resolved. The resolution, however, is only temporary and comes up again in different form in the middle forties.

Restabilization after the Transition

Persons who successfully transcend the "Catch 40" transition usually find life on the other side brighter.[9] Most of the persons interviewed in reported studies indicated that major changes for the better had taken place in their lives as a result of the transition period. They achieved a new level of stability, which lasted from the early forties to the middle forties, when a new crisis period occurs.

The restabilization described in this period seems conceptually close to Becker's description of situational adjustment and commitment as two important processes in middle life.[10] Persons in their early forties may have become proficient at either situational adjustment or at being mavericks who operate just barely within the acceptable parameters of the system. Hence, there is decreased anxiety about the unknown. One knows how to operate within the multiple systems of work, family, and community so that relative stability can be enjoyed. A solid repertoire of behaviors has been amassed from which the person can pick and choose in many different situations. A sense of relative proficiency and self-assurance has been achieved.

Commitment refers to the consistency with which people act in their situational adjustments. Even though major changes do occur over the course of each decade in the adult years, the person is still very recognizable by his behavior patterns. He is both changing and consistent. This seems a paradox, but it does exist.

Becker defines consistency as the phenomenon wherein a person pursues consistent patterns of activity in varied situations over time.[11] Concurrently, committed people reject or ignore other stimuli or alternative actions in a fairly predictable manner. If asked about this patterned behavior, the person might indicate that the actions being pursued are those best suited to his purpose or that he has found that these behaviors get desired results.

Neugarten found that persons in this age group saw themselves as being in a period of maximum capacity.[12] Her sample related their ability to handle a complex environment and a highly differentiated self. Very few of these persons expressed any wish to be young again. One subject cogently elucidated the difference between wanting to feel young and the desire to be young. He indicated a desire for the former but did not want the latter. Middlescents want to maintain the authority, the autonomy, and the self-confidence they have achieved through experience and situational adjustment. One key feature of the so-called flowering that occurs for people over 40 is sensitivity to self as an instrument by which one can achieve personal goals. Neugarten refers to this as "self-utilization" as contrasted to "self-consciousness" in the adolescent.[13]

People in this age group know how to use their time, how to delegate authority, how to make decisions, how to make policy, and how to administer systems. Persons who do not possess these capacities will probably never learn unless some outside source of learning impinges heavily into the life space that can successfully alter old behavior patterns. Examples of such late bloomers exist but are not common. They seem to be most common among women who move from passive home life-styles or submissive occupational positions into managerial or other responsible positions later in life. Similar phenomena may occur for other minority group members as well.

Mid-40s Inferno

The middle of the fourth decade is a paradoxical time. The 45-year-old is self-assured, competent, and respected. Family life, work life, and social life are relatively settled, and everyone knows the rules and the patterns. But somehow the stability comes crashing down, and many people in their middle forties find themselves in a terrific struggle with themselves, their significant others, and the world at large. One 45-year-old put it this way:

> I really had my life together until about 18 months ago. My children were doing well as teenagers; my spouse and I were getting along fine. My career was progressing well. Now I'm in a horrible mess. I just can't solve any of my problems anymore. My spouse's parents are having health problems, and there's a lot of confusion about whether they're following doctor's orders. One is supposed to be on a special diet, but he cheats. Both of them have several prescriptions, and we don't know if they are taking the medications properly. We suspect that they get them mixed up. It's such a worry for us!
>
> My father died last year, and I worry a lot about my mother, who lives about 800 miles from here. I just can't do very much this far away and, even when I do visit her, there doesn't seem to be anything permanent I can do. I come back home feeling so uptight.
>
> My teenagers are never around at the right times. All they want is money for clothes, and now my son wants a motorcycle. I'm so nervous already; I could never stand the realization that he's out somewhere on a motorcycle. I'd never get anything done worrying about him all the time.
>
> My spouse is in the same age category as me and is nearly crazy with concern about our parents and our children. We're not much help to each other. We're both so caught up in all this turmoil. It's just a terrible load. I think that soon my in-laws may need a live-in caretaker, or perhaps they should move in with us—God! The kids would really be impossible then—or maybe they should go to a rest home. No, we couldn't do that. The rest of the family wouldn't tolerate that. It's really difficult for my spouse and I because both sets of our brothers and sisters expect us to take care of family problems and make decisions. But if they don't like the decision, they rant and rave and make us feel guilty. I wish they'd do something for our parents sometime instead of expecting us to do everything!
>
> I changed employers about three years ago because the place where I work now had a national reputation and much more opportunity. Now I'm sorry; they're really clamping down on promotions. New policies require more education for promotion, and so some of the younger employees are getting promoted over ones in my age group. I just can't take on the extra burden of going to school with all the other hell in my life.
>
> What I really can't understand is how my life could have been in such good shape only a couple of years ago and be in such a mess now!

The inferno of the generation in the middle is well expressed in this example. The specific situational crisis mentioned may not be unique to the middle forties; different people may experience such problems at other ages. However, there are indications that people react to such problems with a great deal more stress during the forties. One biologic variable operative here is the wide hormonal swings and imbalances that occur in both men and women during these years. The hormonal swings begin some period of time before the classic symptoms of the climacteric become evident. The early hormonal swings may produce enough biologic imbalance to make otherwise competent people feel overwhelmed. Notice that all except one of the problems mentioned in the illustration above concerned somebody else's life. The only problem that the person actually had control over was the decision about further education. The stress experienced on behalf of the teenagers, the spouse, the mother and in-laws, and both sets of brothers and sisters concerned the lives of other people. Later in this chapter there is a rather detailed description of the double bind people put themselves in when they assume too much resonsibility for managing other people's lives. The inferno of the middle forties is undoubtedly a necessary experience which pushes a person toward the major change in values that becomes evident in the core adult restabilization period at age 49 or 50.

THE MIDDLE OF THE WORK TRAJECTORY

An article in *Time* magazine several years ago described the "command generation." The article stated that the United States has a ruling class composed of one-fifth of the population—the people who are between the ages of 40 and 60.[14] Neugarten was particularly impressed when her studies showed that people in their late forties perceived themselves as generally competent and self-assured.[15] The ideal middlescent was characterized as being self-aware, competent, and possessing a wide repertoire of intellectual skills and knowledge—in other words, in command.

Work has a great deal of meaning in the life of middlescents and may even occupy the central focus of their life space. The meaning of work to an individual probably varies in proportion to the inherent attractiveness of the functions of the job, the flexibility and variety of activities, the sense of achievement, the status of the work, and the monetary rewards received. For the middlescent, work may not mean as much as it did at age 25, or it may mean more because of the commitment made to it. For some persons work is the means; for others it is both the means and the end.

Work may be viewed as a means of developing and maintaining personal, social, and economic security. The meaning of work usually is not limited to economics alone. Work (1) provides structure and social continuity to daily living, (2) links individuals and families to the society/community, (3) provides a means of self-expression, and (4) relates to feelings of self-worth and self-esteem.

Attitudes toward work are influenced by the expectations one brings to the work. If these expectations are met, attitudes are likely to be positive. People with jobs having lower occupational status (which is usually related to education) tend to be more concerned with extrinsic satisfactions, ie, money, job security, fringe benefits, and working conditions. They tend to be satisfied if these expectations are met. The emphasis is on more immediate rather than long-range goals.

College-educated people generally will have gravitated to employment consistent with their educational levels. Their attitudes toward work are influenced by how the work meets their expectations. They tend to have more complex expectations of the work situation; ie, they expect it to give them opportunity for self-expression, development of a variety of skills and interests, and perhaps a place to meet like-minded people and to form friendships.

With a higher occupational status, the individual tends to incorporate his occupation into his self-concept. The job has more psychologic significance for him, and with personal involvement the individual experiences more ego satisfaction. However, there may be greater dissatisfactions as well; these may be considered intrinsic factors with regard to the meaning of work.

Work affects other areas of life and vice versa. It has a significant influence on family and social relationships. The nature of one's work sometimes dictates the extent to which community participation is expected. For some career-oriented persons, work becomes a pseudoreligion. Work is the god, and they believe in the power of science or technology to the virtual exclusion of philosophic or other nonscientific pursuits.

Much of the literature and research on work has focused on the early years of the work trajectory, when the issue of matching individuals to suitable jobs is paramount. A well-developed literature has also emerged during the past two decades on the preretirement and retirement phases of the work trajectory. Few people have looked at work as a longitudinal process that covers 45 or more years in the life cycle.

Studs Terkel's interviews with workers offer much useful information to both social scientists and health care professionals about the maturational crises encountered during all phases of the adult years relative to work. Terkel got considerable information about how the interviewees perceived their work cycle through the years, as well as gut-level reactions of how they saw their present situations and how their trajectories were likely to evolve in the years in the work force remaining to them.[16]

Young persons typically enter a work setting at the lowest rank and move up. If they start a business of their own, they start with something small and build. Children of the very rich may be exceptions, but this process holds for most others.

By middle age, most people will have become seasoned employees.[17] That means that they will have had large doses of on-the-job experiences which led to the acquisition of knowledge bases and skill repertoires valuable to employers. The value of the employee may be measured in terms of the uniqueness of the knowledge and skills he possesses, the difficulty required to inculcate them into younger employees, and the importance of them to the successful operation of the organization. The value is highest for professionals and lowest for unskilled laborers.

In some instances, the knowledge base of the middle-aged expert may be to his detriment in the career ladder sense. He may be passed over for promotion because his technical expertise at the operational level cannot be duplicated.[18]

Promotions do occur for the majority, although only a very few ever reach the top job in an organization. Every promotion necessitates a transition period for both the supervisor and supervisees to become adjusted to their new relationships. Although each position has certain stable functions inherent in it, each incumbent will also bring a degree of uniqueness to the position. Middle-aged people with stable work histories typically invest heavily in their occupational position(s), and their occupational selves become integrated as part of their total sense of self-worth, or pot as it is called in Chapter 4.

Wilensky's research about orderly and disorderly work patterns provided an enlightening insight about the relationship between progress along the work trajectory and people's sense of self-worth.[19] His work histories of 678 white males between the ages of 21 and 55 provide information about the relationships between occupational success or failure, community participation, and general integration or nonintegration of individuals into the society. Jobs that provided an orderly work trajectory, in which one position normally led to a higher status-position until the worker topped out at some level, were held by persons with strong ties to work and to the larger social systems of society as well. These people also tended to see less distinction between work and leisure. The two tended to merge together somewhat, and there were connections and overlaps between work and leisure-time pursuits. No cause–effect direction can be determined from this study because it is impossible to say whether the orderly work trajectory was the cause of the societal integration or whether integration-prone people seek jobs with orderly trajectories.

Those persons who had jobs with little worker freedom, minimal status, low pay, and little or no personal contact with people showed nearly opposite profiles. Worker commitment and personal integration tended to be much lower. Those who had a work history riddled with disorderly job changes and lengthy unemployment periods tended to be less integrated and had less attachment to work as an element of positive self-worth. These people also saw work as sharply split from leisure, which for them was really recreation rather than leisure in the Aristotelian sense.

While there is a great deal of variation in people's work styles, at the same time there are fairly generalizable patterns that can be described. Several illustrations are given here in order to present some sense of the variety of work trajectories and simultaneously to show extreme forms of some general patterns.

Frank is an entrepreneur trash and garbage collector who has contracts in four small villages on the outskirts of an urban center. He owns three trucks designed for various, flexible uses. In addition to the collection of wastes, he also repairs streets and clears snow in the winter. Frank is authoritarian, and he establishes fairly rigid policies that must be met by the citizens or he will not pick up their wastes. He embodies a unique paradox because he has a low-status job, but he has propelled himself into a position of power and influence based on his control over the rules about garbage and trash collection in the villages. His nickname is Dutch, and he operates with stereotypic stubbornness and inflexibility.

He has all that he can handle with the assistance of transient hired help, usually consisting of college students or young persons wanting unskilled labor for short periods of time. Expansion is not in his future because it would mean buying more trucks and hiring persons who would have to be trusted to drive them. Frank could not be in two places at the same time. Four villages represent the limit of his direct supervisory capacity, so he has not expanded.

Carlton is a top-level executive in a corporation. He got to this position by a well-organized and well-executed plan, which he developed shortly after graduating from college in 1952. He judged that television was the best bet for a high-growth industry and decided that he was going to grow with it. He started at the bottom and learned many aspects of the technology, from camera work to producing. He changed positions within one organization or changed organizations whenever it was to his advantage. By the time he was 45, he was on top and he felt very comfortable and competent at that level. It was what he had wanted, and he liked the position now that he had it. His recommendation to other ambitious young people is to search for an industry that is in its infancy but that has a high probability of rapid growth: "Join the industry and learn everything about it; pretty soon you will be considered an expert because nobody else will know anything. You'll be able to write your own ticket. Don't join a company; join an industry. That way you're free to change companies whenever the opportunity arises. Also, don't get into any industry that has already seen its heyday. All the top jobs will be filled. Too many people will know all about the industry, and you'll never get anywhere."

Jake is an assembly line worker. He has been working for the present company for six months. It is his fourteenth job in 20 years. He has tried his hand at outside jobs with big machinery; he has worked underground in the mines; he has worked in heavy industry; and now he has gotten into lighter industry in an assembly plant. His purpose for working is to get a paycheck. He has no sense of commitment, interest, joy, or fulfillment from this job or from any of the previous 13. When he talks about his life, he talks about his family and his bowling score. His ambition for many years has been to become competent enough to win bowling tournaments. He won $1000 and a trophy once, but his score is not consistent enough to fulfill his dreams of being a recognized bowling pro.

All three of the foregoing examples are of men on purpose. The point is to show variation among people, not among sexes. Three parallel examples of women follow.

Estelle, the head of the personnel division in the county welfare department, is comparable to Frank. She has no post-high-school education. She has come up through the ranks for 25 years. She wields a great deal of political power in the county and a good bit of organizational power in the welfare department. The director would not dare depose her. He would like to kick her up to a higher-paying, more prestigious job where she would have less operational-level influence. His rationale is that she runs the personnel department with outmoded methods; the work could be done in one-third the time if modern systems-flow principles were applied. Like Frank, she limits the size of her department to what she can supervise directly.

Carlotta might be comparable to Carlton. As a youth, she became a high-fashion model, moved to a successful career in the movies, then to a successful career as a television personality, and currently is president of a cosmetic company.

Kathy might be comparable to Jake. A waitress who has worked off and on for 20 years in mediocre to poor restaurants and lunch rooms, she takes very little interest or pride in her work. She is mainly concerned about the condition of her feet. She has served so many nondescript meals to so many people in so many places that they are all a blur, and she cannot even remember what year she worked in what restaurant. The central focus of her life is her son. Her major goal is to put him through college. She buys lottery tickets hoping to win the jackpot someday.

Frank and Estelle represent self-limited success stories. They have achieved much. They could achieve even higher statuses if they would be willing to supervise *indirectly* and thus increase the size and complexity of their responsibility. Both of them are limited by their fear of taking risks and distrust of employees not under their direct supervision.

In contrast, Carlton and Carlotta show patterns of high risk taking. They were always ready to move from a concrete success to an unknown situation in hopes of achieving a new success. They apparently did not view any of the steps along the way as having intrinsic value. They were merely steps along the way.

Jake and Kathy represent the alienated workers, all the persons for whom work is purely a means to some end. The job is necessary in order to make a living. It is not an integral part of living from their perspective. They would like to win a large amount of money and forget about working. This attitude toward work partially explains the high popularity of games of chance among blue collar workers.

The work trajectories represented in these illustrations are grossly oversimplified. These six people are in a sense caricatures; real people have more complexities than these illustrations imply. However, they are useful to show patterns. Nor are the three patterns described here exhaustive. Other distinguishable styles could be described.

Leisure Time Increases

Leisure is an elusive concept, as discussed at length in Chapter 3. Every time one thinks that one is in touch with what it means, the definition or example falls flat or could also refer to a form of work for someone. The designation of any specific type of activity as leisure seems to lie totally within the perception of each individual. Any phenomenon that defies generalization cannot be operationalized and studied in a systematic manner. If leisure is a totally individualistic phenomenon, then it cannot be studied. But people have studied it and have presented cogent treatises on it. A section of Chapter 3 is devoted to some of these views of leisure.

Leisure takes on significance during middlescence because some of the busyness and tenseness of young adulthood dissipates. Middle-aged adults have more time to spend in leisure. For middle adults in the professions or in other high-status businesses, frequently there is a lack of distinction between work and leisure. The two may tend to blur and blend together. For persons in jobs that they dislike, work and leisure are often very distinct. Some people have even reported that they put themselves into a numbed state during the work period so that they will not have to fully experience the drudgery of the job.[20] They "live" during the nonwork hours of the day.

Leisure is not discussed consistently in the literature of each decade, but only in times when there is plenty of leisure time available for a significant number of people. During periods of rapid national growth or during wars there is no discussion of leisure time and how best to use it. Leisure generally has been discussed in times of relative affluence, in times of depression or unemployment, and most recently with regard to the older age groups who have large amounts of time on their hands. In the middle years the individual or couple begin to have more and more time on their hands. This occurs because children are grown and caring for themselves and technology is used to facilitate the tasks of daily living. Thus, the days are not as hectic as they were formerly.

Pfeiffer and Davis found that the middle-aged persons in their study of 261 men and 241 women were essentially unprepared for the use of their new leisure time.[21] Vacations were institutionalized events that generally involved a trip lasting two to four weeks. Otherwise these people spent 12 (men) and 14 (women) hours per week watching television and about 8.5 hours per week reading. Sports, hobbies, and volunteer work took up minimal time. They reported spending about 3 hours per week just sitting around.

The general finding of most research on this subject is that the career-oriented middlescent's focus is still on work as the major activity and motivating force of life. Havighurst found that the leisure-time activities of middle-aged persons were consistent with their overall personality and style of life, including their career pattern, even though free time slowly becomes more available during these years.[22] Unfortunately, there is no systematic method that people can use to learn new skills, develop new interests, or broaden their knowledge base. Identification of a need for a mechanism to fill this gap is beginning to produce results. In recent years, several corporations have begun to train their personnel for leisure in preparation for forced retirement. Also the adult education movement, particularly the popularity of night courses in crafts, has had some impact on the lives of persons in this age group. It is difficult to tell how many persons are involved in learning the skills of leisure. Certainly there are many opportunities for participating in adult education classes, and many of the teachers are well-qualified persons with appropriate credentials. The commitments required are often only for one night per week for four to six weeks.

The increasing popularity of family camping trips and of tennis as a sport for the middle-aged middle class and the resurgence of interest in colossal amusement parks represent just three concrete attempts to fill nonwork time in enjoyable ways. The following single illustration of changes in the amount and use of leisure time during the middle years does not do the topic justice. The reader should think of several examples that would suit different interests and life-styles.

> Roger and Mary Lynn, a couple in their late forties, have begun to realize that life is not as hectic as it was earlier. They have time to do things they previously put off. Vacations are no longer frantic periods of traveling with small children. Last year they vacationed alone at a lake and found it very restful and refreshing. This year their teenage children went along on a trip to the Grand Canyon, and the family enjoyed periods of talkative togetherness mixed with periods of separateness.
>
> Roger enjoys working with wood and spends more time now in his basement shop. Mary Lynn also spends time in a contiguous basement area with her hobby. The family are members of a country club, and they enjoy playing tennis and golf, swimming, and chatting with friends. They characterize their life as more balanced now between work and leisure. They say that they are enjoying life more now than when they were younger. Acquaintances agree that they both seem calmer and more relaxed.

FAMILY LIFE CHANGES IN THE MIDDLE YEARS

By the middle forties, most American couples enter a new phase of family life, which will last for 20 years or more. They find themselves without any small children underfoot. This phase of family life holds heretofore unknown challenges and opportunities for members of this age group. Married couples can adapt in a positive way by developing or reclaiming intimacy in their relationship; they can grow increasingly farther apart and end up with chronic loneliness; or they can search for replacement relationships with new significant others.

Stress from the dyadic isolation of the marital couple leads many marriages to failure during the core adult years. American couples have few cultural guidelines on how to change their relationship after the child-rearing years have passed their peak. It should not be so surprising that divorce, depression to psychiatric proportions, psychoactive drug dependence, alcoholism, obesity, and other compulsions become so prevalent during this phase of life. These problems might usefully be viewed as signals of maladaptation in the middle years. Coping has been inadequate, and new alternatives have not been found to handle new circumstances.

Marital relationship problems in the middle years are compounded by the presence of teenage or young adult offspring who want material assistance from parents but decision-making independence from them. They may want to live at home but not be considered a part of the family with familial responsibilities. Much the same is true of aging parents. They need some kind of support and physical assistance but will resist and resent attempted takeovers of their decision-making rights or other aspects of their personal independence. The middle adult is caught in a bind with little preparation. He has been taught to nail down every deal and make it tight. This attitude does not work with adolescents or the elderly. They operate better when they are given help without power tactics or perceived constraints. They resent being nailed down like a business deal. They hate being treated like inanimate commodities.

The middle adult who can change some long-standing habits in his interpersonal relationship style has the best chance of living peacefully in the middle. There is a saying that captures the essence of the prescription for middle adult behavior very well: "Whatever you love, hold with an open hand." North Americans find such advice foreign to their habit patterns. In the Great American Dream orientation, one must hold very tightly in order to fully possess and control that which is owned or loved.

Framework for Change

Watzlawick, Weakland, and Fisch developed a framework that is extremely useful for putting the above saying into a scientific framework.[23] They suggest the relatively simple ideas of first-order change and second-order change.

First-order change is ordinary problem solving as it is practiced in business, industry, government, and family life. It consists of defining the problem, deciding on a solution that will eliminate the problem, and implementing the solution. Unfortunately, in some instances, first-order change does not work. In fact, ordinary problem solving often makes matters worse because the solution becomes a problem in its own right. For example, consider a couple in their early forties who have three teenage children. One of the adults or one of the teenage children begins to show bothersome habit changes that the others react to negatively. The bothered family members may define these new behaviors as a problem and decide to irradicate them through a traditional problem-solving approach. Examples of solutions might include telling the person to stop the behavior, punishing the behavior, begging, nagging, or other emotional attempts at behavior control.

Quite often, these solutions will be ineffective, and the undesirable behavior will persist or even become more frequent. In addition, the attempt at finding solutions or of applying more and more of one solution will go on at an increasingly frantic pace. Eventually the solution itself will become a problem; that is, the tactic that was supposed to solve the problem will itself produce stress within the family system, and the result will be two problems instead of one. Often the second problem is even more undesirable than the first. Nagging is an example of an attempt to change someone's behavior in which the solution becomes a distinct problem in its own right. Nagging may persist as a habit pattern long after the original problem it was supposed to irradicate has disappeared.

This type of ineffective problem solving goes on in family life routinely. Parents try to control children's behavior, spouses try to control each other's behavior, and children try to control each other's behavior. Everybody tries to control grandparents' behavior and vice versa. Even the pets are targeted for control and behavior change. Generally the result is the same. The behavior persists and, in addition, the would-be controller has succeeded in making himself feel even worse by failing in his attempt. He feels defeated, frustrated, and resentful because his attempt at exerting influence failed. The target of the attempted solution may feel pushed, discounted, distrusted, resentful, and full of self-pity. Other family members will also be affected negatively.

Second-order change requires that the definition of the so-called problem be reframed.[24] Usually a paraoxical framework fits most easily. An example is the saying presented earlier: "Whatever you love, hold with an open hand." This line contains a paradox. Reframing is an illusory process. One can never be sure about the accuracy of the reframe until afterward. The following guidelines are useful in reframing for second-order change: (1) If this situation were looked at through a different set of lenses, would it look like a problem situation or a useful situation? (2) If traditional problem solving is used in this situation, is the solution likely to hurt me or others? That is, will the solution turn into a problem in its own right? (3) Instead of determining to solve the problem by changing another person's behavior, reframe the situation in terms of personal ownership of the problem. The problem is owned by the person who is *bothered* by the behavior rather than by the person who *enacts* the behavior.[25] Hence, the one bothered must solve *his* problem, which is now personally owned. The substance of this problem amounts to one's feelings about or reactions to the other's behavior. The question becomes, "What am I going to do to change my reactions to his behavior?" rather than "What am I going to do to change his behavior?"

The first of the three guidelines mentioned above deserves further elucidation because it is so difficult to practice and so difficult to explain to others. How can a person look at a bothersome or fearful situation from a different frame of reference? How can one get outside oneself enough to do that? Actually, it becomes somewhat of a habit if it is believed in and practiced regularly.

Mark Twain's Tom Sawyer reframes a particularly troublesome situation in this way: Tom Sawyer was being punished for some offense and was assigned to whitewash a large fence. He particularly dreaded the ribbing that he would have to face from his cronies as they were walking by on their way to the swimming hole. When the first crony came into sight, a wonderful idea came to Tom and he started painting with great intensity. The other boy started his expected teasing but was nonplussed because Tom made much to-do about the privilege of whitewashing a fence. Eventually, all the boys in the neighborhood were paying Tom to have a turn at painting the fence. Thus, a problem was reframed and became a triumph.

Most people are not as clever or as insightful as Tom Sawyer. The following illustration shows some of the behavioral characteristics of a man in the middle years who is still trying to control his environment with first-order change. The incident occurred at the bus stop of a large metropolitan airport.

A shuttlebus destined for a specific parking lot came around the bus stop for the third time in ten minutes. A man carrying a briefcase and a bulging suitcase came across the street toward the bus stop and alternately ran and walked the distance to the stopped shuttlebus. Just as the man came up to the back of the bus, the bus began to pull out. The would-be passenger yelled, cursed, and slapped the back of the bus with his luggage. The veins of his face were grossly distended and he appeared close to rage, which seemed out of proportion to the situation. Parking lot shuttles in large urban airports make rounds approximately every three to five minutes. What was so compelling about making this bus?

The bystander who observed this scene was quite impressed with the apparent importance to this man of controlling time and of controlling the environment. Without any information about his family relationships, one can only conjecture about how he might react to situations in which the perceived behavior of others is contrary to his expectations of how they should behave.

The following example is of a middlescent couple who live together yet apart. They have settled into this pattern and find it useful for them.

> Margaret earned a college degree at an age much older than is average for most persons today. She already had children in their latter teenage years. After graduation, she decided to take a job about 1000 miles away from home. Her husband elected not to go with her, so they remained married but lived apart. After a few years, Margaret accepted a temporary transfer near the city where her husband still lived. They lived together more consistently during this time and got along as well as they ever had, but in general he led his life and she led hers. After two years in this temporary situation, the woman returned to her permanent job and reinstituted her commuter marriage; the couple maintained their marriage by visiting each other on weekends once or twice a month.

This illustration raises several questions that cannot be answered because of the scanty data. We do not know if the marriage was always a distant relationship or even whether it is distant at present. We do not know anything about the parental backgrounds of the marital pair. Perhaps the mode for this type of life was set in an earlier generation. Notwithstanding all these and more unknowns, it is interesting that the marriage did continue, that both spouses seemed satisfied with the relationship as it was, and that the woman was the mobile member of the family because of career commitments. Perhaps this is actually an example of second-order change. The family may have reframed their relationship at some point from a traditional to a nontraditional family life-style.

An example of first-order and then second-order change in a family system is presented in the following illustration. The middle-aged couple in this illustration is trying to solve a family problem that involves an elderly parent, themselves, and their offspring by using first-order change.

> Annabelle, aged 79, has recently moved in with Hank and Judy and their teenage children. The experience of having three generations under one roof is new to everyone, and no one is really sure about the compromises that will be required. Annabelle is aghast at the way the teenagers dress and cannot comprehend why their parents do not exert more control

over what they wear. In turn, the children are annoyed about having to share "their" bathroom with her and about her putting things away where they cannot find them. Hank and Judy react to these conflicts by urging the teenagers "to be more accepting of Grandma." Of course, this does not solve the problem; it only adds guilt to the list of uncomfortable feelings. Hank and Judy try alternative after alternative to decrease the animosity between Annabelle and her grandchildren. None of the alternatives works, and furthermore these "solutions" are producing even more turmoil in the household. The children are upset with their parents, Annabelle is upset, Hank and Judy are fighting with and blaming each other for the situation, and a crisis is imminent.

Judy and Hank seek outside help and are introduced to the concepts of first- and second-order change and to the notion of "ownership of the problem." Eventually they sort out the mess in their family and try to reframe it. They reframe it as follows:

The responsibility for how the relationship goes between Annabelle and the children rests with each of them. When one of them has a complaint about something another is doing, it is the responsibility of the "bothered" party to communicate his feelings to the "botherer." No third party mediation is permitted. Under this reframe, the family rules must be changed. Hank and Judy will no longer assume responsibility for solving problems that they do not own. Annabelle's annoyance with the children's apparel must be taken up with the children. Their annoyance with her for putting all their things into drawers and closets where they cannot readily find them must be worked out with Annabelle. Finally, Hank will not act as a go-between for Judy, and she will not act as a go-between for him in relating to Annabelle or the children.

This illustration is but one variation of myriad family troubles that are made worse by attempts to use first-order change. The husband–wife relationship is an area where attempts at first-order change are repeatedly made and repeatedly fail. Widespread understanding of the principles of second-order change is sorely needed.

Sexual Behavior in Middle Life

Many studies of sexual behavior have followed the precedent setting work of Kinsey, Pomeroy, and others of the late 1940's and early 1950's.[26,27] The studies have consistently shown that sexual activity occurs most frequently in the early years of cohabitation but that the frequency of coitus declines from an average of three times per week in the early twenties to about once per week in the forties. This behavior is consistent with the male's sexual peak, which is purported to occur between the late teens and age 25. The female's sexual peak occurs between 30 and 40. Thus, it is generally believed that the man's decreased sexual desire promotes

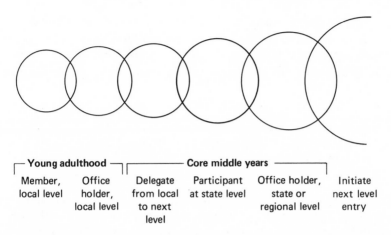

Young adulthood		Core middle years			
Member, local level	Office holder, local level	Delegate from local to next level	Participant at state level	Office holder, state or regional level	Initiate next level entry

FIG. 1 Progressive broadening of community participation from young adulthood through the core middle years.

the decrease in frequency of sexual intercourse among persons with one sexual partner.[28]

One might postulate that under these conditions women might seek other forms of sexual gratification when coitus is less frequent and their sexual desire is at the peak. The research findings indicate that, during the twenties, about 90 percent of the female's gratification comes from intercourse, but by age 45 this percentage has decreased and self-stimulation has increased. Perhaps self-stimulation is used to fulfill unmet sexual needs when social or personal pressures militate against seeking additional sexual partners.

The prevalence of extramarital sexual relationships among married persons changes on the basis of sex and of educational level over the years between the early twenties and late fities. Males of lower socioeconomic levels generally report more extramarital affairs in young adulthood with a marked decrease over the middle years. College-educated men more often begin having extramarital sex during the middle years, when their self-image may be in some transitional turmoil and/or their marital relationship is strained. Women in all socioeconomic and educational groups report lower prevalence of extramarital sexual activity than men, but the prevalence does increase with age. The highest incidence occurs during the late thirties and the forties regardless of socioeconomic or educational background. This time period is consistent with the female's peak of sexual drive.

Perhaps it would be more biologically reasonable for 30-

year-old women to marry 18-year-old men. Thus, their sexual development would be more parallel. Furthermore, they would have a
higher probability of dying about the same time. Thus, women
would have less probability of spending the last 12 years of life as
widows.

COMMUNITY PARTICIPATION DURING THE MIDDLE YEARS

Middle-aged persons frequently accept greater community
responsibility than younger or older adults. This holds true for both
men and women. For some the community-centered activity may be
a part of their pattern of leisure activities, while for others it may be
closely aligned with or may actually become a second career.
Lawyers, for example, frequently use their young adulthood to set up
law practice; then during their middle years they become involved
in politics, eg, in the legislative or judicial branches of government.
Middle-aged health professionals accept memberships and appointments to health organizations or health-related government
boards. Businessmen join Jaycees, Kiwanis and Rotary clubs, and
many other organizations for general and specific purposes of a
community-oriented nature. Noncareer married women are particularly evident in their community action activities during these years.

Keep in mind that, while the North American middle aged
live in a society that is oriented toward valuing youth, it is a society
controlled and implemented by the middle aged. Middle adults are
the norm bearers and decision makers for both the young and the elderly. Their participation in community life is essential for the ongoing progress of this society. Other societies operate with the very old
in positions of leadership. The United States generally favors the
middle aged for high-level decision-making positions.

Persons at all levels of North American Society seem to increase their community-mindedness and usefulness during the
middle adult years. The visibility of their work may differ and so
may the level of impact, but that does not change the basic tenet.
Persons in rural or low-income urban neighborhoods may have a
discrete geographic sense of community that is determined by their
immediate physical environment. Thus, assistance to close
neighbors or to relatives constitutes the enactment of their community service. Often community service is closely tied to church mem-

bership, and it is difficult to draw a line between religious responsibility and community responsibility in a general sense.

Those with more education, a broader definition of the scope of community, and a wider repertoire of language and social skills can participate in community at a different level. Often community service is closely tied to special interests or competencies. The middle section of Figure 1 shows the progressive broadening of community participation that characterizes the businessman, professional person, or housewife who moves from local to increasingly larger social system levels as a member of organized groups or associations. Although Figure 1 specifically relates to a model of movement along geographically defined levels, it should be interpreted as illustrative rather than exhaustive. That is, the circles could also be enlarged to indicate that a person has increased participation over the years from membership in one group to membership in many groups or organizations, even though they all remain at the local level. Also a person may move from being a committee member in an organization to holding an office in that organization. It is common for persons to be at the local level in one group and at other levels in other groups at the same time. The overall pattern is for persons to progressively increase the scope of their impact in community affairs through the middle years. The couple in the following example illustrate this progression:

John and Jeanine have been married for 23 years. They have three children. Two are married and live in other states; the youngest is enrolled in an eastern university. Both John and Jeanine have been active participants in community affairs during their entire adult lives.

As a young man John began to participate in local political campaigns and has been a successful campaign manager for several candidates running for either local office or national congressional seats. Since he is self-employed, many of his community interests have enhanced his business success. He is a board member of several voluntary and charitable associations, belongs to the Chamber of Commerce, and has recently become a board member of a local bank.

Jeanine never held an outside job after her marriage but has devoted comparable amounts of time and commitment to community participation. She has always been interested in art and music and over the years has worked long and hard to raise money and increase interest and participation in a wide variety of activities related to the local symphony orchestra, theater, and art museum. As a complement to John's political interests, Jeanine has always been an active member and frequent officeholder in the League of Women Voters. She has participated in church affairs and has also held offices there. Recently she was elected state president of the garden club that she joined at the neighborhood level when she and John moved into their first house in the suburbs.

Both John and Jeanine are committed to their community activities and state that they are grateful for the many experiences and opportunities that have resulted from their participation over the years.

An interesting phenomenon regarding community participation of low-income persons and racial minorities has resulted
from the dictates of the federal government. Federal programs
funded to improve health, welfare, education, and housing of the
poor require that local residents share in the decision making with
professionals. Advisory boards, concerned citizen groups, and other
such bodies became commonplace in the myriad inner-city programs of the 1960s. The majority of these attempts to make planners
and decision makers out of persons from the local neighborhoods
failed. In some cases attendance was a problem from the start. In
other instances, attendance was high and so was participation, but
few decisions could be made because the art of compromise had not
been learned. In still other instances, decisions were made that
favored a particular segment of the minority population, and
backlash resulted. No mechanisms existed for choosing or electing
community representatives. Often volunteers or persons known to
the local professionals were appointed to these posts. The local residents thus had no real say in who was to represent them. Yet they
were told repeatedly that "their representatives" had voted for a particular action.

After several years of trial and error, some of the indigenous
groups have become successful representatives of local needs.
Others have failed as evidenced by lack of attendance when meetings are scheduled or the absence of meetings altogether. In some
agencies, the citizen's advisory committee or its counterpart has not
met in months. The error in the federal regulations resides in the attempt to use a middle-class style of community decision making
among people with no background for operating in this mode. The
responsibility and in some cases the authority is put on persons who
lack the experiences that would help them develop a repertoire of
knowledge or skills to rise to the occasion.

Persons like Jeanine and John, on the contrary, move
through an apprenticelike process of learning by watching others
who are older, more experienced, and more knowledgeable about
the intricacies of community activity. By participating first at a level
of local membership, they are able to develop slowly and make mistakes under the guidance of senior people. While this method appears slow to the anxious outside observer, it is the method seen

most often in the natural evolution of social systems. Perhaps a viable alternative would be systematic training in the theory and process of community participation. If such a training program was implemented, it could accelerate the process of minority participation in community decision-making.

HEALTH-RELATED SITUATIONAL CRISES

All manner of situational crises impinge on middlescent persons. Some hit middlescents directly. Others occur in the family system—to children, to the spouse, to aging parents, or to other close relatives. The crises may emanate from a death, setback or disappointment in career progress, marital or financial problems, or many other situations. However, the only type of situational crisis that is examined in this chapter is acute and chronic illness during the middle adult years.

Acute Illness

Accidents continue to be a major source of acute medical problems during the early portion of middlescence. Annoying minor health problems include colds, flu, muscle and joint aches and pains, menstrual discomforts, headaches, and intestinal problems. Most such discomforts come and go without any professional treatment. Little is known about the relationship between chronic conditions in the later years of life and the untreated minor complaints of the thirties.[29]

Specific acute problems that require medical intervention during the middle years include accidents, such as broken bones, burns, lacerations, or imbedded foreign bodies; infections, such as bronchitis, pneumonia, or cystitis; and conditions that are treated by surgery, such as hemorrhoidectomy, cholecystectomy, or hysterectomy. Such conditions may be serious, but usually they are temporary crises that come and go in a few weeks or months. Much of medical science, education, and practice caters to these acute, easily reversible conditions. Many persons can be taken care of through a rapid input–output cycle; the process is neat and tidy, and everyone is relieved when it is over. This category of problems can be illustrated by the following example:

Alice, a 46-year-old mother of four, has had episodes of cholecystitis, and the decision has been made to remove her gallbladder. She comes into the hospital after seeing that her family will be taken care of during her absence. She goes through the usual battery of tests, she is prepared for surgery, the surgery is performed, and she goes through an uneventful postoperative period. The period of continued recovery at home is rather trying because the children want her to meet their needs and reject the temporary caretaker. Alice is still weak and tires easily, but after a few weeks her vitality is close to normal. This illness has been a learning experience for the whole family. Alice learned something about her physical limits and the feelings of pain, weakness, and fatigue. Her husband learned something about his methods of coping with family illness and what it is like to handle the family in her absence. The children learned about their mother's vulnerability to illness and about their resources for managing family life in her absence. Overall, it has been a trying but useful experience. Family members have matured a little as a result of this crisis. They are all very glad that it is over.

Chronic Illness

The experience of chronic illness is very different from the tidy picture drawn of acute illness. There is an incalculable but usually lengthy time between input and output through the health care system with no guarantee that professional health care will help the person get better. While chronic conditions are relatively rare in the middle years, they do occur, and their incidence increases as persons get older. Some chronic conditions include diabetes, cardiovascular disorders, cancer, chronic respiratory disorders, multiple sclerosis, and rheumatoid arthritis. Certain of these conditions are more disabling than others, but all affect the entire family system when they occur, not just the person who is diagnosed as having the disorder. All produce major changes in family life. Further, these conditions persist for long periods of time. The illness becomes a permanent part of the family system.

When middle-aged adults, whether men or women, continuously feel sick or become progressively disabled, the positions they hold within the family system undergo changes. Children and the spouse may take on functions heretofore performed by the ill person. Marital relationships and parent–child relationships often become distorted. For example, a man with progressing disability from multiple sclerosis will eventually drop out of the work force, cease to be a breadwinner, narrow the list of household chores he performs, participate less in child-rearing practices, have difficulty performing as a sexual partner, and increase behavior related to being a sick, helpless invalid. Simultaneously, the significant others will be picking up some of the functions he dropped and thus reinforce his new status. Eventually, the roles of husband–wife, father–son, and father–daughter will become distorted. The father–son role, for instance, may be revised in terms of authority, deference, task, and even affect. Conflict can easily arise if the ill person wants to retain or regain his former status but others resist or sabotage his efforts. Or conflict can arise if a teenager has assumed many adult male responsibilities and wants the attendant authority. In the deference dimension, the father's needs come first because he is ill. Affect is changed to pity plus a combination of anger and guilt.

The husband–wife role is perhaps the most distorted. This relationship becomes more care giver/care receiver than wife–husband. Such a role change can have devastating effects on the self-image and morale of the ill person. At the same time, the spouse will feel overburdened and alone with all this responsibility. He could share the wife's burden by participating in problem solving and decision making, but neither of them is open to this option because they are locked into the care giver/care receiver bias. Too often physically disabled persons are treated as if they had lost their intellectual capabilities, sight, and hearing as well.

Finally, the mother–son and mother–daughter roles change. The children assume functions and responsibilities normally performed by adults. The mother may seek their advice or participation in making important decisions. Conflict arises when the mother vacillates between expecting them to perform like adults at times and demanding that they comply with her rules like children at other times.

Essentially the same outcomes result when a female is the ill person. Financial distress may be less severe, since most men are paid higher salaries than women. However, the types of role distortions described above also occur when the ill person is the wife–mother. It is fortunate that chronic illness during the core middle years is unusual, considering how disruptive it can be to the family system when it does occur. Family therapy is not usually available or suggested for such families because they do not have a psychiatric problem. Thus, health care professionals go on treating the single individual who has the chronic illness medically and ignore the family system dysfunction or label the family as a problem family. A family system orientation has gained acceptance in community mental-health programs, but it has not had any appreciable impact on the treatment of long-term medical problems.

References

1. G. Sheehy, Catch 30—and other predictable crises of Growing Up Adult. *New York* 7 (18 February, 1974): 30–44.
2. Ibid.
3. Ibid.
4. Ibid.
5. R. Gould, "Adult Life Stages: Growth Toward Self-tolerance," *Psychology Today* 6 (February 1975): 74–78.
6. M. E. P. Seligman, "Fall into Helplessness," *Psychology Today* 6 (June 1973): 43–48.
7. Ibid.
8. Ibid.
9. G. Sheehy, "Catch 30."
10. H. S. Becker, "Personal Change in Adult Life," in *Middle Age and Aging*, ed. B. L. Neugarten (Chicago: University of Chicago Press, 1968).
11. Ibid.
12. B. L. Neugarten, "The Awareness of Middle Age," in *Middle Age and Aging*, ed. B. L. Neugarten (Chicago: University of Chicago Press, 1968).
13. Ibid.
14. "Command Generation," *Time* (29 July, 1966): 50–54.
15. B. L. Neugarten, "The Awareness of Middle Age."
16. S. Terkel, *Working* (New York: Avon Books, 1974).
17. H. S. Becker, "Personal Change in Adult Life."
18. Ibid.
19. H. L. Wilensky, "Orderly Careers and Social Participation: The Impact of Work History on Social Integration in the Middle Mass," in *Middle Age and Aging*, ed. B. L. Neugarten (Chicago: University of Chicago Press, 1968).
20. S. Terkel, *Working*.
21. E. Pfeiffer and G. C. Davis, "The Use of Leisure Time in Middle Life," *Normal Aging II*, ed. P. Erdman (Durham, N. C.: Duke University Press, 1974).
22. R. J. Havighurst, "The Leisure Activities of the Middle Aged," *American Journal of Sociology* 63(1957): 152–162.
23. P. Watzlawick, J. Weakland and R. Fisch, *Change* (New York: Norton, 1974).
24. Ibid.
25. T. Gordon, *P.E.T.: Parent Effectiveness Training* (New York: Weyden, distributed by David McKay Co., 1970).
26. A. C. Kinsey, W. B. Pomeroy, and C. E. Martin, *Sexual Behavior in the Human Male* (Philadelphia, Saunders, 1948).
27. A. C. Kinsey, W. B. Pomeroy, C. E. Martin, and P. H. Gebbard, *Sexual Behavior in the Human Female* (Philadelphia, Saunders, 1953).
28. G. Sheehy, "The Sexual Diamond: Facing the Facts of the Human Sexual Life Cycles," *New York* (26 January, 1976). Vol. 9 No. 4 pp. 28–39.
29. N. L. Diekelmann, "The Young Adult: The Choice is Health or Illness." *American Journal of Nursing.* 76:(Aug. 1976) 1272–1277.

Suggested Readings

Davitz, J., and Davitz, L. *Making It from 40 to 50*. New York: Random House, 1976.

Gould, R. "Adult Life Stages: Growth Toward Self-tolerance." *Psychology Today* 8 (1975):74–78.

Neugarten, B.L. "The Awareness of Middle Age." In *Middle Age and Aging*. Edited by B. L. Neugarten. Chicago: University of Chicago Press, 1968.

Sheehy, G. *Passages. Predictable Crises of Adult Life*. New York: Dutton, 1976.

Strauss, A.L. *Chronic Illness and the Quality of Life*. St. Louis: Mosby, 1975.

Watzlawick, P., and Weakland, J. *Change: Principles of Problem Formation and Problem Resolution*. New York: Norton, 1974.

9

MIDDLESCENCE II: THE NEW MIDDLE YEARS

The evolution of the human system continues through all of life; that is, development is still going on through the fifth, sixth, seventh, and later decades of life. Even as physical decline is becoming evident, emotional maturation is continuing toward the goal of finding personal meaning in human life. Gould reported that adults continuously seek permission from themselves to keep on developing.[1] Unfortunately, there is no way of knowing whether this finding reflects a basic human phenomenon or whether it is an artifact of societal attitudes. As children, North Americans are taught to believe that being grown-up is one long static plateau that lasts until old age, and this belief is reinforced regularly. Such early assumptions have not been dispelled in the educational processes to date, so people carry false assumptions about adulthood into their middle years. Gould found that the growth work described by middle-aged persons in his samples was toward more self-tolerance, a greater appreciation of the world around them, broadened awareness of their own internal complexity, and acceptance of their heterogeneity (unique characteristics) when compared to others.[2] Individual respondents realized that they were continuing to mature during middle life; however, they did not generalize continued maturation as normal human behavior for the whole adult population. Explicit consciousness raising and educational tactics would most likely be required for the modification of these infantile stereotypes and false beliefs in light of the facts about adult development.

VALUE REORIENTATION OCCURS

By age 50, both men and women consistently report that they experience a mellowing effect in their emotions, feelings, and relationships with others. Uncomfortable feelings are not taken so seriously and thus exert less control over the person's internal milieu; comfortable feelings are savored and remembered. As an explanation, they report the realization, after years of struggle, that extremes of anger, resentment, or jealousy really only hurt themselves. As a result, they show more patience and tolerance in their interpersonal relationships, particularly their marital relationships. In contrast to 40-year-olds, who focus on what they must hurry to accomplish in order to fulfill their personal goals, 50-year-olds focus on what they have learned and how they evolved during the half-century of their existence. These people appear to be intent on living in the present. They express sensitivity to humanistic experiences related to such feelings as joy, sorrow, humor, tenderness, affection, sense of wonderment, curiosity, faith, and trust. Men show a definite change from their earlier focus on masculinity, virility, power, and success. Both sexes report fewer instances of grappling with intense anger, jealousy, hatred, resentment, or self-pity. These feelings certainly do occur, but not over trivial matters as in earlier life, and they say that the episodes are resolved more swiftly when they recall the senseless discomfort they are causing themselves. Hence, the feelings can be de-energized even though the precipitating event has not been resolved.

An interesting study done in the early 1960s revealed the biases of the researcher, but the results are nonetheless applicable here. The title of the report contains the conclusion that there is a decline in the intensity of emotional experience in the decades from 50 to 90+. Dean reported that there is a steady decline in feelings of irritation and anger as people become older.[3] The conclusion drawn from these results, that affect decreases with age, is open to severe question. Only uncomfortable feelings were studied, so no information was collected on comfortable feelings. Further, an alternative interpretation of the findings could be that older people change their orientation toward other people; they stop trying to control others and as a result are less prone to become irritated or angry when others do not fulfill their expectations.

The gradual change in attitudes, feelings, and behaviors from the mastery-oriented uptightness of the thirties and forties to the "living for today" attitude of the fifties and sixties can be viewed as a shift over time on the value orientation paradigm of Table 3, Chapter 1. Recall that according to the dominant North American value orientation man is good, his focus is on the future, the priority behavior is doing, the relationship to nature is master–slave, and the man-to-man relationship emphasizes individual freedom. However, as life progresses, there seems to be a gradual but definite shift toward the value orientation labeled in Chapter 1 as Live and Let Live. The findings of several researchers as summarized above would support this contention, although their interpretation of the phenomena is not necessarily consistent with the one presented here.[4,5] In order to visually depict the hypothesized change in values over time a further adaptation was made of the value orientation paradigm. In this adaptation, shown in Table 1, the columns are rearranged and a time dimension is added. The purpose is to show movement from left to right over the course of the adult years.

Young persons are taught to believe that man was created as the highest creature in the animal kingdom and that man's right and responsibility are to discover the secrets of nature through science and become the master over nature through technology. From this basic belief arises the future-oriented planning and goal setting of young adulthood. Young people work in the now as preparation for the future. Their thought life is directed largely to this weekend, next month, next year, or five years from now. Today is not impor-

TABLE 1.   Value Orientation Shift during Adult Life.

Adult Phases	Young Adulthood	Core of the Middle Years	The New Middle Years	Late Adulthood
Value Orientations	"The Great American Dream"		"Live and Let Live"	
Human nature	Good→		Neutral or mixture of good and evil	
Man–nature– supernature	Mastery over→		Harmony with	
Time	Future→		Present	
Activity	Doing→		Being-in-becoming	
Relational	Individualism→		Collaterality	

tant except for what can be done toward attainment of long-term goals.

The shift in value orientation is a slow process. It would be grossly inaccurate to conceptualize people as waking up one morning in their 55th year and finding that their values had changed overnight. On the contrary, there is much stress, ambiguity, and unevenness in this process. Someone may come to value harmony with nature but remain highly committed to mastery over the spouse, offspring, or work situation. It takes many years to achieve reintegration in the Live and Let Live orientation. Some people never try; others die of stress conditions before they are mature enough to save themselves. However, the majority apparently are engaged in working on this process during most of the new middle years.

Research data that support the model of value shift presented in Table 1 include Gould's study of 524 men and women in seven age-graded groups. Subjects between 50 and 60 indicated that for them "marriage has been a good thing," that they try to be satisfied with what they have and not covet things that they probably will never get, that they very much depend on a few close friendships, and that their spouses are extremely important in their lives.[6] These responses of persons in their fifties contrasted dramatically with those of subjects in their forties and thirties or younger. Subjects between 50 and 59 allotted minimal importance to the following item: "I don't make enough money to do what I want." Most of them said they had learned to live within their means. Younger subjects attached considerable importance to this item. For younger persons, the self is more important than the spouse, but the spouse was consistently rated as more important than the self by persons over 50. Such responses by persons in the new middle years synchronize with being-in-becoming, living in the present, and collaterality of relationships in the Live and Let Live value orientation.

Much more research about these years is needed before the value shift model in Table 1 can be put forth in any more than a tentative manner. Many of the interview questions asked by researchers thus far are grossly biased by the researchers' underlying values of doing, controlling, achieving, and power. Thus, the responses of persons over 50 show up as deviant, deficient, or pitiable in contrast to those of the younger age groups. Indeed, many researchers characterize them in just that way when they write their conclusions. Different kinds of questions need to be asked in order to tap the dimensions of life that are significant to people in the later decades. Bias of the researcher must be taken into account when reviewing the findings and conclusions of all research but especially when reviewing cross-generation comparative studies.

The 20 years included in the new middle years probably have decade transition crises and more stable middle periods in much the same pattern as the young adult years and core middle years. However, research data have not been analyzed in such a way that transitions would show up, if they do exist. The section included here on transitional crises is therefore open to reinterpretation since it came from extrapolation of available data and must be tested by rigorous research.

Following the section on crises and integration in each decade of the new middle years, the work–leisure issue is discussed, with emphasis on retirement. As in the previous age periods, there is a section devoted to family life and one to community participation. Specific maturational crises that occur during the new middle years, besides retirement, include such things as female and male menopause, the midcentury life inventory, and widowhood. Health-related situational crises are discussed under the topics of acute and chronic illness conditions.

CYCLES OF CRISIS AND INTEGRATION

The cyclic pattern described in Chapters 7 and 8 of over-the-decade transitional crises followed by calmer periods in the middle of each decade may be culturally determined rather than biologically determined. The transition from one decade to the next has a great deal of societal meaning; the struggles of the decade transition could be a response to this societal interpretation. Whatever the underlying causative dynamics, research subjects report that the crises were real and, surprisingly, that they were growth-promoting experiences. This finding is reminiscent of childhood developmental crises in which integration at a given stage is followed by a period of ambiguous struggle from which the child emerges with a growth spurt.

Naturally, only people on the post hoc side of decade transitions look back at their experiences and see the progress that emerged from the turmoil. People in the midst of a transition crisis do not have this perspective. Pretransition sensitization is a viable possibility that could help ease the ambiguity and sense of alarm if not the actual stress of the developmental processes.

Specifics of what issues are dealt with over the 49 to 52

transition or over the 59 to 62 transition have not been explicitly documented by research. Most of the transition research to date has concentrated on the years from 20 to 45. Nearly all the gerontologic research has focused on the years after 60 or lumped together the years 55 and older. Knowledge about the developmental processes that occur between 45 and 70, particularly about ministages and transition periods, is simply not available. The few data that are available come from the few subjects that comprise the lower age limits of studies about the aged. It is difficult to find studies that actually focus on persons between 50 and 70. Even Neugarten, who has done more than most others in this field, often divides her samples in a way that obscures the new middle years.* It is hoped that the time will soon come when studies of persons in the fifties and sixties will be done with the goal of describing the growth processes that occur during these years. For the time being, tentative names have been given to four miniphases in the new middle years as an incentive for researchers to test their appropriateness.

The period between 49 and 52 is called the half-century transition. The major task of this transition period appears to be the 50-year inventory, which has been described in the literature and is discussed at some length later in this chapter.

The name applied to the years between 52 and 59 is the solid gold restabilization period. People in this phase hold most of the prestige positions in society. The average age of people in the top levels of business, government, religion, and community affairs (mostly men at present) is 54. At this age, persons in formal organizations have the highest seniority or hold the highest position of their lifetime. For persons in the middle and upper-middle class, this is usually the most financially rewarding decade. Children are grown and living on their own; many of the debts accrued in early marriage have been paid off. At the same time, the 55-year-old's salary is often at its peak. For some, there is a last-minute attempt to invest money for the retirement years. However, the primary reason for calling the fifties the solid gold restabilization period is not economic; it is that they appear to be the most stable years of the entire life cycle. One research subject summed it up by saying, "We just keep on keeping on." To observers they appear to be solid as rocks. Their juniors look to them for experienced judgment. They serve as

---

*For example, dividing the sample into young (20 to 29), middle aged (30 to 55), and senior (55 +) subjects obscures the data on persons in the new middle years.

mentors to young adults. But younger persons often become exasperated with their slow decision making and their attitude that "things will take care of themselves if you wait awhile." Young people value their wisdom and competence but also want speedy decisions, rapid resolution of problems, and fast change in social systems. Hence, the relationship between young adults and new middle agers is paradoxical and often strained.

The period between 59 and 62 is tentatively being called the preretirement transition. It is perhaps a mistake to elevate retirement from work to the level of a maturational crisis, but in North America it has come to be that. It is also risky to name a period after an experience that involves men more often than women. It is true that many women in this age group do not work, but little is known about what they experience through this transition except for information about their reactions to having husbands around the house all day. The percentage of women in this age group who do work has grown tremendously in recent years, so more and more women are and will be retiring in the years to come. The general topic of retirement and its antecedents and consequences is discussed in the section on work and leisure.

The middle of the sixth decade is difficult to name; one might call the period between 62 and 69 the three score restabilization period, except that for many it is not stable. The reality of being in retirement makes some people unstable, at least for a time. Postretirement changes in residence are often made, and this adds to the coping requirements. Some persons become age-isolated with moves to retirement villages, and this often creates another type of stress. Discomforts of chronic health problems ignored during the working years may become enhanced and present still another problem to be dealt with. One major difference between this and all the other mid-decade periods is the societally induced loss of a major status-position. This unique feature of the sixties presents special challenges for future research. Nevertheless, people who cultivate acceptable substitutes for the work roles in their lives and who have adequate internal coping resources report that this period is a most enjoyable one. They have minimal restrictions on their time and can pursue interests without the interruption of going to work. Some choose the Aristotelian forms of leisure. Others choose the industrial-consumer forms. Still others do not engage in additional leisure but simply trade one set of work roles and obligations for another set.

Reflection in the Fifties

The fifties represent an important turning point in the perceptions of self. Neugarten reports that during these years introspection, contemplation, reflection, and self-evaluation characterize the thought life of people. Neugarten calls this change increased interiority.[7] A careful reading of Neugarten's several papers and research publications brings to light the subtle, but consistent sense that increased interiority is not a good thing, that it is indicative of self-centeredness and disengagement, which are the unfortunate lot of the aged. Neugarten implies decline and hopelessness in this change rather than growth and hopefulness. The most concrete example of self-reflection in the fifties is the 50-year inventory.

Fifty-Year Inventory. The personal inventory taken in the fifties should not be confused with the life review of persons approaching death.[8] The term "life review" has been defined as the final inventory of life, which results in the readaptation or final integration process of persons in the period immediately preceding their own death. Some 50-year-olds may go through this experience if they are dying, but usually the life review takes place in the later decades now that people are living into the seventh and later decades. The 50-year inventory refers to a process of reflection on one's past life in order to organize it, put the achievements and failures into perspective, and then face the future with reorganized priorities that better suit the individual's wishes rather than society's expectations. People in the fifth generation are coming to grips with time and with themselves. In Buhler's analysis of biographies, she found that well-adjusted persons reviewed their past without regret. They put their mistakes and accomplishments into perspective and reached the conclusion that their lives had been generally successful and they were, on the whole, satisfied with themselves.[9]

Masculinity and Femininity Blur. Sheehy states that in the twenties the motivating phrase is "I should"; in the thirties it becomes "I want"; and in the forties it is "I must."[10] Perhaps the phrase that best sums up the fifties is "I am." The behavioral distinctions between men and women become less clear as the dependence on external motivators and societal approval wanes. Men show more nurturant behaviors, and women show more assertive and self-assured behaviors. Of course, the timing of these changes in behavior roughly parallels the diminished production of testosterone in males and estrogen in females. Diminished male sex hormone production in men allows the normally insignificant female hormones to exert more influence. Diminished female sex hormone production in women allows the normally insignificant male hormones to exert more influence.* Thus, there is an interesting blurring of possible influencing variables, which, from a wholistic approach, simply indicates that mind, body, and emotions are not divisible even for abstract analysis. Future generations may show a different behavioral curve as a result of the Women's Liberation Movement. Researchers have recently begun to find measurable increases in the testosterone levels of young females in careers that reinforce aggressiveness and risk taking. It will be some years before comparative data from preliberation 50-year-olds alive today can be contrasted with postliberation 50-year-olds of the future. Results of such a comparison should be most enlightening.

The Diamond Decade

Neugarten observed that life histories of people must be interpreted in the context of the historical periods that paralleled those lives and the social definitions of age-appropriate behaviors during the course of those lives.[11] The modal biologic condition of people in each older age group has changed appreciably since 1900. People in their sixties today are biologically less aged than people in their sixties in the 1905 to 1915 era, when today's 60-year-olds were small children. As children, they learned that 60-year-olds were "old people," and indeed they probably seemed ancient because that was about as old as most people became. With this assumption in their memory banks, present-day 60-year-olds may believe that their continuing good health and physical agility make them an exception and that the age group in general is as old as they learned to view them in 1910. Such persons may choose to live according to the out-dated social norms formed in their childhood. These norms mandate that they "act their age," which translates to "act old," even if it is contrary to their good physical condition. One excellent example is cessation of sexual intercourse because "it's shameful to be interested in sex when you are over 60." Another example is, "it's harmful to swim, play tennis, or dance when you get this old."

*Note that both sexes normally produce small amounts of the opposite sex hormones all through life.

The new middle years turn into a missed opportunity if people persist in acting like late adults several years before their biologic clocks reach that stage in the life cycle. Simon values learning to grow older in a new way. She says that the opportunity exists to find ways to be more fully loved and loving, more sexual, useful, leisurely, beautiful, and employable *with* gray hair and wrinkles. As a person in this age group herself, Simon conveys the excitement of an explorer as she contemplates growing older in a new way, a way that is different from how her mother, her father, and their contemporaries or her grandmother, her grandfather, and their contemporaries went through the sixth decade.[12]

These new years offer opportunity in several spheres: (1) There are additional years of married life with the developmental thrust favoring deeper and more relaxed interpersonal relationships between the marital pair; also during these years, sexual intimacy can be enjoyed free of contraceptive concerns and devices. (2) Grown offspring are usually well settled as separate adults, and the opportunity exists for interdependence, respect, mutual aid, and love among four generations or perhaps even five generations.[13] (3) There is little chance even for the diehards to deny the overwhelming evidence that intellectual capacity does not decline and that several forms of cognitive functioning actually improve until shortly before death. Under the impact of such evidence, there can be no logical reason to feign being too old to learn, and the opportunities for formal education and informal experiential learning are limitless. Thus, for the open-minded, the decade of the sixties can be a new age, one never experienced in the same way by previous generations—a diamond decade.

WORK AND LEISURE CHANGE PLACES

Men and women who are career oriented see their life line and their career line intimately bound together. They take stock of the career trajectory during the "Catch 40" transition and then again during the half-century transition. Disparities existing between career aspirations and actual achievements can be dealt with either by a last-ditch effort to meet the original goals or by reassessment of what is important now and delineation of a more relevant set of goals.[14]

Those with a disorderly career pattern are faced with the possibilities of being laid off, phased out, or fired all through their adult life. However, finding the next job becomes increasingly difficult during the new middle years. Employers are reluctant to undertake the expense of retraining a worker who has only five or ten years to give to the company and who will be eligible for retirement benefits without having made substantial contributions to the fund. Very often unskilled workers do not retire in the formal sense. Rather, they get laid off from one job and never succeed in getting another.

Persons sometimes pass up job opportunities during the new middle years even when the alternate job would offer a better salary or better working conditions. Becker suggests that this may be indicative of commitment to several things in the old job: Persons may have valued friends there and dread having to develop new sets of work associates; they may have large pensions built up that would be jeopardized; they may not want to change cities or even the part of the city that is the work site; or they may not want to acquire reputations as job hoppers.[15] Thus, by this time in life, there are many issues besides salary, chance for advancement, and working conditions that enter into a decision about taking a new job. Commitment has the effect of narrowing the range of viable choices that persons allow themselves to take seriously.

Retirement

Retirement is a process that begins long before the acutal event occurs. Persons anticipate retirement ahead of time and, at least to some extent, work through the changes and ambiguities that this new status in life brings before it happens. This form of anticipatory socialization is being integrated into many employee preretirement programs sponsored by business and industry.

At first thought, it might seem an easy matter to determine who is retired and who is not. However, there are a variety of ways to define retirement, and each produces somewhat different statistics. In order to be maximally inclusive, one might choose to include all persons over 60 who did not work 35 or more hours per week, 48 or more weeks during the previous year. A less stringent measure would be the number of persons receiving some type of retirement benefit (public and private). Still another method would be to include only those who did not work at all last year or perhaps those who did not work during the last six months. Each of these measures would contain errors. The first would exclude all retired persons under 60 and all persons over 60 who worked 34 or fewer hours or 47 or fewer weeks, even though those near the cutoff are working nearly as much. People receiving retirement benefits often work in addition, as long as they do not earn beyond some fixed amount. Persons who did not work for one year or six months would include the sick and disabled regardless of age. So no one method is totally satisfactory. The percentage of retired persons over 65 ranges from 75 to 95 percent, depending on which measure of retirement is used.[16]

Although persons in higher-paying occupations have more retirement resources, they are less likely to retire than persons in lower-paying jobs. The former are more likely to continue working either full time or part time. Supposedly, this occurs because the higher-paid persons have more interesting job prospects and greater commitment to their work. In addition, these persons generally enjoy better health for a longer time than those in lower socioeconomic groups.

Persons retire for various reasons. Compulsory retirement age, illness or disability, laid off one job and unable to get another, tired of working, family crisis, and personal desire to do other things are probably the main ones. Whatever the reason for retiring, the most immediate impact for the worker and the family is economic. Even for persons with middle and upper-middle incomes, the difference between the preretirement income and the retirement benefits is significant. Further, this gap increases each year due to inflation, so that persons have less buying power each year of their retirement. Aggrandizing the inflation problem is the fact that more people are living longer after retirement, and they are faced with more years to fall farther behind inflation. When retirees are oldest and most in need of physical assistance and medical treatment, they have the lowest purchasing power.

Retirement is more than an economic matter; it is also a highly personal social event.[17] The magnitude of this social event differs among individuals. It is more significant for persons with valued roles and positions tied into their occupational situs and who invested considerable self-identity in their work. It has less significance for persons who worked only as a way to earn money. A surprising percentage of persons indicate disinterest in finding post-retirement jobs.[18] Some writers maintain that this lack of interest in further work may result from nonintegration of work into the total social milieu of certain work groups.[19] This interpretation well fits the attitude expressed by several persons in the Terkel interviews.[20] They saw their jobs as nothingness; work time was a period of boring physical maneuvers from which they detached themselves into a fantasy thought life. Such a work life does not lead one to view retirement with dread. On the contrary, it is viewed with great anticipation, as freedom at last from boring drudgery.

For some persons, particularly professionals and managerial types, work does have great personal meaning. After retirement, such persons would be expected to pursue alternate careers, become more active in voluntary or political enterprises, or continue their styles in some other way. The extent to which this actually occurs is unclear, but people who do switch to new careers or remain active in community affairs after retirement generally come from the professional, managerial, and military ranks. Even in retirement, persons continue to live according to the trajectory they set earlier in life. They act more like themselves than in any stereotypic fashion reflective of their total age group. Thus, it becomes more erroneous to make general statements about the behavior of an entire age group with each succeeding developmental group under discussion.

Retirement is a socially induced and defined milestone that serves a purpose in the industrial nations. The purpose is to keep input and output of workers flowing in the economy. Obsolescence is built into man-made products so that the latest model can constantly be sold. The rule of built-in obsolescence has been transferred to human workers as well. Older workers must be retired so that younger workers with more agility, speed, and more up-do-date scientific or technical knowledge can take over. In more primitive cultures, people work as long as they can, and they are accepted as long as they are contributing. When they can no longer contribute to the community they withdraw and go away to die alone.

North Americans view such desertion of the aged as cruel and inhuman, blind to the fact that these cultures would view our arbitrary determination of human obsolescence at a precise age as cruel and inhuman. Primitives value having people function until their biology gives out; death should then be swift. Industrial peoples value having people spend their later years as "kept citizens", out of the mainstream of society, apartheid.

Retirement has been described by Carp as consisting of three distinct, although not separate aspects. First it is an event, and as such it marks a transition point—from "middle age" to "old age," to use the common vernacular. Second, "retired person" is a distinct status-position with attendant norms, roles, and functions. Third, retirement is a resocialization process that begins earlier in life and includes thinking about retirement, planning and setting up financial arrangements for retirement, and working toward acceptance of retirement in the context of the self-image. When the event actually occurs, the new status-position starts to become implemented and integrated at various system levels (self-system, family system, and relevant larger social systems.)[21] This process is approximately the reversal of the youth's process of socialization into the status-position of worker. Further, there is a direct correlation between the intensity of the two socialization processes. Persons who were deeply socialized (heavily committed) as workers have much more changing to do during the resocialization process to retired persons. Those who were never committed to the worker position have little changing to do. Hence, the repeated findings are that persons with more education, higher incomes, and orderly career trajectories tend to retire later, find part-time jobs, and report dissatisfaction with retirement and, conversely, that persons with minimal education in low-paying, low-status jobs and disorderly career trajectories retire earlier, do not miss the job, and indicate satisfaction with sitting, watching television, or visiting with cronies.

Maddox elaborates on the status-position of retired persons. He points particularly to the fact that retirement usually involves a dramatic drop in role relationships and functions. A narrowing of the life space is practically guaranteed unless the retiree substitutes new roles and functions for the discarded ones.[22] In this context, retirement is a negativity-generating event in so far as it communicates what to stop doing and where to stop spending time, severs role relationships, eliminates functions, and decreases responsibilities. So it is different from most status-passages in life, which generate increased roles, functions, and responsibilities and thus lead one toward a broader life space. Retired persons who value maintaining a broader life space can certainly find ways to replace the relationships and activities that went with the job, but, by definition, retirement is a negatively oriented process.

Leisure

The point has been reiterated several times that heterogeneity of human beings increases as they get older; through the years people make their own mark on their experiences just as their experiences make a mark on them. People remain themselves, at the very least, and perhaps even become more individual (less like carbon copies of others) as the years pass.[23] Consequently, making statements about the collective behavior of persons in the new middle years is risky. Even more risky is making statements about the collective leisure behavior of this age group since leisure is such an individually defined experience.

The most consistent observable difference between younger adults and older adults is pace. Young adults are always trying to beat the clock, are on a tight schedule, are slaves to the dictates of their lists of things to do. In contrast, persons in the new middle years move more smoothly and calmly. Rushing is the pace of the immature; sauntering is the pace of the more mature.

The sharp contrast in overall demeanor of people in their twenties and thirties compared with those over 50 can be observed unobtrusively in public places. One such observation took place during a return flight from a conference in southeastern Florida:

> Weekday plane rides between major cities follow relatively predictable patterns. Further, the persons on board roughly fit into predictable behavior patterns. Parents with children are uptight and vigilant lest a child do something annoying, embarrassing, dangerous, or loud. The commuting executives, consultants, and salespeople spend their time reading newspapers and news magazines or buried in their briefcases. Those in the tattered blue jean generation look out the window, read paperbacks, or sleep. Late adults make concerted efforts to engage people around them in conversation. These descriptions are caricatures and admittedly ignore the individual differences among people, but they are based on multiple observations.
>
> The flight going north from Florida was different. One could feel the difference from the moment one stepped into the air terminal waiting area. The room was filled with people representing various age ranges, but the vast majority were in the new middle years. The colorful clothing, the suntans, and the communication networks bombarded all the senses at once. The clothing virtually shouted the word "leisure," and the suntans put an exclamation point after it. Persons chatted enthusiastically. Everyone seemed to be eager to converse with everyone else, and apparently there was plenty to talk about. When the time came to board the plane less than half the people got on board! This fact shocked the observer. Viewing an airport as a setting specifically used for social interchange and camaraderie was foreign. That so many people were taking so much time to see their friends off was extraordinary.
>
> After the plane had taken off and the "No Smoking" sign went out, yet another startling event occurred. Packs of playing cards appeared, and within a few seconds multiple card games were in progress. The body postures, the conversations, and the tones of voice generally conveyed the unmistakable pace of leisure. This pace of leisure, of unhurried living in the now, presented a sharp contrast to the usual character of air travel and of air travelers. Typical air travelers merely put up with plane rides as a necessity in order to get from here to there. Their focus is on resuming life

when the plane has landed at their destination. The Florida group was living fully *during* the plane ride.

According to history, Greek males comprised a leisure class. Later European kings and their courts represented the leisure class. Still later aristocratic women were supposedly the fortunate group. Today, at least in some places, the people with the time, the skill, and the attitude to enjoy leisure appear to be a segment of the Live and Let Live generation in the new middle years.

Housing for the New Middle Years

Much criticism and advocacy surround the apartheid housing craze of recent years. The production of targeted housing projects has spread dramatically with the growing popularity of apartment and condominium communities for swinging singles, housing developments targeted for families in specific stages of the family life cycle, and various types of separate communities for older people. Apartheid housing is rapidly becoming an American institution. Segregation on the basis of race is viewed as something to be eradicated; segregation on the basis of age, marital status, or stage of family life is a highly valued breakthrough in the evolution of American society.

A particularly noticeable by-product of the homogenized neighborhood is congregate recreation. Both spontaneous and formally organized group activities at the block, neighborhood, or community level flourish. Practically everybody is the same age; many people have similar interests, and so time spent outside the actual dwelling increases in proportion to the time spent inside. Outside refers to congregate areas—pools, tennis courts, party houses, court yards, and other community land areas. Inside refers to inside one's own house or apartment.

Persons in the new middle years may or may not move from a developmentally mixed neighborhood to a residential setting that caters to their age group. Those who do seek such housing have a range of social styles available to them about as diverse as the architectural styles. Some people want peace, quiet, privacy, and safety. Others want an active social climate with sports, clubs, parties, and an "open-house" atmosphere. Social isolates are free to become more socially isolated by choosing a compatible housing situation; socially active persons can become maximally involved by moving into a community that suits their style.

Imagine two high-rise apartment buildings that are comparable in price, layout, and other basics. The percentage of occupancy in the two buildings is about the same. While touring one, no residents are observed. The halls are empty, the lounges are empty, and the atmosphere is sedate. During the tour, the manager concentrates on showing the elegant furnishings and wall coverings and lauding the soundproof walls between apartments. Touring the other building is quite a different experience. It takes longer because there are interruptions to meet residents. The basement and first floor lounges are alive with activity, and bulletin boards are full of notices. This kind of contrast can be found in any form of housing—condominiums, single-home developments, or apartment complexes. One is not simply choosing a place to live; one is also choosing a way of life. By the time they reach new middle years, people know who they are, what their preferred style of living is, what they can and cannot tolerate, and whether they want a high level of social activity or just to be left alone. Plenty of options are available for the choosing.

THE NEW YEARS OF FAMILY LIFE

Collaterality was presented as the model form of human interaction during the new middle years. While friendships are important all during life, there is more time for and, according to research findings, more commitment to nurturing a few deep friendships during these more leisurely years. The most important friendship is reported to be the one between spouses.

The mellowing of feelings and the increased emphasis on humanistic experiences of persons over 50 portend well for marital relationships in the new middle years. Men in particular report higher commitment to their spouses and greater reliance on their marital relationships than they felt earlier in life.[24] Cross-sectional comparisons corroborate this finding. Older persons cherish the spouse and the marital relationship to a greater degree than younger persons.[25]

Studies done 20 or so years ago reported gradual but consistent declines in marital satisfaction from early marriage to the postparental years.[26-28] Studies done more recently consistently show high levels of satisfaction in the postparental years.[29,30] The shift in findings may be due to an actual change in satisfaction levels, or it may be due to differences in sampling techniques or investigator bias in the presentation or interpretation of data.

Certain changes in society have occurred in the last 30 years that might account for the increase in satisfaction if the shift in findings is real. Since more people in the current population of 50- to 70-year-olds have been divorced and remarried there could be an actual increase in marital satisfaction; that is, couples who were originally compatible stayed married and maintained or perhaps even improved their marital relationships. Many couples who were not compatible got divorced. Most of them remarried, hypothetically to more compatible partners, since the divorce rate for second marriages is comparatively low. Following this line of logic, more married couples in the new middle years would be satisfied with their marital relationship now than several years ago. The following illustration depicts an atypical case of a professionally guided change in the marital relationship of two persons in their fifties. It is presented here to specify in concrete terms the more subtle but nevertheless real changes that are effected by many marital couples working on their relationship alone, without professional guidance.

Corey has recently turned 54. He is a successful corporate lawyer, serves as a councilman, gives lectures at a university, and is a powerful member of his political party. He is on the board of several voluntary organizations and service clubs. Last month he won his party's nomination for the congressional seat in his district.

Corey and his 52-year-old wife Lou Ann have been married for 31 years. He says that through many of those years they were far apart and could have divorced several times, but they agreed that it would be detrimental to the children and hard on Corey's political aspirations. Their three children are living on their own, in various stages of independence, so Corey and Lou Ann no longer have to stay together for the sake of the children. Other politicians have divorced and remarried without ruining their credibility with the voters. The couple's old reasons for staying together are no longer relevant.

Corey says that 3 years ago they found themselves with nobody but each other in the house. After several weeks of awkward silences and embarrasing attempts to be honest and talk about the mess their relationship was in, both of them realized that it would take more work to rebuild their marriage than to dissolve it. Corey was surprised to discover that he did not want to be free of Lou Ann. After years of telling himself that he was staying for the children's sake, for her sake, or for the sake of his career, he finally admitted to himself that he had stayed for his own sake. He did not want a divorce.

Open communication between the pair seemed impossible because they did not trust each other enough to share feelings and because they each had so many habituated ways to block or distort what the other was saying. By what Corey described as a minor miracle, Lou Ann happened to read a magazine article that described their situation and explained that it was not an infrequent dilemma for people in their age group. The author listed several of the common communication hangups couples develop over the years and suggested that a competent professional could help such couples recognize their problematic habit patterns and teach them more effective ways to communicate with each other.

Lou Ann placed the article where Corey would be sure to see it; she was too much of a placater to openly ask him to read it. He had always resented this habit of hers, and this instance was no exception. Usually he would glance through the material but hide the fact as a way of punishing Lou Ann for being so underhanded. He was oblivious to his own underhandedness in this and the many other games that they played.

As usual, he felt anger when he saw the magazine lying open at the appropriate page near his favorite lounge chair. As usual, he tried to think of a way to pretend that he had ignored it. As usual, he began to scan it, despite his annoyance. But the game ended there, because he became fascinated with the article. He immediately related to the close parallels it drew to his own marital experiences. When he finished reading and rereading he told Lou Ann that he had read the article and said he was willing to seek professional help if she was. Lou Ann beat around the bush, rationalized for awhile, and then finally admitted that she was scared and embarrassed to describe their problems to anyone. Eventually, she decided it was worth the risk, and they began searching for a "competent professional." It took a period of searching, but just having made the decision to get help seemed to help them a great deal. They were acting as partners in the search for a therapist; that in itself was something they had not done for years.

Finally, they heard about a husband—wife team that held group sessions in their family room on Tuesday evenings. Lou Ann was even more frightened of talking in front of other couples. She was assured that she would not be pushed into saying anything until she was comfortable enough to do so. In the beginning, Corey and Lou Ann listened and learned from the other group members. They had homework exercises to do between group sessions, audio tapes to listen to, tapes to make and hear of their conversations with each other, and simulation games to discover their own and each other's problematic communication patterns. They worked hard; they took turns getting frustrated and deciding to quit. Fortunately, they were never both in despair at the same time, so they repeatedly talked each other into continuing. In one sense, progress was slow and painful; in another sense, the sharing of these intense experiences was in itself progress. They were each growing separately, they were both growing together, and their marital relationship was moving into a dimension that neither of them ever dreamed possible. They were becoming friends who trusted each other, enjoyed each other's company, and understood what the other was saying but at the same time respected needs for privacy, separateness, and individual freedom. They were developing into sexual partners with each concerned about the satisfaction of the other rather than manipulation and exploitation for self-centered reasons.

Corey and Lou Ann are quick to acknowledge that they have a long growth process ahead of them. They also say they do not want to skip any of it, because sharing in the growth process itself is their vital link to each other.

Sexuality in the New Middle Years

When people experiencing the new middle years are asked about changes in their sexual lives over the decades, they give varied answers. But then heterogeneity is the norm for persons who have lived for more than 50 years. Neugarten's sample of women expressed more satisfaction with their sex life in the postmenopausal years.[31] Pfeiffer and his colleagues found that their male subjects were still sexually active and satisfied with their sexuality; however, 98 percent of them had living spouses. Only 71 percent of the women in the same study had living husbands, and 20 percent of these husbands had a chronic illness or disability, which the female subjects said made them unable to perform sexually.[32] There was a sharp contrast in the responses to questions about sex life from the women. Most of them indicated little or no interest in sexual relationships. Other studies support the notion that both healthy men and women have the capacity for a relatively active and satisfying sex life long after the climacteric. For some of them, this capacity is contrary to what they believe is normal for their age group, and so they ignore it. Others have no acceptable opportunities because they have no accessible partner. Still others buried their sexual urges earlier in life and never think about themselves in terms of sexual desires. While the capacity for active sexuality is not eliminated by the climacteric, there are definite changes that result from the hormonal decreases in both men and women. Testosterone in men and estrogen in women diminish during the new middle years. Nevertheless, researchers have found that nearly everyone still has enough of these and other sex hormones; they simply do not have the oversupply that younger persons have.

The Climacteric.   Both sexes experience the climacteric sometime between the forties and the late fifties. The female climacteric has been studied for decades, and a large amount of literature is readily available on the newsstands so that most women have access to more or less pertinent information about symptoms and their meaning, sources of temporary relief, and, most important, the fact that it also happens to other women. The male climacteric has not been seriously researched until fairly recently. Most men have not been informed that they, too, may experience symptoms such as mood swings (intermingling of depressions, rages, and highs), insomnia, lassitude, morning fatigue, decreased sexual potency, and several of the circulatory symptoms previously associated only with female menopause: dizziness, chills, hot flashes, sweats, headaches, palpitations, cold hands and feet, and numbness or tingling.[33] These symptoms reportedly last about two to three years, and afterward men report considerable relief, as women do after the height of their menopausal symptoms.

Recent literature indicates that only about 10 percent of menopausal females really experience serious difficulty from their menopause; similarly, the male climacteric experts are also projecting that the percentage of men who experience severe drops or swings in testosterone levels and consequently have severe symptoms is probably only 10 to 15 percent.[34] It is currently impossible to judge this percentage accurately since so few physicians are sensitive to the symptoms and so few men tell their physicians about changes in moods or sexual desires when they are undergoing a physical examination.

As more persons get into the area of research on the male climacteric, consciousness raising will most likely occur, and both physicians and their patients will be more likely to consider the male climacteric as one of the possible explanations for the set of symptoms many of them now pass off as flu, the virus, or some other vague malady.

Widowhood

Both men and women can become widowed anytime during the marriage years. Widowhood in young and middle adulthood is rare but does occur. Usually it is a sudden thing resulting from an accident, war, suicide, homicide, or acute disease. During the forties more persons, mostly women, are widowed because of cardiomuscular or renal pathologies, but in general widowhood is not a common event during the young or core adult years. Only about 15 percent of all widowed persons are aged 45 or less.

Primarily women are apt to become widows sometime during the new middle years. While remarriage for widowed men is high, remarriage for widowed women is relatively low. Since so many more men die, there are more widows than widowers available; widowers have more access to unattached women through acceptable channels of friends, church, and business, and they tend to marry younger women. Widows have more societal sanctions on their behavior and more self-imposed sanctions brought forward from their early upbringing. They are more likely to have a lower income than widowers, so they have less capacity to travel.

Black females have the highest incidence of widowhood throughout the adult years, but the increase is especially dramatic between the ages of 55 and 75. White women have a dramatic increase in widowhood between the ages of 64 and 75. By age 75, about 78 percent of black women and 65 percent of white women are widows. During the new middle years, the percentages are about 35 percent of black women and 20 percent of white women.[35] This represents a significant increase since 1900 of women widowed during the new middle years.[36] Men, including black men, have a low rate of widowhood throughout life. Even those men who survive past age 75 have a widowhood rate of only about 38 percent for blacks and 22 percent for whites.

Widowed persons were the heads of households 80 percent of the time in the 1970 census.[37] Those who become widowed spend more years as widows or more years in the next marriage than widows of the 1900s. This is true in spite of the fact that the death rates for widowed persons indicate that their physical and emotional health is less stable than that of other groups. Widowed persons have higher rates than any other marital-status group of deaths from fire, falls, and motor vehicle accidents. The suicide incidence is high for white widowers.[38] It has been suggested that these causes of death indicate that widowed persons have even more personal problems, more loneliness, and fewer resources to help them cope than divorced persons.

The various authors who have attempted to differentiate phases of the grief process are in relative agreement, even though some wording may differ. These phases include (1) fixation of thought life on the lost person; (2) guilt, self-pity, anger, and hostility toward the lost person or others; (3) despair, withdrawal, depression, and disorganization of the self; and (4) reorganization and acceptance of the loss.[39] This process takes about one or two years. Some persons become fixated somewhere in the process and never reach acceptance. Kübler-Ross wrote what so many widowed people say: The worst time is after the funeral, when everybody is gone and one must start to pick up the pieces alone.[40] A friend or confidant who can make visits and be available to decrease the loneliness appears to be one of the pivotal resources. Without this resource, the grieving person is left to his or her own resources or to transient encounters with several people, which carries the danger of superficiality. With it, there is greater chance of working through the events leading up to the death and working through the stages of grief.[41] Thus, the probability of a successful resolution of the grieving process is enhanced.

COMMUNITY PARTICIPATION AT ITS ZENITH

Kelly subsumes community participation under nonworking time, which he classifies into three types of leisure and a fourth category comprised of recuperation from and preparation for work. Kelly specifies community participation as complementary leisure. He says it is independent from but complementary to one's occupation.[42] In this context occupation is the primary status-position, and all nonwork is viewed in juxtaposition to it. Thus, participation in the arts, civic clubs, unions, professional associations, or political/nonpolitical citizen groups would be viewed as forms of leisure that complement one's occupation. This occupation-centered view is too narrow and deterministic. However, if the bias regarding occupation can be ignored, the approach has merit.

It seems logical that persons who are attracted to certain professions or occupations would likewise be attracted to certain kinds of community participation. But this correlation does not signify a cause–effect relationship. Multiple personal attributes and preferences and serendipitous opportunities to become involved in certain things at a point in history are some other variables of the community participation style of people.

Whatever the personal preferences for specific types of community participation, the level of leadership and thus the span of influence is highly correlated with age. With few exceptions, the top offices at the regional, national, and international level of community organizations are held by persons in the new middle years. A few top leaders may be in their thirties or forties and a few are in their seventies or eighties, but the vast majority are between 50 and 70. Figure 1 contains a schematic representation of the influence exerted by persons at the height of their community influence. As in the discussions about earlier phases of adult community participation, the example in Figure 1 is unidimensional and is only meant to be illustrative. It depicts increasing influence on the single dimension of geographic area. Thus, the circle representing the new middle years stipulates national or international leadership. Most com-

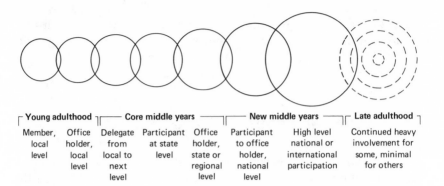

┌ Young adulthood ┐┌── Core middle years ──┐┌── New middle years ──┐┌ Late adulthood ┐

| Member, local level | Office holder, local level | Delegate from local to next level | Participant at state level | Office holder, state or regional level | Participant to office holder, national level | High level national or international participation | Continued heavy involvement for some, minimal for others |

Fig. 1 Broadest participation in community affairs during the new middle years and variations of late adult participation patterns.

munity organizations have multiple committees and multiple levels or positions, so a person could spend a lifetime in various leadership positions at a local geographic level. Conversely, a person may be respected and sought out for advice and become an informal source of influence without ever formally holding office. The important point is that persons in the new middle years assume major responsibility for the continued viability and strength of the community, the nation, and the world.

HEALTH-RELATED SITUATIONAL CRISES

Acute Illness

Acute illness is largely a figure of definition during this and later stages of life. As indicated in the discussion on the climacteric, many so-called acute illnesses may actually be episodes of hormonal swings that are only acute exacerbations of normal human development and not illnesses in the usual sense at all. Still other symptoms of illness may be early indications of chronic health problems. The true acute illnesses and injuries in this phase are probably some infectious diseases—primary pneumonia (pneumonia that is not a complication of some chronic respiratory condition) and various nonallergic upper respiratory infections and flus. As in the previous life stage, certain conditions such as hemorrhoids, gallbladder problems, simple gastric problems, hernias, and various nonmalignant cysts, tumors, or growths can be removed or symptoms alleviated on a relatively permanent basis.

Accidents continue to be a source of problems for persons in the new middle years, although they are not as prevalent as in the earlier, more rapid-paced, and impatient years of life. Death from accidents is lower in this age group than for any of the younger groups.

The following illustration is presented to show that an acute illness of a person in the new middle years can be a useful learning experience for the patient and the other family members:

Elsie and Jessie had been married for 22 years, and they had six children. Their oldest child was married, the next two were away at college, two others were in high school, and the youngest was in the fourth grade. Elsie had been a nursing student, and in her junior year had married Jessie, who was an intern in obstetrics. She had been unable to finish school because of the then-prevailing rule that no nursing student could be married.

Elsie was hospitalized for a hysterectomy and bladder repair. She was friendly and cooperative and seemed extremely sensitive to the need to be a good patient since she was a physician's wife. Most of the staff believed that she knew all about the procedure and the aftercare, or that she should, and so everyone stayed away from sensitive topics. Most of the conversations could be categorized as chatty talks about the weather, current events, or what was playing on television.

Underneath the false front, Elsie was scared and resentful because her feelings were being discounted both by the staff and by her husband. She wanted to know more about what was going to happen to her, what the chances of her having cancer were, and what ramifications the repair would have on her sexual functioning and response.

Jessie was also putting up a false front that had at its base feelings of fear and dread about what the cytology findings might be. He feared for Elsie's well-being, but he also feared for his own future if he were left with three children to rear.

Unfortunately, neither spouse shared their feelings with each other. Further, none of the staff members probed beneath the superficial chitchat to uncover what lay below the surface.

Elsie's surgery was uneventful, and she was released in record time. It took her several months to process the meaning of the psychologic trauma that she had experienced. Eventually, she came to realize that some of the developmental ramifications of the experience were (1) that her life was temporary and would eventually end, (2) that she needed to give more consideration to what life meant to her as an individual human being and as a wife and a mother, (3) that she had received little or no support from her husband during the experience, and (4) that she had given little or no support to him or to her children during the experience. Realization of all these facts helped Elsie to make several decisions about ways that she wanted to change her life. There were differences that seemed desirable in her relationship with her husband, with her children, and, most of all, with herself.

Crises are usually viewed as undesirable occurrences to be avoided in every way possible. But crises are quite often growth-promoting experiences. They get us off a plateau of inattention to what is important to us; they motivate us to take stock and make decisions about our lives.

Chronic Illness

The long-term health deviancies that people must learn to live with rather than cure become more prevalent through the decades of the new middle years and are present in perhaps 85 percent of the late adult population. Findings on the health habits and unattended symptoms of young adults may be indications of the chronic health deviations that they will develop later in life. Slow-growing viruses are microscopic organisms currently under intensive research as the potential causative agent(s) in several chronic diseases. Whether this avenue of research proves to be productive remains to be seen. Other researchers are pursuing ways to appreciably slow down the processes of aging in hopes that this will also delay the onset of chronic illnesses.

Chronic health problems more often than not require changes in the habit patterns and life-styles of not only the ill person, but the rest of the household as well. Particularly in the lower socioeconomic and racial minority groups, the incidence of chronic conditions is high, and both spouses may have one or more chronic conditions with which to cope. Complex adaptations requiring high levels of planning, decision making, and knowledgeable compromises are required from persons who usually do not have the educational background or the habits of planning and decision making that would be required to blend two maintenance regimens into a package that the family can live with.

When two persons in the new middle years live alone with only occasional visits and help from grown offspring, much of their daily life may be fixated around the symptoms and regimens of each of them. Interviews and observations in such cases often show that the couple are unaware of what they could be doing, what forms of help are available, and what potential they do have for a less stressful existence. Instead, they are so focused on their fears and the so-called necessities of their care regimen that they are only marginally alive. The quality of their lives is open to serious question.

Reversing the spiral of negativity is a most difficult undertaking. Health care professionals are at once in a good position to undertake such a goal and at the same time the least likely to do so because they are so concerned with the negative themselves. Illness care is essentially negatively oriented. The focus is on what people are not allowed to do or not able to do. The focus is on special diets, special exercises, special treatments, and special medications, all of which have a schedule requirement and take much time away from normal activities of daily life including family life, work, and leisure. The following illustration portrays many of these things vividly:

A man named Ralph with multiple sclerosis was a husband and father in a family system consisting of his wife Annie, their daughter Samantha and son Dennis, and Ralph's mother Grayce. Ralph was 52, Annie was 47, Samantha was 15, Dennis was 14, and Grayce was 73. They lived in a lower-income neighborhood in an old house that was in need of major repair work and painting.

Ralph had been diagnosed nine years ago and had physically deteriorated in a slow, but consistent manner since then. He had minimal use of his left side, his speech was difficult to understand, he spent all day in a wheelchair, and he was beginning to have skin breakdown over the bony prominences.

Annie was the breadwinner, and Grayce cared for the house and took care of Ralph's needs while the others were gone. During family assessment, it was reported by Annie and the children that Grayce fed Ralph and did other activities that she was not supposed to do while they were gone. Ralph could feed himself, but it pained Grayce to watch him so she tried to take over whenever she could. There were many areas of stress and conflict within the family system. Annie and Grayce were in conflict about who was head of the house, about Grayce's attempts to increase Ralph's dependence, and about Grayce's disciplinary tactics with the children. Annie and Ralph were having difficulty with the changes in the husband–wife relationship, and the children were having conflicts about the discrepancy between how their father fulfilled his position in relation to them compared with the fathers of their friends.

Ralph's sense of the world was extremely constricted and self-centered. He rarely spoke about concerns for the children's future or how they were doing in school or in sports. His major focus was on his own immediate needs and wants. It was never determined whether this was a new behavior pattern that emerged with the progression of the disability or whether he had always acted this way. Grayce often spoke of him as her baby, and he said that he was spoiled because he was her youngest child. Annie usually agreed with this and said she had three children to take care of instead of just two.

When the family was first visited by the nurse, Annie was not working. Ralph said that he had asked her to stop working so she could care for him. In order to make some money, she had started to work as a Fuller Brush representative. This made it possible for her to set her own hours to a greater extent than a 40 hour per week job would allow. During the second session with the nurse, the family discussed in depth the issue of Annie's need to bring in a more dependable salary. At the end of the session, they had come to an agreement that she did need to find a regular job. By the following week, she was working at a checkout counter in a large discount department store.

Ralph was not very happy because he had to do more things for himself. Grayce was delighted because the situation gave her more control in the home. The children were ambivalent, but they knew that this was the only way they could get new clothes and money for school functions. Samantha continued to baby-sit and talked a great deal about starting to work on a part-time basis in a local quick-food restaurant after her six-teenth birthday. Annie had mixed feelings as well. She was glad to see people outside the home and church. She liked being able to count on a predetermined salary every two weeks with time and a half or double time on occasion. She disliked having Grayce recapture so much influence rela-tive to Ralph's care and decision making about the children during her daughter-in-law's working hours. All the family members realized that they had little choice but to accept the fact that Annie must continue to work if they were to continue living together as a famly. This was a compromise that they accepted in order to make the best of their situation.

Compromise, bargaining among family members, and ac-tive, open decision making are activities that can deter a family with a chronic illness from the spiral of negativity. Unfortunately, these activities occur infrequently in such families. More typically, the communication pattern is one of secrecy, decision making either by default or by one adult without consultation, and persistent feelings of anger overlayed with guilt. Such family situations are ripe areas for preventive health care by professionals through family therapy, family teaching, and active participation by all the family in deci-sion making and compromise setting related to the maintenance re-gimens and care needs of the chronically ill person.

Much can be gained by such an aggressive therapeutic ap-proach. In particular, it may be possible to help people who would ordinarily stop maturing because of their own or their spouse's chronic illness get back into a direction of positive growth. Further, the potential benefits to the children are significant, since their emo-tional scars are often severe when they grow up in a home with both a chronically ill parent and a chronically dysfunctional family system.

References

1. R. Gould, "Adult Life Stages: Growth Toward Self-tolerance," *Psychology Today* 8 (February 1975: 74–78.

2. Ibid.
3. L. Dean, "Ageing and the Decline of Affect," *Journal of Gerontology* 17 (October 1962): 441.
4. Gould, "Adult Life Stages."
5. B. L. Neugarten, "Dynamics of Transition of Middle Age to Old Age: Adaptation and the Life Cycle," *Journal of Geriatric Psychiatry* 4 (1970): 71–100.
6. Gould, "Adult Life Stages."
7. B. L. Neugarten, "Adult Personality: Toward a Psychology of the Life Cycle," in *Middle Age and Aging*, ed. B. L. Neugarten (Chicago: University of Chicago Press, 1968), pp. 140–141.
8. R. N. Butler, "The Life Review: An Interpretation of Reminiscence in the Aged," in *Middle Age and Aging*, ed. B. L. Neugarten (Chicago, University of Chicago Press, 1968), pp. 486–496.
9. C. Buhler, "The Course of Human Life as a Psychological Problem," *Human Development* 11 (1968): 184–200.
10. G. Sheehy, *Passages: Predictable Crises of Adult Life* (New York: Dutton, 1976).
11. B. L. Neugarten, "Dynamics of Transition."
12. A. W. Simon, *The New Years: A New Middle Age.* (New York: Knopf, 1968).
13. P. Townsend, "The Emergence of the Four-Generation Family in Industrial Society," in *Middle Age and Aging*, ed. B. L. Neugarten (Chicago: University of Chicago Press, 1968), pp. 255–257.
14. B. L. Neugarten, "The Awareness of Middle Age," in *Middle Age and Aging*, ed. B. L. Neugarten (Chicago: University of Chicago Press, 1968), pp. 93–98.
15. H. S. Becker, "Personal Change in Adult Life," in *Middle Age and Aging*, ed. B. L. Neugarten (Chicago: University of Chicago Press, 1968), pp. 148–156.
16. U.S. Bureau of the Census, "Some Demographic Aspects of Aging in the United States." *Current Population Reports*, series P-23, no. 43, Washington, D.C. U.S. Government Printing Office, 1973.
17. G. L. Maddox, "Retirement as a Social Event in the United States," in *Middle Age and Aging*, ed. B. L. Neugarten (Chicago: University of Chicago Press, 1968), pp. 357–365.
18. L. A. Epstein and J. H. Murray, "Employment and Retirement," in *Middle Age and Aging*, ed. B. L. Neugarten (Chicago: University of Chicago Press, 1968), pp. 354–356.
19. G. L. Maddox, "Retirement as a Social Event."
20. S. Terkel, *Working* (New York, Avon Books, 1974).
21. F. M. Carp, ed., *The Retirement Process*, U.S. Dept. of Health, Education, and Welfare Publication 1778 (Washington D.C.: U.S. Government Printing Office, 1966).
22. G. L. Maddox, "Retirement as a Social Event."
23. D. C. Kimmel, *Adulthood and Aging* (New York: Wiley, 1974).
24. R. Gould, "The Phases of Adult Life: A Study in Developmental Psychology," *American Journal of Psychiatry* 129 (November 1972): 33–43.
25. Ibid.

26. J. H. S. Bossard and E. S. Boll, "Marital Unhappiness in the Life Cycle," *Marriage and Family Living* 17 (February 1955): 10–14.
27. C. W. Hobart, "Disillusionment in Marriage and Romanticism," *Marriage and Family Living* 20 (May 1958): 156–162.
28. P. C. Pineo, "Disenchantment in the Later Years of Marriage," *Marriage and Family Living* 23 (February 1961): 3–11.
29. B. C. Rollins and H. Feldman, "Marital Satisfaction Over the Family Life Cycles," *American Journal of Marriage and the Family* 32 (1970): 20–28.
30. B. L. Neugarten, "Dynamics of Transition."
31. B. L. Neugarten, V. Wood, R. J. Kraines, and B. Loomis, "Women's Attitudes Toward the Menopause," *Vita Humana* 6 (1963): 140–151.
32. E. Pfeiffer, A. Verwoerdt, and G. C. Davis, "Sexual Behavior in Middle Life," *American Journal of Psychiatry* 128 (1967): 1262–1267.
33. R. Hull and H. J. Ruebsaat, *The Male Climacteric* (New York: Hawthorn Books, 1975).
34. S. Kent, "Sex After 45. Impotence: The Facts versus the Fallacies," *Geriatrics* 30 (April 1975): 164–171.
35. U.S. Bureau of the Census, "Marital Status and Living Arrangements." *Current Population Reports,* series P-20, no. 242, Washington, D.C. U.S. Government Printing Office, March 1972, p. 373.
36. P. H. Jacobsen, "The Changing Role of Mortality in American Family Life," *Lexet Scientia* (1966): 121.
37. U.S. Bureau of the Census, "Marital Status and Living Arrangements." *Current Population Reports,* series P-20, no. 242, Washington, D.C. U.S. Government Printing Office, March 1972, p. 373
38. "Suicide Rates by Age and Color in the United States, 1964." National Center for Health Statistics, Vital and Health Statistics, series 20, no. 5, Washington, D.C. U.S. Government Printing Office, 1967, p. 5.
39. J. Bowlby, "Grief and Mourning in Infancy and Early Childhood," *Psychoanalytic Study of the Child* 15 (1960): 9–52.
40. E. Kübler-Ross, *On Death and Dying* (New York: Macmillan 1969).
41. L. Caine, *Widow* (New York: Morrow, 1974).
42. J. R. Kelly, "Work and Leisure: A Simplified Paradigm," *Journal of Leisure Research* 4 (1972): 50–62.

Suggested Readings

Butler, R. *Why Survive? Being Old in America.* New York: Harper, 1975.
Davitz, J., and Davitz, L. *Making It from 40 to 50.* New York: Random House, 1976.
Kimmel, D.C. *Adulthood and Aging.* New York: Wiley, 1974.
Simon, A.W. *The New Years: A New Middle Age.* New York: Knopf, 1968.

10

EPILOGUE—SO WHAT?

The final task of any book seeking to point out observable patterns that are largely unnoticed can be stated succinctly as the So what? task: What does it all mean for you and me? What is to be done if what this book says sounds worthwhile? First, it should be reiterated that this book is a report of what individuals have been experiencing but have been keeping to themselves, mostly because they believed such experiences were exceptions to "normal" patterns of adult life. In addition to reporting, an attempt was made to synthesize, organize, and build conceptually coherent generalizations about these experiences. Recommendations were made in Chapter 1 in the form of developmental tasks. These are intended to serve as both goals and standards of growth. Individual persons can use these ideal statements to guide them in moving from phase to phase. They can also use them to measure personal progress through each phase. The tasks are not generalizations about the average behavior of persons today. Rather, they represent a higher level of emotional and mental evolution than is currently normative. Adults of today are developmentally disadvantaged. They are left to develop on their own with no organized goal-oriented guidance. Is it any wonder that each one suffers through a particular maturational crisis alone and often unaided even though surrounded by family, friends, and co-workers?

A recent publication by Joel and Lois Davitz entitled *Making It from 40 to 50* is filled with incidents that poignantly depict the plight of individuals who, because of ignorance about their own growth processes, suffer far more than if they understood and accepted what was happening to them. These people triple the pain that might otherwise accompany one of the maturational crises: They suffer a valid amount from the actual situation; they suffer a surplus amount because, in their naiveté about adulthood, they do not realize that their crisis is developmental and hence temporary, so they add the fear of permanency; finally, they too often suffer alone, either because they blame significant others for the situation and thus alienate them or because they are ashamed to acknowledge their need for support and so suffer alone in stoic silence.

Adulthood is a period of human development equal in importance to the periods of childhood and adolescence. The growth of adulthood differs in details and types of experiences from child development, but not in essence. The growth of childhood is, of course, easy to see because of the concretely measurable increase in size and weight. However, growing plants and animals grow in size and weight. The essence of the human dimension of child development is from uncontrolled random behavior to controlled, goal-oriented behavior. This increase in humanness is readily visible in the growing child because we have been alerted to its existence, sensitized to observe it as it happens, and anxious to aggrandize it to the extent that we can.

The essence of development in the adult years is from externally motivated behavior to internally controlled, value-integrated behavior. This change is noticeable to the person experiencing it. In order for it to become readily visible to others and for people in general to notice the growth taking place in their friends and neighbors, something more is needed. Two components necessary to this something more are consciousness raising and society's permission.

Consciousness raising is necessary in order for people to remove their blinders and reverse their tendencies to discount the possibilities of change and growth in themselves and their contemporaries. A significant advance will be made when people no longer say, "Well, that's just his personality; he'll never change," or "You'll just have to learn to accept that that's how he is." Statements such as these deny the potential of human development and goal-oriented change in the adult years. Our everyday conversation is full of such expressions.

Permission to grow might be phrased better as encouragement to grow. Currently, adults grow in spite of all the sociocultural pressures against growth. In a more enlightened society, adult development not only would be recognized and tolerated but also could be actually encouraged as a normal and desirable part of human life. Under the aegis of such a social milieu adult development would flourish. Logically, one might predict that, in a system that nurtured adult development, people would move over the course of several generations into heretofore unknown realms of human evolution. The So what? task of this book, then, is both to report facts about what people in their adult years already acknowledge about their own development during this time of their lives and to encourage and provide direction for those who are floundering in the absence of a permission to grow.

SO WHAT FOR EDUCATION?

Small clusters of people in social psychology have taught about life-span development for years. While this sounded positive in book and course titles, the reality of what was inside the books and courses did not fulfill the promise. Generally, the so-called life-span developmental approach consisted of discussions about growth and development up to the early twenties and then some sections on family and career development followed by sections on aging that were either subtly or blatantly antidevelopmental in tone and content.

An educational system based on a truly positive approach to life-span development ideally would begin in the preschool years with early inculcation of the fact that the preschoolers' parents and teachers are also growing up, although differently from the way children grow up. As early as possible children should learn to accept lifelong growth and change. This means acceptance of human beings as open systems during childhood but as closed systems whose personalities are carved in stone during adulthood.

In an educational program about lifelong development, curriculum materials, while important, are only part of the requisites for successful learning. The pivotal factor for success or failure of the effort is consistency between what is presented didactically and what the children experience from interacting with real adults, particularly their parents and teachers. Too often, the classroom materials present a particular concept as true and both teacher and parent may verbalize that it is true but then act as if it is not true.

For example, a high school social studies unit might be directed toward the phases of adult life with emphasis on psychosocial maturation. The students would be given an assignment to interview ten adults whose backgrounds varied in terms of sex, marital status, age, occupation, and amount of education. The interview results might or might not coincide with the material presented in the didactic materials. Even if all the interviewees verbalized that they were still developing, still learning new things, and cognizant of their flexibility, very little attitude change would be accomplished with the students if the behaviors of their teachers, school administrators, parents, and other significant adults denied what the written materials and the interviewees said. Teenagers are told in dozens of behavioral ways every day that their parents, teachers, and so on are in a static stage of ultimate maturity. This message is conveyed by authoritarian modes of setting rules and making decisions, especially ones that regulate the lives of teenagers.

Even young children are subject to hypocritical behavior from their significant adults. An incident that occurred in a church that had both an active preschool program and a senior-citizen program points up this type of hypocrisy. The children from the preschool program had various informal, random contacts with sporadic participants of the senior-citizen program. Occasionally the seniors would converse with one or two children when they met in the halls. At other times, one or two seniors would push children on the playground swings. This went on, seemingly unnoticed, for almost three years. However, the new kindergarten teacher was presenting a unit on the elderly and suggested that there be more contacts between the children and the seniors as a way of making the classroom experiences real. The children's parents were vehemently opposed. They did not want those smelly old people touching their children. The parents had positive atattitudes toward the classroom lessons on the elderly as long as the lessons remained abstract. They were unwilling to have the abstract learning translated into real experiences between the children and the readily accessible senior citizens in their midst. Consistency is very important with the very young and with elementary school, high school, and college students as well. Didactic presentations that are denied by actions only serve to undermine the credibility of the adult world.

Adults are sorely in need of factual information about lifespan development. Television would be the most efficient medium to reach the majority of the adult population with information. However, the most viable mechanism for in-depth study and discussion about this important topic appears to be adult education courses or programs. Most high schools, many churches, and certain voluntary organizations like the YMCA regularly offer short courses on topics of interest to adults. This would be a useful way to have groups of adults read and discuss the literature. Over time group members would have the opportunity to evaluate what they read in light of their personal experiences and the shared experiences of other adults in the group.

SO WHAT FOR THE HEALTH CARE PROFESSIONS?

One of the most frequently used phrases in medical practice is "for your age." Usually this phrase is attached to some sentence about the client's physical condition such as, "You're in good physical shape for your age," or "You have a few abnormal tests, but overall you're doing pretty well for your age." These and similar statements are pejorative. They tell clients that they cannot or should not expect anything better, that they are doing as well as can be expected "at your age." This approach to health maintenance is topsy-turvy. Instead of using the positive aspects of what one person has achieved or retained beyond the average for the age group, this approach pushes the exceptional person into the normative mold. Health care professions were bred and raised within a cultural milieu. Their body of knowledge, skills, and technologies are culture bound. Just as the general culture uses a self-fulfilling prophecy to keep middle-aged people down, so health care professions generate and maintain self-fulfilling prophecies that give people expectations of aches, pains, and other symptoms just because they have reached a particular phase in life. Another form of the putdown comes when clients ask about physical exercise. Many times they are warned to take it easy, to not overdo, to build up slowly, and so on. While this approach is the conservative way to prevent heart attacks in unconditioned people, it probably errs on the side of too much care and negativity. The underlying tone of caution most often carries the connotation that "at your age" walking around the block a few times is about all that is safe. Spouses and grown offspring help to reinforce these cautions and thus become an extension of the health care professional at home. A spouse may harass the exercising partner with cautions, threats, scare tactics, and any power plays that come to mind. Often a spouse will beg and cajole the partner for months to get into an exercise regimen and then panic when the partner gets into a routine that goes far beyond the plan envisioned by the cajoling spouse.

Reversal of this negative approach, which is spawned by negative attitudes toward changes over the life-span, will require slow but dramatic change. Major attitude changes, major curricular changes, and major changes in clinical teaching will be required to do the job. Medicine will most likely be the last profession to change because medicine is most intimately bound to focusing on illness, disability, and other forms of pathology. Higher-level wellness and life-span development, as important topics for medical school curricula, would involve a deep-seated change of philosophy and orientation about the essential focus of medical practice.

Nursing curricula have incorporated courses on human growth and development for many years. The major changes that will be required are either going beyond adolescence, in those schools where the courses stop there, or, in schools where the whole life-span is treated, reversing whatever negative orientations remain and making teaching comparable to the positive approach used from conception through adolescence. Unfortunately, in many instances, nursing courses focus on normal growth and development up through the young adult years and then take a distinctly geriatric turn and emphasize all the losses, signs of deterioration, and illnesses of the middle and late adult years. It is hoped that this pattern will be changed soon since so many nurses and teachers of nursing are becoming oriented to primary care, to expanding school health programs, to family health care, and to neighborhood health clinics. All these trends in health care work against the biased view nurses previously had of the world when they saw only institutionalized representatives of each age group. Today, nurses have the opportunity to see active, alert, and independent late adults functioning well in their own dwellings and to contrast them with other late adults in their case loads that represent various levels of dependency, including those in nursing homes. This exposure to the variety of ways that people go through the phases of life, including late adulthood, gives a much more realistic view than the one-sided intra-institution view in which nurses learned by association that all old people were geriatric patients suffering from chronic brain syndrome.

The allied medical professions would follow along very rapidly if medicine's orientation would change. Change by one or more of these groups will be slow if they are acting alone because most of them are still tightly tied to medicine's apron strings. They depend on physicians' orders for their practice, and they depend on medical literature as the basis of their curricula.

Physical therapy may be one allied medical profession that will move whether or not medicine moves. It has this potential because it has links to exercise physiology, which is a specialty area combining traditional physiology and the active athletics components of physical education. Physical therapy can move away from dominance by medicine and begin to do research in its own right and/or pursue some of the avenues of research opened up by exercise physiology. It can expand this to older age groups and those with physical impairments. Then the stage can be set for a positive attitude toward physical development, exercise, and rehabilitation all through life.

Occupational therapy has a similar opportunity. As more positions become available for occupational therapists to work with healthy senior-citizen groups in neighborhood recreation programs, they, too, will gain a better perspective of the wide range of ways that people move through their later years. The growing popularity of new middle and late adult volunteers assisting with activities in nursing homes and other inpatient facilities should also help to correct the stereotypical view of people in the new middle and late adult years. Healthy late adult volunteers present sharp contrasts to the inpatients they serve. Therapists, administrators, families, friends, and the residents themselves will observe the volunteers and should begin to appreciate the heterogeneity of persons in the new middle and late adult years.

The United States does not have a health care system; it has an illness care system. In any illness care system the resources and energies are directed toward curing or caring for disease or dysfunction. This approach, by nature, aggrandizes negativity. The emphasis is on deviations, problems, symptoms, and pathologies. In the last chapters of Part III, distinctions were made between acute and chronic health-related situational crises. Negligible developmental damage results when an illness-oriented care system is engaged to assist a person with a short-lived, reversible pathology. The sick person recovers and then goes on with his maturation unhindered by either the pathology or medical personnel. Unfortunately, chronically ill and disabled persons are not so fortunate. They must depend on and comply with the therapies dictated by illness care personnel for the rest of their lives. The focus of the therapies is either on what they should not do that normal individuals can do, or on what they should do that normal individuals need not do. The emphasis is placed on their deviancy; the pressure is to conform toward more deviancy and dependency. Family members are encouraged to act or are even coerced into acting as protectors or watchdogs to see that the deviancy is maintained for the remainder of adulthood.

Hence, the chronically ill person has a double load of the illness plus the connotation of deviancy and the aggrandizement of dependency. So the innate thrusts toward continuing emotional and intellectual maturation have to overcome a heavy counterforce. Significant persons can make growth virtually impossible for the chronically ill person. It is vitally important that health care professionals, family members, and the chronically ill person develop a balanced view of the illness and put its negativity into developmental context. In particular, the significant others should grant the person the right to maintain his humanity, intelligence, and right to grow.

SO WHAT FOR THE MEDIA?

The media have a continuous and strong influence on what people believe about the world outside their personal experience. If national television stations present the stars of every program as young, good-looking, athletic superheroes and heroines, members of the viewing audience who do not have these physical characteristics are subtly being told again and again that they are "out of it;" they are exclusions from the in-group. They are more villain or victim than hero or heroine. Mass media are the most influential attitude shapers in the United States. In the past, they took society's negative attitude toward aging and aggrandized it so that ours became a culture that worships youth. Americans see youth as the standard against which all else is contrasted. Middle age is an undesirable stage because it is different from the standard; late adulthood is the most undesirable stage because it is farthest away from the standard. Mass media have been the most virulent enemy of adult development, yet they have the potential to become the most influential champion of adult development. The pivotal issue, of course, is whether a positive orientation toward middle and late adulthood will sell products.

In recent years, new advertising models have been added to the television scene. These models are called the uglies. They are middle or older adults, usually with some physical characteristic that can be caricatured; examples are baldness, distorted facial features (particularly large or crooked noses), obesity, and comical or irritating voices. Ugly models advertise mundane items that have no intrinsic glamor: instant coffee, dish soap, laundry soap, shaving cream, beer, over-the-counter drugs, deodorant, and other hygiene items. Young, glamorous, and virile models still advertise items like wine, liquor, cigarettes, cosmetics, perfume, clothing, cars, household furnishings, travel, and sporting goods. The difference would seem to be that beautiful people promise us that our fantasies will come true with those commodities or services that are not required as mundane necessities of everyday living. The uglies do better advertising those things that are part of everyday responsibilities, like washing clothes or personal hygiene. Thus, the traditional stereotypes remain and are constantly reinforced by the media; beautiful, young people have fun and do the things that the uglies can only fantasize about. The drudgery and menial tasks of daily living are done by the middle-aged ugly people. The uglies are always portrayed as foolish; they are always subtly or overtly laughable characters. This is the general approach of mass media to portray, and thus fashion, the attitudes of both children and their elders toward adulthood. Our culture has never moved beyond the stage of ancient Greece in the worship of the seminude muscular body of the virile young Greek. Mass media and the advertising industry have done their part to maintain the potency of this ideal among the American people.

Changing the media orientation will be most difficult in one sense and very easy in another sense. The media are inanimate. *People* have the ideas, write the scripts, and hire the actors. Thus, if there were a revolution that reversed the youth worship cult, the media would sooner or later become responsive to the adjusted attitudes of audiences. However, this kind of one-sided action—reaction never occurs in open systems. What occurs instead are multiple rounds of incremental change with small actions and small reactions. Thus, changes in a positive direction toward seeing man as constantly growing though all the years of life would both affect and be affected by the media. Special-interest programs and the educational networks already have devoted time to life-span development. The news media and the talk shows usually are the second group to pick up newer trends and to try to convey them to audiences. The most recalcitrant components of the media are the situation serials and commercials. Commercials are the least likely to change because they thrive on an appeal to secret or subliminal desires of the consumer public.

A projection can be made with little fear of contradiction

that any one-hour special about life-span development in man will be effectively washed out by thousands of minutes of contradictory messages from sensual young adults in romantic scenes discounting the possibility that there could be life after 30. Notwithstanding this washout probability, any programmatic trend in the desired direction would be a welcome first step. It is ironic that the middle aged own, operate, and finance the communication systems of this nation and yet these media tenaciously perpetrate the worship of youth and the negativity of postyouth.

SO WHAT FOR FUTURE GENERATIONS?

The children born into a culture where there is a fairly clear and consistent orientation toward lifelong development would probably be different from today's children in their outlook on life. They would have a different attitude toward their elders, a dynamic rather than the current static view. They could be less uptight about themselves insofar as all their growing and developing and perfecting of defects would not have to be done by age 18 or 20. All the years of their lives could be used to learn, grow, and change. If these children then lived to the conservative 120 years projected by some scientists or to 800 years as projected by others such as Dr. Johan Bjorksten, a chemist at the University of Wisconsin, Madison, they would have even more time to develop into the persons they want to be. It would be extremely unfortunate if middle adulthood continues to elongate, but society's beliefs remain fixated on the notion that human growth and development are complete by the early twenties.

SO WHAT FOR YOU AND ME?

And now the 'So What?' question comes around full circle. The answer is: Everything that really matters to you and me as human beings could change if we changed our attitudes about ourselves. If we gave ourselves the chance for lifelong change, if we had a built-in expectation that age is not a barrier to self-improvement, we would be open to being transformed as a species. While this transformation would initially be intellectual and attitudinal, it would doubtless have physical ramifications before long. Open, enthusiastic people will have bodies that feel and behave with more vitality. Why wait for education, the health care system, or the media to convince us? Let's give ourselves and each other permission to grow! Starting right now!

Index

Note: Boldface page numbers indicate material in tables or illustrations.